BLOOMSBURY
LONDON · OXFORD · NEW YORK · NEW DELHI · SYDNEY

River Cottage
easy

HUGH FEARNLEY-WHITTINGSTALL

PHOTOGRAPHY BY SIMON WHEELER   ILLUSTRATIONS BY MARIKO JESSE

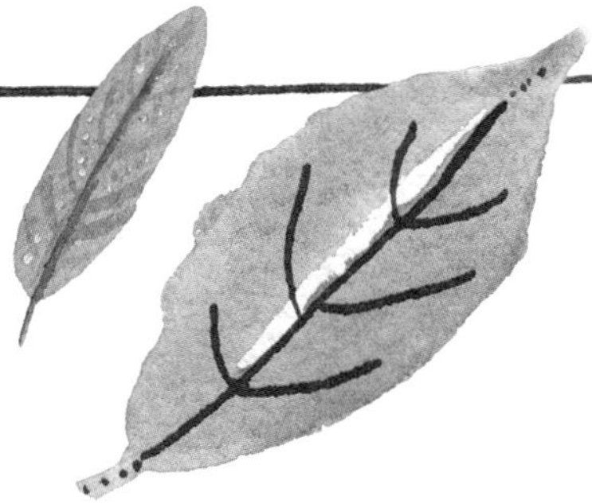

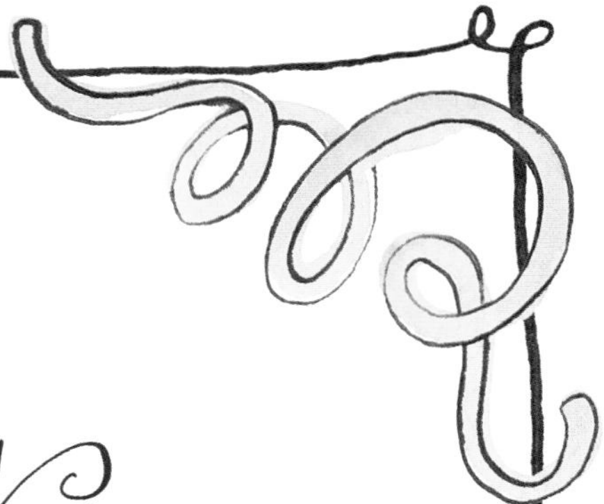

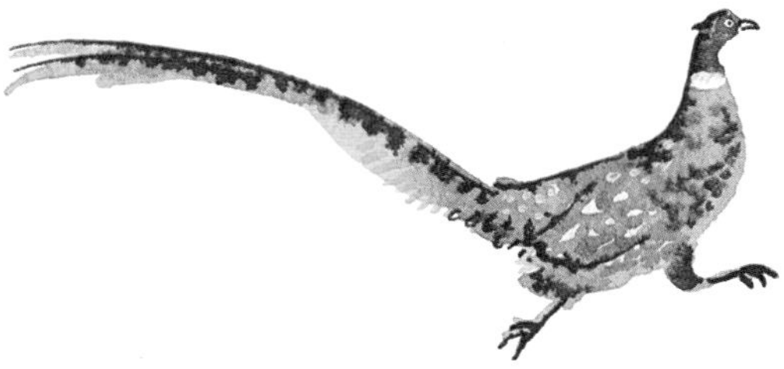

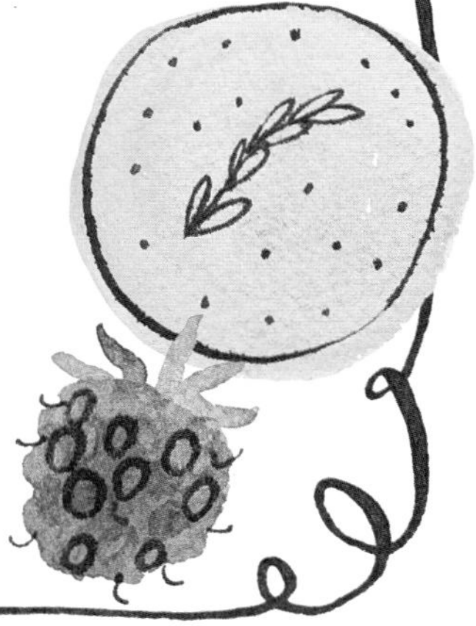

If you love cooking, but sometimes struggle to carve out the time or summon the energy to do it, then this ridiculously simple cookbook is aimed at you. And if you feel your food is stuck in a rut, or your repertoire of recipes is a little tired, I think I can help with that too.

I hope to set you off in a fresh creative direction, reinvigorate your cooking, bring you a new level of culinary satisfaction – all with the minimum of effort, sweat and angst. This book is about cooking 'smart'. My approach has nothing to do with cheffy techniques or exotic ingredients. It's conceptual: a simple idea about how to put a dish together that will set you on the road to success.

I love to cook – of course I do – and, on occasion, I will put aside an entire afternoon to make a special dish or a celebratory meal, and relish every minute of it. But increasingly, like so many busy people, I look for the least demanding meal solutions I can find. The good news is that those easy eats can be just as delicious and satisfying, if not more so, than long-winded recipes.

I am just about organised enough to ensure that when I want to 'throw something together' for supper or pack up a tempting lunchbox in a matter of minutes, there are potential ingredients to hand. My armoury is based on store-cupboard staples, a line-up of lovely leftovers, and whatever seasonal fruit and veg I have recently harvested or bought. Making sure you have a reasonably well-stocked kitchen is one way to ensure your meals punch above their weight. But the thing that's fascinated me lately is the principle that guides my hand as I make my selection from the available assortment of ingredients. I didn't even realise what that principle was at first – it was quite unconscious – but I've come to see that it's absolutely key. And it's as simple as one, two, three.

In my quest for food that's as easy as it is delicious, it has struck me that so many of the recipes I create at home, and indeed many that I enjoy cooking or eating from other writers and chefs, have something in common. They are little more, and little less, than three good things on a plate. It's a simple pattern that underpins many well-loved dishes. At the most unreconstructed level, there's good old 'meat and two veg'! But consider also tomato, avocado and mozzarella; pasta, cream and bacon; ham, egg and chips; rhubarb, crumble and custard; a humble jacket potato, baked beans and grated Cheddar... They all work, don't they? Even with more elaborate dishes, there are so often three primary ingredients holding the fort.

Of course, there's a bit more than that to these satisfying dishes. They are not only three things on a plate – there are seasonings, perhaps oil or vinegar, some spices, maybe a starchy carbohydrate on the side or an egg to finish things off. One of the 'things' might be a plain sponge cake or a slice of bread or a scoop of ice cream –

something that already contains other ingredients within it. But the core 'triple template' is extremely useful – so useful that I've built this book around it.

So here you will find salads built upon a trinity of ingredients – fennel, orange and watercress, or celeriac, lentils and raisins – augmented with the simplest of dressings. There are satisfying snacks that march to the beat of three – broad beans, spicy meatballs and flatbreads turned into a sumptuous wrap, or potatoes, cheese and thyme fried into irresistible little cakes. I've cooked up easy main courses truly worth coming to the table for (chicken thighs with plums and soy, pasta with juicy tomatoes and blue cheese) and sweet treats that will win you plaudits (cherries, cream and chocolate mousse or ricotta with honeycomb and hazelnuts). All simple, all based on the concept of three.

The recipes here are, I hope, just a beginning: a jumping-off point for any time-poor, hard-pressed home cook. I want you to use them as springboards for your own freewheeling fusions and lovely combinations, with the idea of three core elements as a guideline that is not restrictive, but deliciously liberating. After all, most of the best meals have some personal touch, some element of improvisation, from the cook preparing them.

Of course, you can't just throw any three ingredients together and expect an instant hit. Cheese, chocolate and curry powder might be an experiment too far, while bread, pasta and potatoes would of course be way too bland and samey. More crucial than the number of ingredients is the contrast between them. Thankfully, that's pretty easy to get a handle on: you can usually deconstruct successful dishes into a handful of adjectives that reveal how each ingredient differs deliciously from the others. That might be sweet, sour, spicy; or salty, crunchy, bland. It could be creamy, sweet, crisp or sharp, rich, crumbly. It's not necessary to be a culinary wizard to understand this alchemy. Combining flavours and textures so that each ingredient shines and somehow tastes more 'of itself' is something most of us do instinctively – we naturally reach for the cool, sweet cream to pour over our tangy apple crumble, or the salt and vinegar to go on our chips. Listen to what your tastebuds are telling you, and you'll be on the right track.

My holy trinity idea is not sacrosanct. You might feel you actually need a fourth, maybe even a fifth ingredient to make a dish work. If so, go for it, as long as they harmonise with each other. Just bear in mind that once you start giving a prominent role to half a dozen ingredients or more, you are well beyond 'simple' territory and heading into 'complex', 'multi-layered' and possibly 'confused'.

Indeed, some of the best and tastiest of treats require only two good things: chocolate and nuts, sausage and pastry, greens and garlic, cheese and apples. It's all about the interplay that makes the whole so much more than the sum of its parts – an interplay that I believe anyone who loves to eat will understand without really having to think about it. That's what makes this approach so easy and so much fun. It relies not on what you 'ought' to cook, what you've perhaps been taught, or come to expect, or what you imagine other people might cook. It's all about exactly what you want to eat – what your appetite and experience tell you is going to be delicious.

When you find a combination that works, play with it. One of the lovely things about keeping your food combos very simple is that they are then also very flexible. With most of the recipes here, just taking the main players and preparing them in a different way – raw instead of cooked, for instance – will give you a whole new dish. If you go a bit further and start swapping new ingredients in (celery for fennel, pollack for mackerel, plums for peaches), then the sky's the limit. That's why so many of these recipes come with ideas for varying the offering: my 'plus ones' and 'swaps'.

Do yourself a favour by stocking your cupboards, your fridge and your freezer with good basics. You'll then have the option of whipping up all kinds of winning dinners without recourse to the shops. And note that a well-stocked kitchen needn't mean an overstocked one. For me, lining the larder is not about ramming it to the rafters, it's about having my old faithfuls always waiting in the wings. I get nervous if there are fewer than four cans of tomatoes on the shelf, for instance. I like to keep a couple of decent oils to hand, and I always have lemons, garlic and onions, honey, mustard and bay leaves in reserve. Tinned pulses, tinned fish and the aforementioned tinned tomatoes offer me supper security. Pasta, rice and noodles are my starchy standbys and I keep eggs, yoghurt and a bit of decent cheese in the fridge; homemade stock in the freezer. Dried fruit, nuts, brown sugar and chocolate hold up the sweet end of things.

Finally, to do yourself justice, remember that simple dishes demand raw materials of top-notch quality. When there's no lengthy list of ingredients to hide behind, vegetables and fruit need to be at their freshest and/or ripest, while cheeses, fish and meat must be the best you can find. But you will be rewarded: with this kind of pared-back cooking, you can spend a bit more on a great loaf of bread or a top-of-the-range vinegar, safe in the knowledge that you will taste and fully appreciate it in the finished dish. Nothing's going to get hidden or lost – the simple approach is the best way to honour your ingredients. It's also the best way to lessen the pressure on yourself and, I think, to knock out the kind of satisfying, flavoursome, nourishing food that so enriches our daily lives. Great food is not rocket science: just take it easy!

Superbly Simple Salads

The salad bowl is an excellent arena in which to explore simple combinations, and many classic salads neatly make the point that 'three good things' is so often the way to go. Think of the Waldorf (celery, apple, walnut), the Caesar (lettuce, croûtons, Parmesan), the Caprese (mozzarella, tomato, basil). Grasp the guiding principles enshrined within these landmark recipes and you won't go far wrong.

In the most satisfying salads, contrasts of taste and texture abound – the sharp cutting the rich, the crunchy as a foil to the creamy, the leafy set against the farinaceous. Once you have hit on a successful combination you can swap out just one element to arrive at a totally different dish. So beetroot, boiled egg and anchovy (page 40) gives you a hearty summer salad, for lunch perhaps; lettuce, egg and anchovy offers a nice little starter or canapé; and anchovy-topped scrambled eggs on toast becomes that classic gentleman's club savoury known as Scotch woodcock. I'd love to tuck into all of the above!

In most of the salads that get my vote, at least one of the elements is reasonably substantial or full of protein: cheese, nuts or seeds, some leftover meat or fish, a scattering of pulses, perhaps, or chunks of a starchy, rooty veg (probably roasted). There's often something tangy or zesty in the mix – raw fruit being the obvious example. And there's just as likely to be a crunchy, aromatic vegetable like fennel or celeriac, or a punchy herb like parsley, as there is a regular salad leaf.

A good dressing is of course crucial, not as a discernible element (you should never be too aware of a dressing) but as part of the seasoning and coming together of the dish. A dressing can be as straightforward as a glug of good olive or rapeseed oil, a dash of vinegar or lemon juice, and a generous seasoning of salt and pepper. With that handy trio working inside the greater whole, success on the salad front is yours for the taking.

When most of your ingredients are raw, and the 'method' is simply to toss them together, you can be quite daring. You'll find recipes here that combine raw citrus fruit with grilled vegetables and toasted seeds (fennel, tangerine and pumpkin seeds on page 37), but what you get at the end is still unquestionably a salad. You'll come across a quirky mingling of blanched cabbage, ripe avocado and nutty Puy lentils on page 38 (do try it, it's so good), and the deliciously eccentric trio of raw chicory, ripe peaches and black pudding on page 48. But I hope it won't stop there. Please use these recipes as a launchpad for your own ideas. Go on, have a play!

Courgettes, mangetout, lemon

The crisp, sweet crunch of mangetout and vegetal bite of baby courgettes go incredibly well with the tang of citrus fruit in this lovely summery starter salad. Don't be alarmed at the quantity of raw lemon in this dish – the effect is refreshing, rather than mouth-puckering. It is essential, though, to use really fresh, sweet little summer veg, as their natural sugars balance the acidity of the lemon.

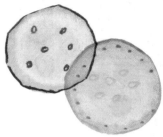

Serves 4

4–6 baby courgettes

A few handfuls of tender young mangetout, or very fresh sugar snaps

2 small lemons

2 tablespoons olive oil

A small bunch of mint, leaves only, torn

A small bunch of dill, leaves only, roughly torn

A few pinches of sugar

Sea salt and freshly ground black pepper

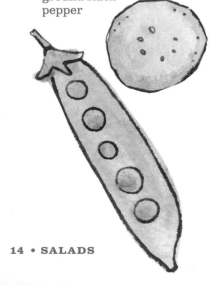

Slice the courgettes into thin rounds, 2–3mm thick. Strip the mangetout or sugar snaps of the thin fibre that runs along the inside seam of the pod. If you're using sugar snaps, slice them thinly on an angle. Put them into a bowl with the courgettes. Finely grate the zest from 1 lemon on to the veg.

Slice all the peel and pith away from both lemons. To do this, cut a slice off the base of each and stand the lemon on a board. Then use a sharp knife to cut down through the peel and pith, slicing it away completely, in sections. Now, working over the bowl of veg to catch any juice, slice the segments of lemon out from between the membranes, dropping them into the bowl. Remove any pips as you go. Taste and squeeze out more juice from the lemon membrane into the bowl if the salad needs more acidity.

Add the olive oil, herbs, a good pinch of sugar and some salt and pepper. Toss well, then leave to stand for 5–10 minutes.

Taste and adjust the seasoning with more salt and pepper and a pinch or two more sugar, if needed, then serve.

PLUS ONE Garnish the finished salad with a scattering of pea shoots and/or pea or borage flowers.

SWAPS Swap orange for lemon. Or, better still, use 1 orange and 1 lemon, instead of 2 lemons. Try using freshly picked raw baby peas instead of mangetout or sugar snaps.

Tomatoes, chilli, parsley

This simple, vibrant salad makes a great light lunch with some good bread – but you can also serve it as part of a spread alongside cheeses, cold meats and/or salads based on pulses, rice or couscous. I always go for a mild or medium chilli here.

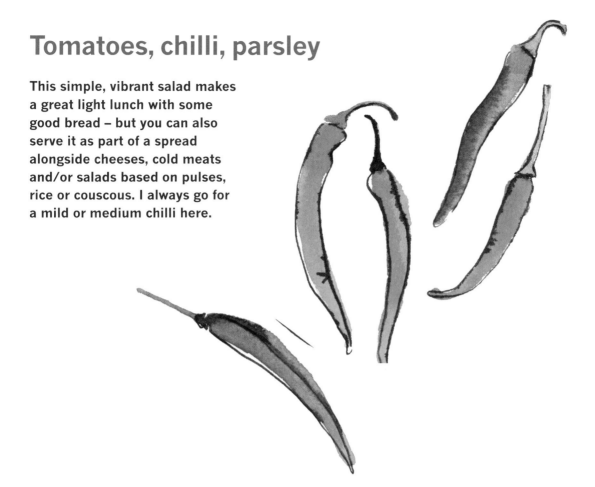

Serves 4

500g ripe tomatoes (ideally a mixture of types, shapes and colours)

1–2 mild red chillies

2–3 tablespoons extra virgin olive oil

A few drops of cider vinegar

A bunch of flat-leaf parsley, leaves only

Sea salt and freshly ground black pepper

Slice the tomatoes across into fairly thin rounds and arrange them more or less in a single layer on a large platter, overlapping the slices only a little. Cut the chillies in half lengthways, scrape out the seeds, then slice finely. Scatter the chilli slices evenly over the tomatoes.

Trickle the whole lot with extra virgin olive oil and sprinkle with the merest few drops of cider vinegar, then season with salt and pepper. Finally, scatter the parsley leaves over the top.

Serve straight away or, for optimum flavour, leave to stand for 20–30 minutes before serving.

SWAPS To give this salad an Asian feel, replace the parsley with coriander leaves. For the dressing, instead of the olive oil and cider vinegar, mix 1 tablespoon rice wine vinegar with 1 tablespoon sunflower oil, 2 teaspoons toasted sesame oil, 2 teaspoons soy sauce and a pinch of sugar.

Fennel, orange, watercress

This is a fantastic summer or autumn salad – perfect to serve before, with or after a roast chicken, or alongside a simply grilled or barbecued oily fish, such as sardines or mackerel. Sweet, sharp orange flesh and crunchy, aniseedy fennel are a great match, and the pepperiness of watercress really brings the dish alive.

Serves 4

2 oranges

2 medium fennel bulbs

1 tablespoon extra virgin olive oil

A squeeze of lemon juice

About 100g watercress

Sea salt and freshly ground black pepper

Using a fine grater, lightly grate the zest from one of the oranges into a large bowl. Now slice all the peel and pith off both oranges. To do this, cut a slice off the base of each and stand the orange on a board. Then use a sharp knife to cut down through the peel and pith, slicing it away completely, in sections. Now, working over the bowl of zest to catch any juice, slice the segments of orange out from between the membranes, dropping them into the bowl. Remove any pips as you go. Squeeze out the remaining juice from the orange membrane into the bowl.

Slice the base and tip off the fennel bulbs, reserving any fresh green fronds that are still attached. Remove any tough outer layers, then slice the fennel as thinly as you can. Add to the oranges, along with the extra virgin olive oil, a small squeeze of lemon juice and some salt and pepper. Toss together well and leave for at least 10 minutes, to allow the fennel to soften.

Remove any tough stalks from the watercress and pat dry. Mix the fennel and orange again, add the watercress sprigs and toss lightly. Divide between serving plates and finish with a touch more black pepper and any reserved fennel fronds.

PLUS ONE Try sprinkling the salad with about 50g lightly toasted flaked almonds or other nuts such as cashews or pine nuts.

Beetroot, apple, pecans

Beetroot works beautifully with apples, so this is a particularly good introduction to raw beetroot – if you haven't tried it before. In its simplest form, this salad makes a lovely starter for an autumn meal. Or, for a good light lunch, add some nutty Cheddar, and perhaps a few salad leaves, and serve with some crusty bread.

Serves 4

2 small-medium beetroot (about 200g in total)

2 medium crisp, tart dessert apples

125g pecan nuts (or walnuts), lightly toasted

For the dressing

1 tablespoon cider vinegar

3 tablespoons extra virgin rapeseed or olive oil

½ teaspoon English mustard

A pinch of sugar

Sea salt and freshly ground black pepper

To make the dressing, put all the ingredients in a jam jar, screw on the lid and shake until emulsified. Set aside.

Trim and peel the beetroot. Cut into quarters, then slice thinly into a bowl. Quarter the apples, remove the cores, then slice thinly and add to the bowl with the beetroot. Add the toasted pecans and dressing and toss together.

Arrange the salad on individual plates and finish with a grinding of pepper.

PLUS ONE To make this very simple salad more substantial and savoury, add 50–75g crumbled or coarsely grated Cheddar or other firm, nutty cheese.

PLUS TWO I sometimes like to serve this salad on a bed of crisp green salad leaves too.

SWAPS Use firm pears instead of apples. And if you're going for the cheesy plus one, try blue cheese instead of Cheddar.

Fennel, apple, goat's cheese

As simple salads go, this is about as crisp and refreshing as it gets – and it looks very elegant too. With some crusty brown bread, or toast trickled with olive oil, it's all you need for a light lunch, but it also works well alongside a good baked potato.

Serves 4

2 medium fennel bulbs

2 tablespoons extra virgin olive oil

A good squeeze of lemon juice

2 medium crisp, tart dessert apples

100g fairly mild, firm goat's cheese

Sea salt and freshly ground black pepper

Remove the tough, outer layers from the fennel bulbs and trim off the base and the top, reserving any fresh green fronds that are still attached. Slice the fennel bulbs from top to bottom, as thinly as you can. Place in a bowl with the extra virgin olive oil, a good squeeze of lemon juice and some salt and pepper. Toss well and leave to marinate for about 30 minutes.

Just before serving, quarter and core the apples, then slice thinly. Add them to the fennel and toss together. Taste and add more lemon juice, salt and/or pepper as needed.

Arrange the salad on individual plates. Slice, shave or crumble the cheese over the top and finish with any little fronds of fennel you have and a sprinkling of pepper.

PLUS ONE A scattering of cold, cooked Puy lentils (see page 27), lightly dressed with a dash of olive oil, gives an extra nutty texture to this salad and ups the protein.

SWAP If you're avoiding or cutting down on dairy foods, then you could simply replace the goat's cheese with cooked lentils.

Carrots, yoghurt, coriander

This simple combination of warm flavours from the carrot, orange and coriander is beautifully cooled by the gentle tang of yoghurt. I like to serve it with a clutch of other dishes as part of a mezze spread. Alternatively, served with warm flatbreads, it makes a delicious starter.

Serves 4

A good bunch of young carrots (12–20), trimmed with a little of the green top left on, scrubbed

3 tablespoons extra virgin olive oil

Finely grated zest and juice of 1 orange

4 tablespoons plain wholemilk yoghurt

A small bunch of coriander, tough stalks removed

A pinch of dried chilli flakes or ½ fresh red chilli, deseeded and finely chopped (optional)

Sea salt and freshly ground black pepper

Bring a large pan of salted water to the boil and add the carrots. Bring back to the boil and cook for 4–6 minutes, until almost tender but just firm to the bite. Drain and leave to cool just a little.

Combine half the extra virgin olive oil with the zest and juice of the orange. While the carrots are still warm, toss them in this dressing and season with salt and pepper.

Lay the warm carrots out over a large plate or serving platter and add the yoghurt in dollops. Scatter over whole coriander sprigs, along with the chilli if using, and some more salt and pepper. Trickle over the rest of the olive oil and any remaining dressing.

Serve the salad with warm pittas or flatbreads to soak up all the lovely juices.

PLUS ONE To make more of a meal of this salad, you can add a generous handful of cooked (or tinned) chickpeas. Toss them in a pan with a little olive oil, a sprinkling of paprika and a pinch of salt, then scatter over the warm carrots before dressing with the yoghurt and coriander.

SWAP Flat-leaf parsley works very well in place of the coriander.

Celeriac, lentils, raisins

This side salad has been a family favourite for some time now. The flavours and textures of the three ingredients are very different but the combination is truly harmonious. If you object to dried fruit in salads, the dressed celeriac and lentils alone are a delicious combination – or try them with one of the suggested added extras.

Serves 4

125g Puy lentils

1 garlic clove (unpeeled), bashed

1 bay leaf (optional)

A few parsley stalks (optional)

3 tablespoons extra virgin olive oil

Juice of 1 small orange, or 75ml apple juice

100g raisins

300g celeriac

2 teaspoons cider vinegar

Sea salt and freshly ground black pepper

Put the lentils into a saucepan and cover with cold water. Bring to the boil and boil for 1 minute only, then drain and return to the pan. Pour on enough water to cover them by 1cm or so. Add the garlic, and bay leaf and parsley stalks, if using. Bring to a very gentle simmer and cook slowly for about 25 minutes, topping up with boiling water if necessary, until tender but not mushy.

Drain the lentils and discard the herbs and garlic. Toss with 1 tablespoon of the extra virgin olive oil and some salt and pepper and set aside to cool completely.

Warm the orange or apple juice in a small pan until hot but not boiling. Remove from the heat, throw in the raisins and leave to soak in the hot juice for at least half an hour.

Meanwhile, peel the celeriac, then cut into very thin matchsticks or julienne.

Drain the raisins and set aside, reserving the juice. Mix this juice with the remaining 2 tablespoons olive oil, the cider vinegar and some salt and pepper to make a dressing.

Add the dressing to the lentils, along with the celeriac and raisins. Toss to combine, then leave for at least 20 minutes – up to an hour – to allow the flavours to mingle before serving.

PLUS ONE To add colour and an extra layer of flavour, toss plenty of flat-leaf parsley through the salad just before serving.

PLUS TWO Some thin slices of crisp, sweet-tart dessert apple are a lovely finishing touch – try an Ashmead's Kernel or Orleans Reinette if you can; or a good, firm Cox.

Spinach, mushrooms, blue cheese

Raw mushrooms can be very tasty in a salad, providing they are paired with a good dressing and some robust companions. This example makes a nice starter, and a rather good side dish to a simple pizza. As with all pared-down recipes, particularly where the ingredients are served raw, quality is vital. Use only very fresh, fleshy baby spinach leaves and choose some really fresh, firm mushrooms. I like to use a creamy blue cheese with a hint of sweetness, such as Cornish Blue or Harbourne Blue goat's cheese.

Serves 4

100g baby leaf spinach

100g closed-cap mushrooms

100g blue cheese, cubed or crumbled

Sea salt and freshly ground black pepper

For the dressing

½ garlic clove

½ teaspoon English mustard

2 teaspoons cider vinegar

1 teaspoon clear honey

3 tablespoons extra virgin olive oil

Start by making the dressing. Crush the garlic with a pinch of salt, then put it into a jam jar with the mustard, cider vinegar, honey, extra virgin olive oil and a grinding of pepper. Screw the lid on and shake vigorously to emulsify the ingredients. Taste and add more salt and pepper if necessary.

Place the baby spinach leaves in individual bowls or on one large platter. Trim and finely slice the mushrooms, then add roughly half of them to the spinach, along with about half of the cheese. Trickle over half of the dressing and toss lightly together.

Arrange the remaining mushrooms and blue cheese over the salad, trickle over some more dressing and serve.

PLUS ONE Crumbled cooked chestnuts make a stunning addition to this salad, particularly if you give them a few minutes with a little butter in a hot frying pan first, to lightly caramelise them. Other nuts are good here too – try lightly toasted walnuts or flaked almonds.

Cauliflower, tomatoes, capers

Sweet-tangy tomatoes and salty capers make an excellent foil to cauliflower. I like to eat this salad as a course on its own with some toasted bread trickled with good olive oil, but it also goes very well with a mild cheese, cold meats or a potato dish.

Serves 4

1 small-medium cauliflower (800g–1kg)

300g ripe plum or large round tomatoes

2 tablespoons baby capers (salted are best), rinsed

3 tablespoons extra virgin olive oil

A good squeeze of lemon juice

Sea salt and freshly ground black pepper

A little coarsely chopped flat-leaf parsley to finish (optional)

Trim the cauliflower and chop into very small florets. Bring a pan of salted water to the boil, add the cauliflower, return to a simmer and cook for 2 minutes until just tender with a bit of crunch. Drain and rinse under cold water, then drain again thoroughly and put into a bowl.

Cut the tomatoes in half, remove the seeds and clinging juicy bits, and trim out the white stalky ends. Roughly chop the flesh and add to the cauliflower.

Add the capers, extra virgin olive oil, lemon juice and some salt and pepper to the salad and toss gently. Leave at cool room temperature for at least an hour, or up to 3 hours to allow the flavours to mingle a little, turning once or twice.

Taste and adjust the seasoning with more salt and pepper if you think it is needed, then serve, scattered with a little chopped parsley, if you like.

Celeriac, cabbage, mustard

This is really a cross between a classic French rémoulade and a coleslaw. Remoulaw? Coleslade? Never mind, it's a lovely fresh, crunchy winter treat that you can serve with, before or after just about any dish. I particularly like it alongside meat-and-spud classics such as stew and mash or a shepherd's pie. You can use a good ready-made mayonnaise, adding the double dose of mustard, but this homemade version is very quick and much nicer.

Serves 4–6

300g celeriac
200g white cabbage

For the mustard mayo
½ garlic clove
1 teaspoon cider vinegar
2 large egg yolks
2 teaspoons English mustard
2 teaspoons wholegrain mustard
A pinch of sugar
150ml sunflower oil
100ml extra virgin olive oil
Sea salt and freshly ground black pepper

Start with the mayonnaise. Crush the garlic to a paste with a pinch of salt and put into a bowl with the cider vinegar, egg yolks and both mustards. Add some salt and pepper and a pinch of sugar and stir together. Combine the two oils in a jug. Start whisking them into the egg yolk mixture, a few drops at a time to start with, then in small dashes. You can use an electric whisk or a food processor, but you will still need to trickle slowly and carefully, especially to begin with. Stop when you have a glossy, wobbly mayonnaise. Taste and add more salt, pepper, sugar, vinegar or mustard if you think it needs it.

Peel the celeriac and cut into very thin matchsticks or julienne, or you can coarsely grate it if you prefer. Stir immediately into the mayonnaise so it doesn't get a chance to brown.

Remove any damaged outer leaves from the cabbage and trim away any thick stems, then shred very thinly. Stir this into the mayonnaise too. Taste the mixture again to check the seasoning, then serve.

PLUS ONE OR TWO To make this a slightly more substantial salad, stir through some cooked and cooled Puy lentils (see page 27). Flat-leaf parsley, either coarsely or finely chopped, is another very good addition.

Tomatoes, bread, olive oil

Based on the classic Italian panzanella, this bread and tomato salad is even simpler. You need robust, open-textured bread, to absorb all the lovely tomato juices, and the tomatoes themselves must be good, tasty ones. If you use a mixture of varieties and sizes, the salad looks particularly enticing.

Serves 4

150g sourdough or other coarse bread (1–2 days old)

5 tablespoons extra virgin olive oil

About 500g tomatoes (ideally a mixture of types, shapes and colours)

1 garlic clove, halved (optional)

A good handful of basil leaves

A pinch of sugar (optional)

Sea salt and freshly ground black pepper

Preheat the oven to 180°C/Gas 4. Tear the bread into small, bite-sized chunks. Put them into a bowl with 3 tablespoons of the extra virgin oil and some salt and pepper. Toss well to coat. Scatter on a baking tray and bake for 10–15 minutes until golden. Leave to cool completely.

Meanwhile, cut the tomatoes into bite-sized pieces (halve cherry tomatoes, cut medium tomatoes into wedges, etc). Take a large bowl and, if you fancy a little garlicky tang to your salad, rub the inside of the bowl with the cut surface of the garlic clove. Add the tomatoes, along with the remaining 2 tablespoons olive oil. Tear about two-thirds of the basil over the tomatoes and add some salt and pepper. Toss well and leave to macerate while the bread is cooling.

When the bread is cooled, toss it thoroughly with the tomatoes. Taste and add more salt and pepper if necessary, plus a pinch of sugar if you like. Leave for at least 30 minutes – up to 2 hours – so the bread can soften a little. Toss one more time, then scatter over the remaining basil leaves and serve.

PLUS ONE Add some coarsely chopped stoned olives to the salad for extra flavour.

PLUS TWO, THREE AND FOUR Add a thinly sliced red onion, a few anchovy fillets and a scattering of baby capers, and you have pretty much a classic panzanella.

Fennel, tangerine, pumpkin seeds

The freshness of tangerines is the perfect partner to fennel's aniseedy tang. A handful of crunchy pumpkin seeds seals the deal very nicely.

Serves 4

2 fennel bulbs

2 tablespoons extra virgin olive oil, plus a little extra to finish if needed

4 tangerines or clementines

2 tablespoons pumpkin seeds

1 teaspoon cider vinegar

Sea salt and freshly ground black pepper

Preheat the grill to high. Remove the tough, outer layer from the fennel bulbs and trim off the base and the top. Slice the fennel very thinly, from root to tip, then toss with the 2 tablespoons extra virgin olive oil and some salt and pepper.

Spread the fennel out in a shallow roasting dish or grill pan and grill for 10–12 minutes, stirring once or twice, until tender and tinged with brown. Leave to cool completely. (You can also cook the fennel on a barbecue, or in a ridged cast-iron griddle pan.)

Meanwhile, peel the tangerines and slice them across into rounds, about 5mm thick. Set aside the top and bottom pieces.

Toast the pumpkin seeds in a dry frying pan over a medium heat for a minute or so until fragrant and just starting to colour. Tip out on to a plate and leave to cool.

Squeeze the juice from the end pieces of tangerine directly over the cooled grilled fennel. Add the cider vinegar and toss lightly. Taste and add a little more olive oil, salt and pepper if you think the fennel needs it.

Arrange the fennel slices on large individual plates and lay the tangerine slices on top. Scatter the toasted pumpkin seeds over the salad and trickle over any remaining dressing from the fennel to serve.

SWAPS Instead of tangerine slices, use segments of orange or pink grapefruit, sliced out from between their membranes (see page 18). Thinly sliced apple is another alternative. If you don't have pumpkin seeds, then lightly toasted sunflower seeds, pine nuts, walnuts or pecans can provide the required nutty crunch.

Cabbage, avocado, lentils

This unusual combination works superbly. It has become a favourite lunch, and I would happily serve it as a dinner party starter too. It's light and fresh, with a lovely creamy richness from the avocado.

Serves 4

100g Puy lentils

1 garlic clove (unpeeled), bashed

1 bay leaf (optional)

A handful of parsley stalks (optional)

½ small green cabbage, such as Savoy (about 200g in total)

2 avocados

Sea salt and freshly ground black pepper

For the dressing

Juice of ½ lemon

4 tablespoons extra virgin olive oil

1 heaped teaspoon English mustard

½ teaspoon sugar

Put the lentils into a saucepan and cover with cold water. Bring to the boil and boil for 1 minute, then drain and return to the pan. Pour on enough water to cover by 1cm or so. Add the garlic, and bay leaf and parsley stalks, if using. Bring to a very gentle simmer and cook slowly for about 25 minutes, topping up with boiling water if necessary, until tender but not mushy.

Meanwhile, whisk the dressing ingredients together in a bowl and season with salt and pepper. (Or shake in a jam jar to emulsify.)

Drain the lentils and discard the garlic and herbs. Toss with 2 tablespoons of the dressing, add a little more salt and pepper and set aside to cool completely.

Bring a pan of salted water to the boil. Remove the tough stalks from the cabbage and coarsely shred the leaves. Add to the boiling water and cook for 30 seconds–1 minute, no more. Drain in a colander, then immediately refresh the cabbage by holding the colander under cold running water. This will stop the cooking process and helps to keep the brilliant green colour. Drain the cabbage again, then give it a whirl in a salad spinner to remove all water.

When the cabbage and the lentils are ready, peel and stone the avocados and cut the flesh into 2–3cm pieces. Gently toss the cabbage with the lentils and avocado. Divide between individual bowls, trickle over the remaining dressing and serve.

PLUS ONE A scattering of crisply fried bacon is a pretty good way to top this off.

SWAPS This recipe works well with a good crisp lettuce, such as Cos or Little Gem, instead of the cabbage. There's no need to cook the lettuce – just wash it, spin it dry and coarsely shred it.

Beetroot, egg, anchovy

Sweet, earthy beetroot, salty-sharp anchovy and rich, soft-middled boiled egg. Lovely. Even if you're not a fan of the pungent little fish, the beetroot, egg and dressing combo works well in its own right.

Serves 4

400g small beetroot, scrubbed

4 large eggs, at room temperature

12–16 anchovy fillets in oil, drained

A small handful of chives, snipped (optional)

Sea salt and freshly ground black pepper

For the mustard dressing

1 teaspoon English mustard

½ teaspoon sugar

1 teaspoon cider vinegar

¼ garlic clove, crushed with a pinch of salt

2½ tablespoons extra virgin rapeseed or olive oil

Put the beetroot into a saucepan and cover with water. Bring to the boil, then lower the heat and simmer for 30–45 minutes, or until tender. Drain and allow to cool, then rub off the skins. If the beetroot are really baby, leave whole; otherwise, cut them in half or into quarters.

Bring another pan of water to the boil. Add the eggs, return to a simmer and cook for 6 minutes. Drain and hold the pan of eggs under cold running water to stop the cooking. Cool, then peel and quarter them.

To make the mustard dressing, put all the ingredients into a jam jar with some salt and pepper. Screw on the lid and shake to emulsify. Taste and add more sugar, salt or pepper if necessary.

Lay the beetroot and boiled eggs out on individual plates and season well with salt and pepper. Lay the anchovy fillets over the top and trickle over the dressing. Sprinkle with the chives, if using, and serve.

Potatoes, beans, sardines

This simple but substantial summer salad is a crude reworking of a niçoise, with tinned sardine fillets serving admirably and sustainably in place of questionable tuna. All you need add is some lemon juice, salt and pepper. I like to use locally caught Cornish pilchards from The Pilchard Works, but any well-sourced sardines or pilchards will do. If you use whole sardines, rather than fillets, you might want to remove the bones.

Serves 4

500g small new or salad potatoes

200g French beans, trimmed

120g tin sardine fillets (or pilchard fillets) in olive oil

A good squeeze of lemon juice

A little extra virgin olive oil (if needed)

Sea salt and freshly ground black pepper

Cut the potatoes into 2 or 3 pieces each. Put them into a saucepan, cover with water and add salt. Bring to the boil, then lower the heat and simmer for 6–10 minutes until tender. Meanwhile, cut the French beans into 3–4cm lengths and add to the pan for the last 3–5 minutes – they should still have a bit of crunch when cooked. Drain the potatoes and beans well and leave to cool until warm, or at room temperature.

Tip the sardines (or pilchards), with their oil, into a large bowl. Add some salt and pepper and the lemon juice, then use a fork to mash the sardines to a rough purée.

Tip the cooled potatoes and beans into the bowl with the sardines and toss thoroughly so the vegetables are well coated in the fishy dressing. Taste and add more salt, pepper, lemon juice and/or a little extra virgin olive oil as needed, then serve.

PLUS ONE Try stirring a handful of roughly chopped stoned black olives into the mix.

PLUS TWO A hard-boiled egg or two will add further to the salade niçoise effect.

SWAP If you can't get French beans, this salad is also lovely with Little Gem lettuce hearts. You could shred the lettuce or just halve or quarter the hearts.

Beans, ham, tomatoes

This is an example of how a delicious trio of ingredients can be exploited in more than one way to give totally different results – I refer you to the rich bacon, bean and tomato stew on page 272, which starts with the same building blocks as this lovely, fresh salad.

It's important to give the salad time to macerate before serving, to allow the tomato juices to run and the flavours to develop. I give it 15 minutes at the very least, or make it the day before and keep it in the fridge, adding the ham and final sprinkling of thyme at the last minute.

Serves 4

400g tin white beans, such as cannellini, drained

About 200g cherry tomatoes, quartered (or other flavoursome tomatoes, cut into smallish pieces)

2 or 3 good sprigs of thyme, leaves only (optional)

About 50g thinly sliced Parma ham or other air-dried ham

Sea salt and freshly ground black pepper

For the dressing

¼ garlic clove, crushed with a good pinch of salt

½ teaspoon English mustard

2 teaspoons balsamic vinegar

4 tablespoons extra virgin olive oil

A pinch of sugar

To make the dressing, put the crushed garlic and mustard into a bowl and whisk in the balsamic vinegar and extra virgin olive oil, then add the sugar and season with plenty of salt and pepper. (Or shake the ingredients together in a jam jar to emulsify.)

Tip the beans into a bowl, add the dressing and toss well. Add the tomatoes and most of the thyme leaves, if using, and stir in. Leave for at least 15 minutes, so the tomato juices start to run a little, then stir again, taste and adjust the seasoning if necessary.

Serve the bean and tomato salad topped with the salty ham and a final scattering of thyme leaves, if you have them.

SWAPS In place of ham, use crisp-fried, thinly sliced pancetta. Or top the bean and tomato salad with crumbled blue cheese or goat's cheese, anchovy fillets or chunks of tinned sardine.

Squash, ricotta, ham

With its beautiful colours and deliciously varied textures, this is a lovely 'layered' dish of contrasting ingredients. It's a real looker too – ideally served on a big platter in the middle of the table as a starter or component of a main meal.

Serves 4

800g–1kg squash, such as Crown Prince, butternut or kabocha

3–4 garlic cloves (unpeeled), lightly bashed

Several sprigs of thyme (optional)

2 tablespoons extra virgin olive or rapeseed oil, plus extra to serve

100g ricotta

30–40g thinly sliced Parma ham or other air-dried ham

A squeeze of lemon juice

Sea salt and freshly ground black pepper

Preheat the oven to 190°C/Gas 5. Peel and deseed the squash, then cut into big chunks. Put into a roasting dish with the garlic, and a few thyme sprigs, if using. Trickle over the 2 tablespoons extra virgin oil, sprinkle with some salt and pepper and toss to ensure the squash is well coated. Roast for 40–50 minutes, or until the squash is tender and starting to caramelise, giving it a stir halfway through cooking. Discard the garlic and thyme, if used. Leave to cool completely.

Put the roasted squash on individual plates or a large platter. Dot the ricotta over the top. Tear the ham into shreds and scatter these over the squash and ricotta. Tear the leaves from the rest of the thyme sprigs, if you have them, and scatter over the dish. Add a grinding of black pepper, a little sprinkle of salt and a generous trickle of extra virgin oil. Finish with a judicious squeeze of lemon juice, then serve.

PLUS ONE This combination looks and tastes wonderful when served on a bed of baby salad leaves, or scattered with a handful of micro-salad, such as cress.

SWAPS You don't have to use air-dried ham here: any good, thinly sliced ham tastes pretty good, as does cooled, crisp-cooked bacon. For a really quick, very different dish, replace the roasted squash with slices of ripe, juicy pear.

Chicory, peaches, black pudding

This is an unusual but very successful combination of sweet and sharp, rich and savoury, and bitter and crisp. The black pudding turns what would be a very light salad into something deeply satisfying, but not heavy – buy the best pudding you can find, ideally an organic one.

Serves 4

1 large or 2 small heads of red or white chicory

4 ripe peaches

About 400g black pudding

4 tablespoons extra virgin olive oil

A small knob of butter

1 tablespoon red wine vinegar

1–2 teaspoons thyme leaves (optional)

Sea salt and freshly ground black pepper

Trim the base from the chicory, then separate the leaves and wash and dry them. Using a sharp knife, split the larger leaves down the middle.

Halve and stone the peaches, then cut each peach half into 5 or 6 wedges. Peel them if you like.

Remove the skin from the black pudding and break up the meat into large chunks. Heat 1 tablespoon of the extra virgin olive oil with the butter in a frying pan over a medium heat. Add the black pudding and fry until browned on all sides, allowing the edges to crisp slightly. Remove from the heat. Divide the warm black pudding between warm plates.

Add the wine vinegar, remaining olive oil and most of the thyme leaves, if using, to the pan and stir to incorporate the meat juices and make a warm dressing.

Arrange the peach wedges and chicory leaves over and around the black pudding. Trickle the dressing over everything and season with salt and pepper. Scatter over the rest of the thyme leaves, if you have them, and serve.

SWAPS Apple slices, gently fried in a little butter, make an ideal autumnal alternative to the peaches.

ANOTHER TAKE You can make an all-cooked version of this dish, which is a particularly good idea if your peaches are under-ripe. After frying the black pudding, set it aside on a warm plate. Then gently fry the peaches in the pan for couple of minutes each side, until just colouring; remove and set aside. Add a dash more oil if the pan looks dry and lightly wilt the chicory leaves in the hot pan until softened. Make a dressing with the pan juices, adding a dash of olive oil and a splash of wine vinegar, as above.

Apple, mint, lime

This explosive little salad takes its inspiration from a favourite River Cottage cocktail, the apple mojito. Take away the rum, rustle up a simple fruit salad and it's still a super-fresh zinger. You could serve it as a palate-cleanser, or to wrap up a hearty meal after the cheese course.

Serves 2

2 large limes

3 medium-sized, sweet dessert apples

½–1 teaspoon sugar

A handful of mint leaves

Using a sharp knife, slice off both ends of each lime. Put the limes on a board, flat end down, and carefully slice away all the peel and pith from each. Then carefully cut down between the membranes to release each segment of lime. Drop them into a bowl. Squeeze any juice left in the membrane into another bowl.

Peel the apples; set one aside for your dressing. Cut the other two into quarters, remove the core and then cut into wedges. Immediately add to the lime segments and toss to combine.

For the dressing, grate the last apple and squeeze in your hands over the bowl of lime juice to extract all the juice. Whisk the lime and apple juice together with sugar to taste.

Finely chop the mint leaves and toss with the apple and lime segments. Divide the salad between individual plates and trickle over the juicy, minty dressing.

SWAPS You can use lemon instead of lime, pear instead of apple, and lemon verbena instead of – or as well as – mint.

Orange, cucumber, strawberry

This is a simple fruit salad, with the crunch of cucumber – technically a fruit despite its salad veg status – giving a surprising, non-sweet contrast to the oranges and strawberries. You can serve this to start a meal or to end it, or to refresh the palate after a meaty main course and before cheese.

Serves 4

2 oranges

½ cucumber

About 350g ripe, sweet strawberries

10–12 large mint leaves, finely shredded

Freshly ground black pepper (optional)

Slice all the peel and pith off both oranges. To do this, cut a slice off the base of each and stand the orange on a board. Then use a sharp knife to cut down through the peel and pith, slicing it away completely, in sections. Now, working over a large bowl to catch the segments and any juice, slice the segments of orange out from between the membranes. Remove any pips as you go. Squeeze out the remaining juice from the orange membranes into the bowl.

Peel the cucumber and cut it into thin slices, about 3mm thick. Hull the strawberries, then cut each into 3 or 4 slices depending on size.

Add the cucumber and strawberries to the orange segments, along with the mint, and toss all gently together. A twist of freshly ground black pepper is an excellent, unexpected final tweak. Arrange the salad on a large serving platter or individual plates and serve.

PLUS ONE The last of the late strawberries in August sometimes overlap with the first Discovery apples in my garden. One or two of these, peeled, cored and sliced, makes a great addition to this gorgeous fresh salad.

Easy Starters and Soups

The best part of a meal is so often the starter, don't you

think? Frequently I am tempted to order two or three (or even four!) starters in a restaurant, and skip the main course. And at home we increasingly like to tuck into a spread of small, simple dishes, rather like tapas or mezze. So while the recipes in this chapter certainly function as 'starters' in the traditional sense, they also make fantastic 'sharing plates', and I'd like to encourage you to use them (and many other dishes in the book, for that matter) in this way.

The most striking starters often combine three highly contrasting elements. A whole host of time-honoured favourites can be deconstructed thus... The prawn cocktail = prawns, spiked mayonnaise, lettuce. Soupe à l'oignon = onions, bread, cheese. Moules marinières = mussels, garlic, wine. You get the idea.

Fond as I am of these oldies, my recipes come from a rather different place. There are combinations here that I hope will intrigue you – the asparagus dunked in yoghurt and a spice and nut dry 'dip' (page 59), for instance; or seared scallops scattered with summer peas and spring onions (page 72). These are dishes you probably won't have had before. And I'm betting they will bowl you over, not in spite of their simplicity, but because of it.

I've also included several soups. These are a bit of a special case, as they're pretty much the only recipes in the book in which the key ingredients are inextricably combined – often at high speed by a blender – so you might not immediately be able to tell what they actually are. Yet the principle still works. In each of them, something hefty and starchy (potato, bread, barley, white beans, celeriac) is mingled with something fresh and vibrant (tomatoes, apples, leeks) and the whole thing is finished off with something punchy or piquant (peppery olive oil, crumbled blue cheese, crispy bacon, flakes of smoked fish).

Even when those three elements are blitzed into a creamy smooth soup, I'm hoping your tastebuds will still discern the constituent flavours. That's part of the fun (and part of the challenge). I'm a soup fiend, you see, always at it, chopping and blending whatever I have to hand. It's often fresh vegetables, of course, the finest building blocks of great soups. But it can also be storecupboard staples: tinned pulses with a pinch of spice, for example. And I love creating soup from yesterday's leftovers, whether it's leftover veg blended with stock made from a good-quality cube, or a classic broth spun out of a great home-cooked chicken stock, made even more homey with noodles and a handful of shredded greens.

Asparagus, yoghurt, dukka

This makes a great starter or canapé. Griddling asparagus gives it a lovely sweet, caramelised flavour but, if you are short on time, just increase the spell in hot water to cook the spears through (3–6 minutes depending on thickness), then drain and serve. Dukka is a Middle Eastern mix of spices, seeds and nuts, traditionally served as a sort of dry dip.

Serves 4

16–20 asparagus spears

1 tablespoon extra virgin olive or rapeseed oil

150g plain wholemilk yoghurt

Sea salt and freshly ground black pepper

For the dukka

100g blanched whole almonds

1 tablespoon cumin seeds

1 tablespoon coriander seeds

3 tablespoons sesame seeds

1 tablespoon sunflower seeds

½ tablespoon extra virgin olive oil

½ garlic clove, finely grated

½ teaspoon dried chilli flakes

½ teaspoon flaky sea salt

Start with the dukka. Set a frying pan over a medium heat, add the almonds and all the seeds and allow to toast gently, tossing them often so they don't burn. When the almonds are lightly coloured and everything is smelling toasty and fragrant, tip the contents of the pan on to a plate to cool. When cool, transfer to a mortar.

Heat the extra virgin olive oil with the garlic and chilli flakes in the same frying pan over a medium heat for just a few seconds to take the rawness out of the garlic, then add to the seedy mix along with the flaky sea salt. Bash with the pestle but don't overdo it – I like to keep lots of texture in the dukka. Taste and add more chilli and salt if you like, bearing in mind the yoghurt will have a cooling, softening effect on the dish. Transfer to a serving bowl.

Bring a pan of salted water to the boil. Snap the woody ends off the asparagus, then drop the spears into the boiling water. Blanch for about 2 minutes, depending on thickness, until almost al dente; drain well. Toss the asparagus in a bowl with the extra virgin oil and a good seasoning of salt and pepper to coat.

Heat a ridged cast-iron griddle pan until searing hot. Add the asparagus and cook for about 5 minutes, turning from time to time, until tender and patched with brown. Arrange on a plate and serve with the yoghurt and dukka. To eat, dunk an asparagus spear first in the yoghurt, then in the dukka, before devouring.

SWAPS This is an excellent way to serve other char-grilled or barbecued veg: long batons of courgette or aubergine, thin slices of fennel or whole spring onions. These don't need blanching – just griddle or barbecue until cooked. If the veg are too soft for dipping, just arrange on a plate, dot with yoghurt and sprinkle with dukka.

Asparagus, egg, ham

Rich, salty flavours often work well with the intense taste of asparagus. This is an elegant starter, and if you serve this quantity for two rather than four you'll have a very decent lunch or supper.

Serves 4

16–20 asparagus spears

1 tablespoon extra virgin olive or rapeseed oil, plus extra to trickle

4 large eggs, at room temperature

4 slices of sourdough or other good bread

4 thin slices of Parma ham or other air-dried ham, roughly torn

Sea salt and freshly ground black pepper

Bring a pan of salted water to the boil. Snap the woody ends off the asparagus, then drop the spears into the boiling water. Blanch for about 2 minutes, depending on thickness, until almost al dente; drain well. Toss the asparagus in a bowl with the 1 tablespoon extra virgin olive oil and a good seasoning of salt and pepper.

Place a heavy-based non-stick frying pan or griddle pan over a medium-high heat. When hot, add the asparagus and cook for about 5 minutes, turning from time to time, until tender and patched with brown.

Meanwhile, poach the eggs. This is the way I do it: pour a 4–5cm depth of water into a wide saucepan or deep frying pan and bring to a rolling boil. Break each egg carefully into a cup or ramekin. When the water is boiling, turn off the heat and immediately but gently tip the eggs into the water. Put the lid on the pan and leave to cook in the residual heat for 2½–3 minutes. Carefully scoop up the eggs using a slotted spoon and check that the whites are set, with no jellyish clear bits left; if there are any, return the eggs to the water for 30 seconds. Give them half a minute in the spoon to drain and dab carefully with a piece of kitchen paper to help get rid of the water. Trim off any raggedy bits of white.

While the eggs are poaching, toast the bread, cut in half, trickle with a little extra virgin oil and place on warm plates. Lay the asparagus on the plates and scatter over the ham. Add the poached eggs and a grinding of black pepper, then serve.

SWAPS You can use crisp-fried bacon or pancetta in place of the air-dried ham. Or, for a more radical change, replace with kipper or smoked mackerel fillets, broken into chunks. You can also soft-boil or even fry rather than poach the eggs if you like.

Beetroot, feta, walnuts

A rich and beautifully coloured starter or side dish, this is
a gorgeous way to serve beetroot, and a lovely thing to have
on the table – or the rug – as part of a buffet or picnic.

Serves 4

About 500g beetroot

2–3 garlic cloves (unpeeled),
bashed, plus ½ peeled clove

A sprig of thyme (optional)

3 tablespoons extra virgin
rapeseed or olive oil

75g walnuts, lightly toasted

2 tablespoons walnut oil (or
additional extra virgin olive
or rapeseed oil)

75g feta

Sea salt and freshly ground
black pepper

Preheat the oven to 190°C/Gas 5. Scrub the beetroot and cut up
any larger ones into chunks, so the beetroot are all roughly the
same size. Put into a roasting tray with the whole garlic cloves,
thyme if using, 2 tablespoons extra virgin oil and some salt and
pepper. Shake the tray to toss all the ingredients together. Cover
with foil and bake until the beetroot are tender – about 1 hour,
but possibly longer. Discard the garlic and thyme, if used. Leave,
covered, to cool completely in the dish.

Crush the ½ garlic clove with a pinch of salt, using a large pestle
and mortar. Add the toasted walnuts and crush roughly, keeping
some chunky bits in the mix. Add the walnut oil and remaining
1 tablespoon olive or rapeseed oil (or 2 tablespoons olive or
rapeseed oil, if you're not using walnut oil) and stir with the
pestle to amalgamate.

Peel the cooked beetroot and slice into chunky pieces. Arrange on
a large plate or individual plates. Tip the juices from the beetroot
roasting dish into the mortar with the crushed walnut mixture.
Mix well. Taste and add pepper and some more salt if necessary,
bearing in mind that the feta is salty.

Crumble the feta into chunks and scatter over the beetroot, then
trickle or spoon the walnut mixture on top and it's ready to serve.
If you're serving the dish as a starter, accompany with some good
bread – sourdough or flatbreads would be ideal.

PLUS ONE A shot of bright green – in the form of flat-leaf parsley,
watercress, rocket, or just about any other leaf of your choice –
is a delicious fourth element in the mix. Scatter the leaves over
the plate first, lay the beetroot and feta on top and finish with the
walnut mix.

Egg, purple sprouting, garam masala

I love the complex yet delicate flavour of garam masala. This traditional Indian spice mix is often used to add fresh spicy flavours to a dish at the end of cooking and, provided you start with a good-quality blend that is well within its use-by date, it needs little more than a touch of heat to bring it alive. Combined with butter, it makes a gorgeous dressing for broccoli and eggs.

Serves 2

3 large eggs, at room temperature

About 250g purple sprouting broccoli, woody ends removed

50g butter

1 tablespoon extra virgin olive oil

1 garlic clove, grated or very finely chopped

2 teaspoons garam masala

Sea salt and freshly ground black pepper

Bring a pan of water to a rolling boil. Add the eggs, return to a simmer and cook for 6 minutes. Immediately drain and hold the pan of eggs under cold running water. This stops the eggs cooking at the right point: the yolks should still be a little soft when you cut into them. Carefully peel the eggs (under a trickle of cold tap water is easiest) and set them aside.

You can either steam or boil the purple sprouting broccoli. I like to steam it as it retains a little more of its fantastic colour this way and the delicate florets are less likely to get waterlogged. Either way, cook the broccoli for 2–6 minutes until just tender (just-picked home grown spears will only take a couple of minutes, shop-bought ones a little longer). Drain if necessary.

Melt the butter with the extra virgin olive oil in a small pan over a medium heat. Add the garlic, then the garam masala. Turn the heat down low and gently cook the spicy butter for 1–2 minutes. Season with salt and pepper.

Put the broccoli on a large warm plate or individual plates. Halve the boiled eggs and place on the broccoli. Dress the eggs and broccoli with the warm, fragrant butter. Season with a little more salt and pepper and serve.

SWAPS You can use standard broccoli here of course, but also other green veg. Tender young leaves of kale or cavolo nero are delicious, and green beans work well in the summer.

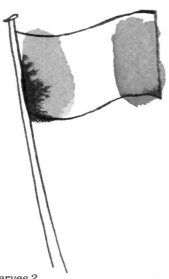

Tomato, mozzarella, basil

This is a great take on the tricolore Italian salad. Roasting the tomatoes and using a fresh basil pesto makes the flavours that much more intense.

Serves 2

About 4 tablespoons roasted tomato purée (see right)

1–2 balls of buffalo mozzarella

Sea salt and freshly ground black pepper

For the basil pesto

75g basil leaves (120g bunched basil, stalks removed)

25g Parmesan or hard, mature goat's cheese, finely grated

1 garlic clove, crushed

30g pine nuts, lightly toasted

A squeeze of lemon juice, or more to taste

Up to 100ml extra virgin olive oil

Make a half quantity of roasted tomato purée (as described on page 89); the finished sauce needs to be fairly thick – at least the consistency of double cream. If yours is thinner, put it into a pan and simmer gently to reduce and thicken. Leave to cool. Taste and add more salt and pepper if needed, then chill. (You'll have more than you need for this dish – what's left over will be wonderful in a sauce, soup or curry; it freezes well too.)

To make the pesto, put the basil, grated cheese, garlic and pine nuts into a food processor. Season well with salt and pepper, add a squeeze of lemon juice and blitz to a fairly fine, but still granular texture. Add the extra virgin olive oil a slosh at a time, pulsing the machine to blend it in, and stopping when you have a loose but still textured purée. Taste and add more salt, pepper and lemon juice if you think it is needed.

Spoon the chilled tomato sauce on to serving plates and add the mozzarella balls – kept whole or just roughly torn in half. Add the basil pesto and a generous grinding of black pepper. Serve straight away.

Artichoke, egg, capers

Globe artichokes are a delight to eat and to grow, but they are rather expensive to buy and a bit of a faff to prepare. This recipe makes the most of a small quantity of artichokes and is a lovely way to enjoy them.

Serves 4

4 large or 6 medium globe artichokes

A good squeeze of lemon juice

4 large eggs, at room temperature

4 teaspoons baby capers, rinsed and patted dry

For the dressing

¼ teaspoon Dijon or English mustard

⅛ garlic clove (a mere morsel), crushed with a little pinch of salt

1 teaspoon cider vinegar

2½ tablespoons extra virgin rapeseed or olive oil

A pinch of sugar

Sea salt and freshly ground black pepper

To prepare the artichokes, remove 3 or 4 rows of the outer tough leaves from around the base of each artichoke and trim the stem back to the base. Bring a large pan of salted water to the boil and add the lemon juice. Add the artichokes and cook until the base is tender to the point of a knife and the leaves pull away easily. Freshly picked young artichokes may cook in 8 minutes; older, larger ones can take 20 minutes or so. Lift the cooked artichokes out with tongs and stand them upside down to drain and cool.

Meanwhile, bring a pan of water to a rolling boil. Lower the eggs into the pan, return to a simmer and cook for 7 minutes. Drain and hold the pan of eggs under cold running water to stop the cooking. Carefully peel the eggs.

For the dressing, whisk the ingredients together in a small bowl or shake in a jam jar to emulsify. Set aside.

Pull the leaves away from the artichokes – the first few may still be rather fibrous, but as you work in towards the heart, the bases of the leaves will become tender and are delicious to nibble. When you've pulled away all the leaves, the fibrous 'choke' on top of the heart will be exposed. Remove this, either by scraping it out with a teaspoon or by cutting the heart in half and cutting out the choke with a small knife. Thickly slice each heart.

Quarter the boiled eggs and arrange on a large plate or individual plates with the sliced artichoke hearts. Scatter the capers over them and then trickle with the dressing. Finish with a grinding of black pepper.

ANOTHER TAKE Cut the artichoke hearts into smaller pieces, roughly chop the eggs and capers, then toss everything together with the dressing. This is particularly good piled on to oiled toast as a bruschetta, or served with warm pitta or flatbreads.

Artichoke, yoghurt, lemon

Preparing these three elements yourself is simple enough, but if you want a near instant version of this dish, you can buy them ready-prepared from a good deli. If you make just one, go for the labneh – it's a doddle.

Serves 4

For the preserved lemons

8 unwaxed lemons

4 tablespoons coarse sea salt

OR

¼ large pickled lemon from a jar

For the labneh (yoghurt 'cheese')

500g plain wholemilk yoghurt

½ teaspoon fine sea salt

Extra virgin olive oil

Freshly ground black pepper

OR

250g ready-made labneh

For the artichokes

4 large or 6 medium globe artichokes

A good squeeze of lemon juice

About 200ml extra virgin olive oil

1 garlic clove (unpeeled), bashed

½ small red chilli, deseeded and finely chopped (optional)

1 small stem of rosemary (optional)

Sea salt and freshly ground black pepper

OR

250g char-grilled or roasted artichoke hearts in olive oil

To salt your own lemons, cut 4 lemons vertically into four, but not through to the ends, so the fruit is joined at the top and base. Pack sea salt into the cuts. Squash the salted lemons into a preserving jar. Seal and leave for a couple of days – the salt will draw out a lot of lemon juice. Squeeze enough juice from the other 4 lemons to cover the fruit in the jar and seal again. Store for at least 1 month before using, turning the jar upside down and back again every now and then. Once opened, store in the fridge – for up to a year if you keep the lemons covered by the liquid.

To make your own labneh, put the yoghurt in a bowl, add the salt and mix thoroughly. Line a sieve with muslin or a thin cotton cloth, place over a deep bowl and spoon in the salted yoghurt. Flip the sides of the muslin over the yoghurt to enclose it. Leave for 3–4 hours, until a significant amount of liquid has drained off and the yoghurt has the texture of crème fraîche. Transfer the labneh to a bowl or tub, trickle with extra virgin olive oil and season with black pepper. Refrigerate until needed. It will keep for a week.

To prepare your own artichoke hearts, cook the artichokes whole as described on page 69. When you've removed all the leaves and the hairy 'choke', quarter the hearts. Put them in a bowl with a little extra virgin olive oil, salt and pepper and toss to coat. Heat a ridged cast-iron griddle pan or heavy-based frying pan over a high heat. Cook the hearts over the fierce heat for a few minutes, turning once or twice, until patched with golden brown. Transfer to a bowl, add the garlic, and chilli and rosemary if using, and cover with extra virgin olive oil. Refrigerate for at least 24 hours, bringing them back to room temperature before serving.

To serve, put a generous spoonful of labneh on each plate, add the artichoke hearts and trickle with some of their oil. Scoop away and discard the soft flesh from the pickled lemon quarter, then slice the rind finely and scatter over the labneh and artichokes. Finish with a grinding of black pepper and enjoy with flatbreads.

Scallops, peas, spring onions

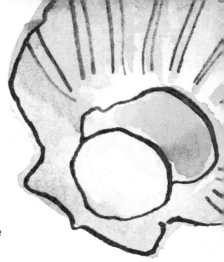

It takes a lot for me to depart from my favourite scallop and chorizo combination (see below), but sweet little peas and spring onions – with a hint of garlic – are a delightful diversion from that meaty path. Use diver-caught scallops if you can. If the orange 'corals' or roes look plump, bright and juicy, leave them attached. Frozen petits pois work well here, but if you happen to have peas growing in the garden, they'll be even better.

Serves 4

1 large bunch of spring onions (150–200g)

100g peas – either frozen petits pois or very fresh baby peas

2 tablespoons olive oil

12 scallops, cleaned, with corals attached if you like

A knob of butter

1 garlic clove, very finely chopped or grated

A squeeze of lemon juice

Sea salt and freshly ground black pepper

Trim off the rooty ends of the spring onions and remove the outer layer of skin. Cut into 5mm–1cm slices, on an angle.

If you are using frozen petits pois, put them into a sieve and pour a mugful of boiling water over them.

Heat 1 tablespoon olive oil in a large, heavy-based frying pan over a medium-low heat. Add the spring onions and let them sweat gently for about 5 minutes, until soft. Add the peas and toss with the spring onions for a minute or two. Season with a little salt and pepper, remove from the pan and set aside.

Wipe out the pan with kitchen paper. Add another 1 tablespoon oil and turn the heat up to high. Season the scallops with plenty of salt and pepper. When the pan is very hot, add the scallops – they should sizzle vehemently when they hit the hot pan. Leave them for about 1 minute, then carefully turn one over: this should reveal a gorgeously golden brown, caramelised underside. If so, carefully flip all the scallops over and cook for another minute until caramelised on the other side.

Reduce the heat to medium-low and return the peas and spring onions to the pan, along with a knob of butter and the garlic. Toss the whole lot together for another minute as the butter melts, then take off the heat. Give the scallops and veg a squeeze of lemon juice, then transfer to warm plates and serve.

PLUS ONE I can't resist saying that nuggets of chorizo or bacon – fried until crisp before you cook the spring onions – add a fine extra element to this lovely dish.

Fish, lime, mint

This delicate pared-down example of a ceviche – a dish where citrus juice is used to 'cook' raw fish – was devised by River Cottage head chef, Gill Meller. The bass is marinated in lime juice which, combined with lots of fresh mint, gives a lovely cool, fresh, uplifting taste. It's almost a sea bass mojito. If possible, use line-caught wild sea bass. Black bream also works well, but again go for line-caught rather than farmed.

Serves 4–6

2 skinless fillets of very fresh wild sea bass or black bream (about 300g in total)

Juice of 4 limes

3 teaspoons caster sugar

A small bunch of mint, leaves only

1 small green or red chilli (optional)

Sea salt and freshly ground black pepper

Using a sharp knife, cut the fish into bite-sized pieces, working across the grain of the fillet. Carefully check the fish for any bones, scales or scraps of skin – you want completely clean flesh. If in doubt, rinse the fish briskly in fresh cold water, then pat dry immediately with a spotlessly clean kitchen cloth.

Put the fish into a bowl with the lime juice and sugar. Season well with salt and a twist of black pepper. Have a taste at this point. If you feel it needs a little more sweetness or acidity, add more sugar or lime juice. Allow the fish to marinate for at least an hour, or up to 3 hours, in a cool place.

Shortly before serving, chop the mint and deseed and very finely slice the chilli, if using. Turn the chilli and/or mint through the marinated fish. Have a final taste and adjust the seasoning – it may need a little more sugar, a pinch of salt or some more mint.

Serve the ceviche on its own, or with a fresh cucumber salad sprinkled with some toasted, crushed hazelnuts.

ANOTHER TAKE I also like a zingy grapefruit and ginger version of this ceviche. Use 1 large pink or ruby grapefruit and prepare as for the oranges on page 18. Put the juice in a bowl with the fish. Finely grate a large chunk of root ginger, wrap the pulp in a scrap of muslin and squeeze out the ginger juice into the bowl. Leave to marinate with the sugar and seasoning. When the fish is ready, add the grapefruit segments too – and the chilli if you like. A little finely diced shallot is another nice addition.

Mackerel, juniper, bay

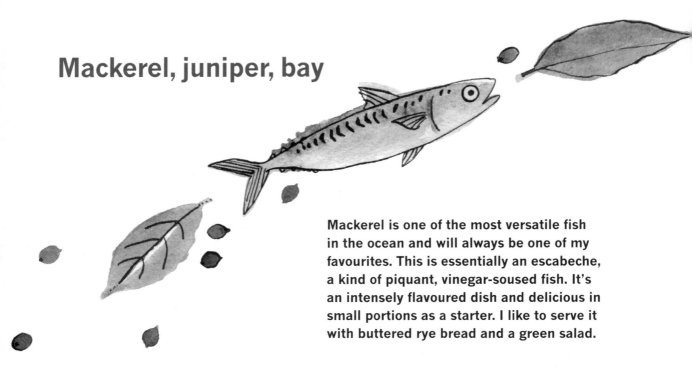

Mackerel is one of the most versatile fish in the ocean and will always be one of my favourites. This is essentially an escabeche, a kind of piquant, vinegar-soused fish. It's an intensely flavoured dish and delicious in small portions as a starter. I like to serve it with buttered rye bread and a green salad.

Serves 4

400g mackerel fillets
(about 4–6 fillets)

100ml cider vinegar

20–30 juniper berries,
lightly crushed

6 bay leaves, torn

2 garlic cloves (unpeeled),
lightly bashed

20g caster sugar

Sea salt and freshly ground
black pepper

Cut the mackerel fillets across into 5cm pieces, on an angle if you like, removing any remaining bones as you go. Season the fish well with salt and pepper.

Put the cider vinegar, juniper, bay, garlic, sugar and 100ml water in a medium saucepan and bring to a simmer. Allow to simmer for 1–2 minutes, so the flavours can infuse, then add the pieces of mackerel, skin side up. Try to make sure they all get a bit of the hot souse – swirling the pan gently to cover them. Cook the fish like this for just 1 minute or until opaque, then pour the entire contents of the pan on to a warm plate or shallow dish. Allow to cool to room temperature.

The mackerel is ready to eat now. Alternatively, you can keep it in the fridge for up to 5 days, bringing it back to room temperature before serving. The juices may jellify slightly, but don't worry, that's the sign of a great escabeche.

PLUS ONE Some strips of thinly pared orange zest included in the souse add a nice scented touch to the liquor. Squeeze a little orange juice over the finished dish too, if you like.

SWAP You can use fillets of extra-large sardines, such as Cornish pilchards, instead of the mackerel.

Venison, lemon, capers

This incredibly simple take on *carpaccio*, which looks amazing and tastes fantastic, is a glorious way to use venison. I like to serve it as a starter for a winter feast – you could even bring it out for Christmas dinner.

Serves 8

About 500g venison loin fillet in one piece, well trimmed

A little olive oil

1 teaspoon finely chopped thyme leaves (optional)

Sea salt and freshly ground black pepper

For the dressing

2 tablespoons baby capers, rinsed and drained

Finely grated zest of ½ lemon and 2 tablespoons juice

½ teaspoon caster sugar

4 tablespoons extra virgin olive oil

To serve

Seasonal salad leaves

Heat a frying pan over a high heat until searing hot. Massage the venison fillet lightly with olive oil, then season well with salt and pepper, and the chopped thyme, if using. Place in the hot pan, leave for about 30 seconds, then turn over. You want to cook only the outer surface of the meat, so keep the heat really high and have the loin in the pan for no more than a couple of minutes, turning it regularly so all sides are browned.

Remove the venison from the pan and set aside to rest on a board for 15–30 minutes, before you slice it.

For the dressing, just stir all the ingredients together in a bowl, then taste for seasoning. It will need pepper, but not necessarily salt because the capers are already salty.

Slice the venison into slivers, about 3mm thick, and arrange on serving plates. Pile the salad leaves into side bowls. Whisk the dressing again and trickle it over the meat and leaves. Serve straight away.

Black pudding, bacon, sprouts

Reluctant as I am to keep on banging the old 'If you think you don't like Brussels sprouts, try this' drum, I feel compelled to do so once in a while. Cook your sprouts lightly, reduce them to a thick, chunky purée with butter, cream, shallots and garlic, then see how you feel. Salty bacon is an obvious companion, and I've recently discovered that adding black pudding works really well too. It has a slightly mealy texture that provides the perfect ballast.

Serves 4

250g Brussels sprouts, trimmed

25g butter

2 shallots or ½ small onion, sliced

1 garlic clove, chopped

50ml double cream

A dash of sunflower, rapeseed or olive oil

8 rashers of streaky bacon

4 good, chunky slices of black pudding (about 125g in total), peeled

Sea salt and freshly ground black pepper

Bring a large pan of salted water to the boil. Add the sprouts and cook for 6–8 minutes, until tender. Drain well.

Meanwhile, melt the butter in a small frying pan over a medium heat and add the shallots or onion and garlic. Cook gently for 5–10 minutes until softened.

Tip the contents of the frying pan into a food processor and add the sprouts and cream. Blitz briefly to a purée – I prefer to keep it fairly coarse. Season well with salt and pepper and keep warm.

Heat a large frying pan over a medium heat. Add a dash of oil, then the bacon and fry for a few minutes, turning as necessary, until crisp. Push the bacon to the sides of the pan, add the black pudding and fry for 2–3 minutes on each side.

Divide the sprout purée between warm plates and top with the black pudding and crisp bacon. Add a sprinkling of salt and pepper and serve.

PLUS ONE To make a real meal of this lovely dish, serve with some toasted sourdough bread or fried potatoes.

PLUS TWO And to make it a deliciously greedy treat, top the black pudding with a fried egg!

Smoked fish, leek, potato

A creamy smoked fish and potato soup, known in Scotland as cullen skink, rarely fails to be supremely soothing and comforting. This very simple but utterly delicious example can be knocked up in little more than half an hour.

Serves 4

300g smoked pollack or smoked haddock fillet

650ml fish or vegetable stock

A large knob of butter

2 large leeks, trimmed, washed and finely sliced

500g potatoes, peeled and cut into 4–5mm cubes

4 tablespoons double cream

Sea salt and freshly ground black pepper

Finely chopped parsley to finish (optional)

Put the fish into a saucepan and add the stock. Bring slowly to the boil, then immediately turn off the heat, flip the fish over in the pan, cover and leave for 3 minutes. Turn the fish over again and check if it is cooked – the flesh should all be opaque and flake easily from the skin. If it's not quite done, leave it in the covered pan for a couple of minutes longer. Once cooked, lift it out of the pan on to a board, reserving the stock. Take the fish off the skin in large flakes, checking for any bones as you go.

Heat the butter in a large pan over a medium-low heat. Add the leeks and sweat gently for about 10 minutes until soft. Add the potatoes and reserved stock. Bring to a simmer and cook for about 10 minutes until the potatoes are tender.

Stir in the cream and flakes of smoked fish. Reheat gently, without boiling, then taste and add salt and pepper as needed. Ladle into warm bowls and finish with a scattering of parsley if you like. Serve at once, with brown bread and butter on the side.

SWAPS If you don't have leeks, but you do have spring onions, or even regular onions, you can happily use them instead. Trim and slice a couple of good bunches of spring onions and sweat for 5 minutes only. Or finely slice 2 large onions and sweat for 12–15 minutes, until soft and tender.

Tomato, bread, olive oil

This dish uses pretty much the same ingredients as the salad on page 34 to produce a very different result: a version of pappa al pomodoro – a coarse, Tuscan bread-and-tomato soup. Providing you've got good, tasty tomatoes and well-textured bread, you'll have a wonderful soup – comforting, yet full of fresh flavours. When fragrant fresh tomatoes are not available you can make a very good version using tinned plum tomatoes.

Serves 4

2kg ripe large tomatoes

2 tablespoons extra virgin olive oil, plus extra to finish

1 large garlic clove, sliced

About 300g slightly stale coarse-textured bread, such as sourdough, crusts removed, torn into pieces

A large handful of basil leaves, shredded

Sea salt and freshly ground black pepper

Put the tomatoes into a large bowl, cover with boiling water and leave for 2 minutes. Take one out and nick the skin with a small, sharp knife; the skin should start to peel away easily. If not, return the tomato to the hot water for a minute or two longer. Drain and skin all the tomatoes. Quarter the tomatoes and scoop out the seeds and clinging juicy bits into a sieve over a bowl. Rub this through to extract the juice. Roughly chop the tomato flesh.

Heat the 2 tablespoons extra virgin olive oil in a large saucepan over a medium-low heat. Add the garlic and cook gently for a minute or two without letting it colour. Add the chopped tomatoes and saved juice. Bring to a simmer and cook to reduce the sauce and intensify the flavour. You may need to do this only briefly, or it might take up to 30 minutes – it all depends on the flavour and juiciness of your tomatoes. Stop when you have a thick, rich, savoury sauce.

Remove from the heat and, while still hot, add the torn-up bread. Stir until it has absorbed the liquid and is starting to soften. You should now have a thick, chunky sort of purée. If it seems very dry, add a little boiling water but go easy: the soup is supposed to be really thick – the kind you can eat with a fork! Add some salt and pepper and most of the basil. Stir again, cover and leave for 15–20 minutes (to allow the bread to soak up the tomato and soften). Taste and add more salt and pepper if needed.

Serve warm, topped with the remaining basil and a generous slosh of very good extra virgin olive oil.

SWAP Instead of fresh tomatoes, use 3 x 400g tins plum tomatoes. Roughly crush the tomatoes in your hands before adding to the garlic and oil, along with the juice from the tins.

Red lentils, onion, bacon

I used to make this soup a lot when I was a student because it was easy, cheap, filling and very, very tasty. All those qualities remain and I still make it regularly today.

Serves 4

1 tablespoon rapeseed, sunflower or olive oil

4 rashers of smoked bacon, chopped

1 onion, chopped

200g split red lentils, well rinsed

1 bay leaf and/or a sprig of thyme (optional)

Sea salt and freshly ground black pepper

Heat the oil in a large saucepan over a medium heat. Add the bacon and fry for a few minutes so the fat starts to run. Add the onion and sweat gently over a low heat, stirring from time to time, for a good 10 minutes until soft and silky.

Stir in the lentils, then add about 800ml water. Add the bay and/or thyme if you have them. Bring to a simmer and cook, stirring from time to time, for about 15 minutes or until the lentils are completely soft and breaking down.

Remove the bay and/or thyme if used. Blitz the soup in a blender or with a handheld stick blender until smooth, adding just enough extra water to get a thick soup consistency. Taste and add salt and pepper as needed, then serve.

PLUS ONE You can finish the soup in various ways: a few more snippets of bacon, fried until crisp, make a lovely sprinkle, as do some simple fried bread croûtons. A swirl of yoghurt would be good, or a generous scattering of chopped parsley. Alternatively, slice another onion and sweat it gently in a little oil while the soup cooks, until very soft and golden. Float a tangle of this on top of the soup before serving.

Barley, onion, tomato

A wonderfully hearty soup, this is also very straightforward.
It relies on some good puréed tomatoes for the base flavour.
I prepare my own, but you could use a good-quality ready-made
passata instead. In this case, you might want to add some bay,
thyme and a whole garlic clove to the simmering soup to boost
the flavour. If you use a little less tomato purée, you'll produce
a risotto-style dish that will be delicious with some melting
mozzarella stirred through, or some slivers of Parmesan on top.

Serves 4

2 tablespoons olive,
rapeseed or sunflower oil

1 large onion, finely chopped

150g pearl barley or pearled
spelt, rinsed

750ml good beef or chicken
stock

Sea salt and freshly ground
black pepper

For the roasted tomato purée

2kg ripe tomatoes, halved

3 garlic cloves, finely
chopped

A few sprigs of thyme

2–3 bay leaves

2 tablespoons rapeseed
or olive oil

OR

750ml passata

To finish (optional)

Extra virgin olive oil

If you're making your own tomato purée, preheat the oven to
180°C/Gas 4. Lay the tomato halves, cut side up, in a single layer
in a large, deep baking tray. Scatter over the garlic and thyme,
tuck in the bay leaves, trickle over the oil and season with salt and
pepper. Roast in the oven for about an hour, maybe a bit longer,
until the tomatoes are completely soft and pulpy, and starting
to crinkle and caramelise on top. Remove and leave to cool off
for half an hour or so. Then tip them into a large sieve and rub
through with a wooden spoon, or use a mouli. Discard the skin
and pips. Your sauce is now ready to use. If you haven't produced
the full 750ml you need here, just increase the quantity of stock
to compensate.

To make the soup, heat the oil in a large saucepan over a medium-
low heat. Add the onion and sauté for 8–10 minutes until soft.
Stir in the pearl barley or spelt, then add the stock and 750ml
tomato purée or passata. Bring to a simmer and cook very gently,
uncovered, until the barley or spelt is tender. Barley should take
30–40 minutes; spelt will only need 20–25 minutes.

Taste and season with salt and pepper as needed, then ladle the
soup into bowls and serve. A trickle of good extra virgin olive oil
on top will not go amiss.

SWAP You can make a risotto version of this dish, replacing the
barley with arborio or carnaroli rice.

Celeriac, sprouts, bacon

I quite often blitz surplus root veg and cooked greens together. Brussels sprouts puréed with creamed celeriac and some stock was a particularly successful improvisation, and now I make this lovely soup from scratch. A handful of crisp, salty bacon bits is a great finishing touch.

Serves 4

30g butter

1–2 tablespoons sunflower, rapeseed or olive oil

1 medium onion, chopped

500g celeriac, peeled and cubed

700ml vegetable stock

200g Brussels sprouts, trimmed and sliced

4–6 rashers of unsmoked streaky bacon or pancetta, cut into small lardons

100ml double cream, or milk (if you prefer a lighter soup)

Sea salt and freshly ground black pepper

Heat the butter and 1 tablespoon oil in a large saucepan over a medium heat. Add the onion and sweat gently for a few minutes. Add the celeriac, stir to combine, then cover and sweat for about 10 minutes to soften.

Add the stock, bring to the boil, then reduce the heat and simmer for 15–20 minutes until the celeriac is tender. Add the sprouts, return to a simmer and cook for 5 minutes more. Purée the whole lot in a blender until smooth. Return to the pan.

While the soup is cooking, heat a trickle more oil in a frying pan over a medium heat and fry the bacon until crisp and golden brown. Drain on kitchen paper.

Add the cream or milk to the soup and reheat gently. Season with salt and pepper and serve, scattered with the bacon.

MINUS ONE For a vegetarian version, just serve the soup without the bacon.

SWAPS Some toasted blanched almonds or crispy, garlicky bread croûtons are great alternatives to the bacon to give the soup a bit of a fancy finish.

Squash, apple, chilli

Spicy chilli oil deliciously balances the delicate sweetness of an autumnal squash and apple soup. The swirl of glowing orange-red oil enhances its appearance too.

Serves 4

About 1kg squash, such as Crown Prince, butternut or kabocha

5–6 garlic cloves (unpeeled), bashed

8–12 sage leaves (optional)

3 tablespoons rapeseed, sunflower or olive oil

About 500g sharp dessert apples, such as Cox or Ashmead's Kernel

Up to 700ml chicken or vegetable stock

Sea salt and freshly ground black pepper

For the chilli oil

6 tablespoons extra virgin olive oil

½ teaspoon dried chilli flakes

A good pinch of sweet paprika (smoked paprika if you like)

½ garlic clove, slivered

Preheat the oven to 190°C/Gas 5. Cut the squash into slim wedges and scoop out the seeds. Put the squash wedges into a roasting tray, skin side down. Scatter the bashed garlic cloves over the squash. Roughly crush the sage leaves, if using, in your hands to release the flavour and strew these over too. Trickle the oil all over everything and season well with salt and pepper. Roast for 40 minutes, checking after 25 minutes to see if any of the sage leaves are starting to look charred; if so take them out, but retain.

Meanwhile, to make the chilli oil, gently heat the extra virgin olive oil, chilli flakes, paprika and garlic together in a small saucepan over a low heat for 3–4 minutes. You want the oil barely fizzing – just hot enough to infuse the chilli. Set aside until needed.

Shortly before the roasting time is up, peel, quarter and core the apples. Cut each quarter in half. When the squash has had 40 minutes, remove the sage if you haven't already and add the apples to the tray. Stir everything around a bit, then return to the oven for a further 20 minutes, by which time the squash should be tender and caramelised and the apples collapsing.

Squeeze the roasted garlic cloves out of their skins into a blender (omit any that are a bit burnt). Add the apples. Scrape the squash flesh away from the skin and add this too. Add any oily juices left in the tray and a few of the sage leaves. Pour about 400ml stock into the blender and blitz to a thick, creamy purée. Add more stock as you like, to achieve a consistency you are happy with. The amount you need will vary depending on the variety of squash: butternut is quite wet, but many other squashes have drier flesh. Transfer to a saucepan and reheat. Add salt and pepper to taste.

Serve in warm bowls, topped with a generous trickle of the chilli oil. You can include a few fragments of chilli and garlic with the oil if you like, or not; it's up to you.

Parsnips, garlic, blue cheese

Pale, smooth, delicately sweet but deeply flavoured, this soup is a perfect winter's lunch. It was dreamt up by my collaborator Nikki Duffy and she recommends using a creamy, softish blue cheese such as Cornish Blue. Dolcelatte works well too, but avoid Stilton, which usually introduces an unwanted bitter note.

Serves 4

500g parsnips

1 medium onion, thickly sliced

2 tablespoons rapeseed, sunflower or olive oil, plus extra to trickle

2 garlic bulbs

About 600ml hot vegetable stock

50g creamy blue cheese, cut into chunks

Sea salt and freshly ground black pepper

Preheat the oven to 190°C/Gas 5. Peel the parsnips, top and tail them, then cut into large chunks. Put them into a large roasting tray with the onion. Spoon over the 2 tablespoons oil, season with some salt and pepper and toss the lot together.

Slice the tops off the garlic bulbs, so the cloves inside are just exposed. Put both bulbs on a piece of foil, trickle generously with oil, add some salt and pepper, and scrunch the foil up loosely around the garlic to enclose it. Nestle the foil parcels in among the parsnips and onion.

Roast for 40–50 minutes until the parsnips are tender and caramelised and the onions are soft, giving the veg a good stir halfway through. Unwrap the garlic. The cloves should be soft and golden inside their papery skins – poke one of the cloves with the tip of a small knife to check. You can always transfer them, still wrapped in their foil, to a smaller roasting dish and cook them a little longer if necessary.

Transfer the parsnips and onion to a blender. Squeeze out the soft garlic cloves from their skins into the blender, adding any garlicky oil from the foil too. Add the hot stock and blue cheese, and purée until completely smooth, adding a touch more stock or water to thin the soup a little if necessary.

Taste and add salt and pepper if needed. Serve piping hot, topped with a grinding of black pepper.

Beans, tomatoes, olive oil

This is a super-simple soup with Italian overtones. Make it in the summer or autumn with good, ripe, flavourful tomatoes.

Serves 4

2 tablespoons olive oil

2 garlic cloves, chopped

2 x 400g tins white beans, such as cannellini, drained and rinsed

1 bay leaf (optional)

1 sprig of thyme (optional)

350g tomatoes, deseeded and diced

Extra virgin olive oil to finish

Heat the olive oil in a large saucepan over a low heat. Add the garlic and cook gently just until it starts to colour. Immediately add the drained beans and enough water to just cover them. Add the bay leaf and thyme, if using. Bring to a simmer and simmer gently for 5 minutes.

With a slotted spoon, scoop out about half the beans into a bowl, along with the bay and thyme. Use a handheld stick blender to purée the beans and liquid left in the pan. Return the reserved beans and reheat gently.

Stir in the chopped tomatoes and heat through, then season with salt and pepper to taste. Ladle the soup into warm bowls and finish with a generous trickle of your best olive oil.

PLUS ONE A handful of basil leaves, roughly torn, won't go amiss. Alternatively, if you happen to have a little good, homemade basil pesto (page 66) to hand, dot a few blobs over the soup.

Quick
Snacks and
Sides

While I will champion until the end of time the tradition of sitting down to a formal family meal, that's simply not how most of us eat most of the time. In my household, certainly, the various members of the family converge on the kitchen at all kinds of random hours, throwing together stop-gap snacks or on-the-run meals as needed. And that includes the adults as well as the children.

But the mayhem of modern life needn't make us slaves to the microwave and the ready meal. There are plenty of delicious 'mini-meals' that can be rustled up quickly with minimal fuss.

Bread-based recipes have a starring role in this chapter. I like playing with classics and, dare I say it, even improving them. Take good old cheese on toast. By sneaking some softly sweated leeks between the toast and the Cheddar, you get a lovely sweetness that properly makes a meal of it (page 116). Or there's my variation on the time-honoured soft-boiled egg with toast soldiers, in which anchovies add a classy, salty tang (page 123).

Sometimes the bread feels very much like a key element in the meal – as in the aforementioned leeks, cheese and bread, or toast, olive oil and honey on page 120. But sometimes it's more the setting, the backdrop, to the really exciting bit of the dish, as in the delicious sandwiches that open this chapter.

I have also included a clutch of recipes that can perhaps best be described as 'nearly meals'. Whilst they could certainly be pressed into service as a snack or even sometimes a starter, they really come into their own when placed beside a simply cooked piece of meat or fish, to complete the plate. Take the lovely fried potato, fennel and onion dish (page 131) – it only wants a fillet of mackerel alongside, or a few strips of leftover chicken sautéed with it, to turn it into a satisfying meal. Likewise the spelt, peppers and raisins combination (page 136) – just add a bit of cold ham or leftover lamb on the side, or even a chopped up omelette (anything more would be a bit much). These combinations are often more memorable than the sausage, drumstick, omelette, chop or fish fillet that they have flattered into a feast; in other words, never underestimate the bit on the side.

Bacon, Cheddar, avocado

This is more than a mere sandwich: it's a magnificent miniature feast, a super-rich and yielding combination captured between hunks of bread. You might want to save it for a weekend brunch or indulgent telly supper *à deux*, and with someone you know pretty well – eating it is no delicate matter (and really shouldn't be attempted while wearing a tie).

Serves 2

A little olive, rapeseed or sunflower oil

6–8 rashers of streaky bacon

Butter for spreading

4 slices of good fresh white or brown bread, toasted if you like

4–6 slices of mature Cheddar or other well-flavoured hard cheese

1 large, ripe avocado

Mayonnaise for spreading (optional)

Freshly ground black pepper

Heat a large frying pan over a medium-high heat and add a scant trickle of oil. Add the bacon and cook for a few minutes on each side until as crisp as you like it.

Butter the slices of bread or toast and lay the bacon and cheese over two of them. If the avocado is ripe enough, I like to mash it first, then spread it on top. Otherwise, you can just slice it and lay it on. Season with black pepper.

Spread your other bread or toast slices with a little mayonnaise, if you like. Place on top of the avocado and apply a little pressure to bed everything down. Cut the sandwich in half and serve straight away.

PLUS ONE A few sliced juicy tomatoes only add to the fun – and the laundry bill.

Sausage, egg, parsley

You can serve this hearty medley as a traditional 'closed' sandwich – and it would make magnificent lunchbox fodder – but I like to serve it open like this in order to show off its lovely, chunky texture.

Serves 2

3–4 cold, cooked sausages

2 slices of good fresh bread

Sea salt and freshly ground black pepper

For the egg mayonnaise

3 large eggs, at room temperature

2–3 tablespoons mayonnaise, preferably homemade (see page 194)

To finish

Finely chopped parsley

Begin by boiling the eggs for the egg mayonnaise. Bring a large pan of water to the boil. Add the eggs, return to a brisk simmer and cook for 7 minutes. Immediately drain and hold the pan of eggs under cold running water to stop the cooking. When cool enough to handle, peel the eggs, then roughly chop them and put into a bowl.

When the eggs are completely cool, add the mayonnaise and mix well. Taste and add salt and pepper if needed. Halve the sausages lengthways, then cut into slices. Fold the sausage slices into the egg mayonnaise.

To serve, spread the sausage and egg mixture over each slice of bread. Scatter generously with parsley and serve.

PLUS ONE A little finely chopped gherkin adds an extra frisson to the egg-and-sausage mix.

Steak, Cheddar, gherkins

Rich, tangy and packed with flavour, this may be the best 'not-a-burger' hot meat sandwich you've ever had.

Serves 2

2 minute steaks – ideally thin slices of rump or topside (125–175g each)

A little olive, rapeseed or sunflower oil

Butter for spreading

4 slices of good fresh bread or 2 crusty warm baguettes, split

2–3 crunchy gherkins, sliced

4 slices of Cheddar or other well-flavoured hard cheese

Sea salt and freshly ground black pepper

The steaks should be no thicker than 1cm. If necessary, put them between two sheets of greaseproof paper and give them a light 'tapping' with a mallet, rolling pin or other similar object, to thin them slightly.

Heat a large frying pan or ridged cast-iron griddle pan over a high heat until very hot. Trickle some oil over the steaks and season them well on both sides with salt and pepper.

Cook the steaks in the searing hot pan for just 45–60 seconds each side – no longer or they may become tough. Remove the steaks from the pan, transfer to a warm plate and allow them to rest for 5 minutes in a warm place.

Butter the bread. Slice each steak neatly into 5 or 6 pieces, on an angle, and arrange over two of the bread slices or the bottom of the baguettes. Top the steak with the gherkins and cheese and sandwich together with the other bread slices or baguette tops. Serve with mustard.

PLUS ONE As with a burger, some form of tomato is always an option. I'd recommend a simple relish of chopped tomatoes mixed with olive oil, a splash of balsamic vinegar, salt, pepper and, if handy, a few baby (or chopped larger) capers.

Egg, parsley, toast

In this recipe, parsley appears not as a garnish or finishing touch, but as a particularly intense form of 'wilted greens'. Its beautiful colour and deep, fresh flavour are a lovely contrast to crisp, hot toast and the richness of a poached egg. I use flat-leaf rather than curly parsley here for its fuller, more refined flavour.

Serves 2

About 100g flat-leaf parsley, washed

A knob of butter (about 20g)

2 large eggs, at room temperature

2 slices of good bread

A little extra virgin olive oil

Sea salt and freshly ground black pepper

Pick over the parsley, removing the coarse stems: you want just the leaves and fine stems attached to them. Put the parsley in a steamer and steam over boiling water for about 5 minutes, or 'wilt' for 3–4 minutes in a pan with a little simmering water. Tip the parsley into a sieve, press with the back of a large spoon to squeeze out excess moisture and let it steam off for a couple of minutes. Place on a board and chop roughly, then put into a pan with the butter and some salt and pepper. Heat very gently, tossing once or twice, just until the butter is melted and mixed with the parsley. Take off the heat, cover and keep warm.

Poach the eggs according to your favourite method. This is mine: pour a 4–5cm depth of water into a wide saucepan or deep frying pan and bring to a rolling boil. Meanwhile, break each egg carefully into a cup or ramekin. When the water is boiling, turn off the heat and immediately but gently tip the eggs into the water. Put the lid on the pan and leave to cook in the residual heat for 2½–3 minutes. Carefully scoop up the eggs using a slotted spoon and check that the whites are set, with no jellyish clear bits left; if there are some, return the eggs to the water for 30 seconds. Give them half a minute in the spoon to drain and dab carefully with a piece of kitchen paper to help get rid of the water. Trim off any raggedy bits of white.

While the eggs are poaching, toast the bread and trickle with a little extra virgin olive oil or spread with butter. Place on warm plates. Top with the parsley, then the eggs. Sprinkle with salt and pepper, then serve.

SWAPS Tender nettle tips, prepared as described on page 174, and cooked in the same way as the parsley, work well here. A heap of buttery, wilted sorrel leaves, softened with a spoonful of cream, is another great swap. And, as you might guess, wilted spinach is excellent too.

Broad beans, meatballs, flatbread

Merguez sausages are a North African speciality, often made with lamb but also sometimes beef, and richly spiced. Really good, authentic, ready-made ones are a little tricky to find, so I tend to make up my own meaty merguez mixture and shape it into burgers or meatballs. Fried until hot and crisp, the meatballs are fantastic with sweet, young broad beans.

Serves 2

750g–1kg young broad beans in the pod

1 tablespoon rapeseed, olive or sunflower oil

A couple of squeezes of lemon juice

Sea salt and freshly ground black pepper

For the merguez meatballs

1 teaspoon cumin seeds

1 teaspoon fennel seeds

1 teaspoon coriander seeds

1 teaspoon caraway seeds (optional)

10–12 black peppercorns

1 teaspoon sweet paprika

A pinch of cayenne pepper

½ teaspoon salt

500g reasonably coarse lamb mince (not too lean)

2 garlic cloves, very finely chopped

OR

About 250g merguez sausages, cut into chunks

To serve

2 flatbreads, pitta breads or slices of sourdough

To make your own merguez meatballs, heat a dry frying pan over a medium heat, add the cumin, fennel and coriander seeds, and the caraway, if using, with the peppercorns, and toast until fragrant, about a minute. Tip into a mortar and leave to cool, then pound with the pestle to a fine powder. Mix with the paprika, cayenne and salt until well blended.

Put the lamb into a bowl, add the spice mix with the garlic, and mix everything together with your hands until well combined. Cover and refrigerate for at least 2–3 hours – or up to 24 hours – to allow the flavours to develop.

Form about half the mixture into small meatballs, about the size of a walnut. Keep the rest in the fridge for a day or two or freeze it for another meal (it's fiddly to make a smaller quantity).

Bring a large pan of water to the boil. Pod the broad beans, add to the pan, return to a simmer and cook for 3–4 minutes until tender. Drain and pop larger beans out of their thicker skins; very small beans don't need to be skinned.

Heat a large frying pan over a medium heat and add the oil. When hot, add the meatballs (or sausage chunks) and cook, turning often, until well browned all over and cooked through, about 10 minutes. Tip in the beans and toss them in the spicy fat. Cook for a minute longer, then give the whole thing a spritz of lemon juice and add a little salt and pepper if you think it needs it.

Warm your flatbreads or toast your bread. Pile the meaty bean mixture on top, along with any pan juices, give it a final squeeze of lemon juice, and serve.

PLUS ONE Thick, plain yoghurt is lovely with this trio: serve as it comes or pepped up with a little crushed garlic, salt and pepper.

Olives, capers, tomatoes

This combination – a kind of coarse, tomatoey tapenade –
is fantastic served with good bread and red wine, or spooned
on to garlic-rubbed toasted baguette slices to serve as canapés.
It's also a superb accompaniment to grilled lamb, and makes
a delicious stuffing for roasted fish. It's best prepared ahead,
to allow time for the flavours to mingle.

Serves 4

100g black olives, stoned
and coarsely chopped

20g baby capers, rinsed
and patted dry

250g tomatoes, deseeded
and chopped

¼ garlic clove, crushed
(optional)

A trickle of extra virgin
olive oil

Sea salt and freshly ground
black pepper

Simply mix the olives, capers and chopped tomatoes together in
a bowl, adding the crushed garlic if you like. Trickle with enough
extra virgin olive oil just to bind everything together and season
with salt and pepper to taste. Leave to stand for an hour before
serving, if possible, to let the flavours mingle.

Brandade, tomatoes, toast

Brandade is a traditional dish from southern France: a satisfying thick purée of salt cod, garlic and mashed potato. Salt cod needs to be soaked for about two days, but you can make a lovely, easy version of the dish using a smoked fish such as pollack or haddock. Serve it with some intense roasted tomatoes and a slab of garlicky toast, and you have a punchy bunch of flavours. It's perfect party food – pass it around with some rosé wine or cold beers.

Serves 4–6

For the oven-dried tomatoes

About 400g smallish, ripe tomatoes

Extra virgin olive oil to trickle

Sea salt and freshly ground black pepper

For the brandade

250g floury potatoes, peeled and cut into large chunks

25g butter

1 garlic clove, finely chopped

300g natural (undyed) smoked pollack or haddock fillets

100ml milk

2 tablespoons extra virgin olive oil

For the garlic toast

6–8 slices of coarse-textured bread, such as sourdough

1 garlic clove, halved

Extra virgin olive oil to trickle

For the oven-dried tomatoes, at least 3 hours before serving (or the day before), preheat the oven to 75–100°C/Gas low. Halve the tomatoes and lay, cut side up, in a roasting tin. Trickle with a little extra virgin olive oil and season with salt and pepper. Place in the oven for at least 3 hours until wrinkly, but still juicy in the middle.

For the brandade, put the potatoes into a pan of lightly salted water, bring to the boil and simmer for 15–20 minutes until tender. Tip into a colander to drain and dry for a few minutes.

Meanwhile, melt the butter in a wide pan over a low heat, add the garlic and sweat for a minute or two. Add the smoked fish, cutting it into pieces as necessary to fit in a single layer. Pour over the milk (don't worry if it doesn't quite cover the fish) and bring just to a simmer. Partially cover with a lid and simmer very gently for 3–4 minutes, or until the fish is cooked through.

Drain the fish, reserving the liquid. Return this liquid to the pan and add the olive oil and a few twists of black pepper. Either push the cooked potatoes through a ricer into the hot liquid or just add them to the pan and mash thoroughly to create a nice loose mash – it will be highly aromatic with the fishy milk and olive oil.

As soon as the fish is cool enough to handle, discard the skin and any bones, and break the flesh into flakes. Mash as well as you can (or blitz in a food processor), then beat the fish thoroughly into the mash. Do this by hand – a processor will make the mash go horribly gluey. Taste and add more pepper if you like.

Toast the bread on both sides. Rub with the cut surface of the garlic and trickle with a little extra virgin olive oil. Pile the warm brandade and oven-dried tomatoes on to the toasts and top with a final trickle of olive oil and a grinding of black pepper.

Leeks, cheese, bread

My culinary history is peppered with variations of the divine combination of soft, sweated leeks, melted cheese and crusty bread. This, I think, is just about the simplest interpretation possible – and arguably one of the very best. I usually toast the bread but if you have a really good, very fresh loaf you don't even need to do that – the tender crumb, soaked with leeky, buttery juices, will be delicious.

Serves 2

25g butter

2 medium leeks (about 350g untrimmed weight), trimmed, washed and sliced

2 thick slices of sourdough or other robust bread

50g strong Cheddar, grated

Sea salt and freshly ground black pepper

Melt the butter in a medium saucepan over a medium heat, then add the leeks. As soon as they are sizzling, turn the heat down quite low and put the lid on the pan. Sweat gently, stirring often, for about 10 minutes, until the leeks are tender. Season with salt and pepper to taste.

Preheat the grill. Toast the bread (or not, if you prefer). Spoon the leek mixture thickly over the bread and top with the grated cheese. Grill until bubbling and golden, then serve straight away.

PLUS ONE A few thyme leaves, stirred into the leeks as they are sweating, will enhance the flavour. A smear of mustard on the toast is delicious too.

SWAPS You can also make a fine version of this with red onions in place of the leeks: finely slice 2 medium red onions and cook them gently in butter for at least 20 minutes until very tender. Lightly fried mushrooms also work very well in a cheesy open toastie like this, in addition to – or instead of – the leeks.

Peppers, sourdough, goat's cheese

Sweet, yielding roast peppers, crunchy fried sourdough bread and creamy cheese with a salty, goaty tang: a superb medley of contrasting flavours. The pepper-infused olive oil is particularly good; any that you have left over can be kept in the fridge for a few days and used in salad dressings or pasta dishes, or just trickled on to good bread.

Serves 4

4 large red peppers

125ml extra virgin olive oil

1 garlic clove (unpeeled), lightly bashed

A sprig of rosemary, lightly bashed (optional)

3 slices of good, light sourdough bread

400g goat's cheese (any kind will do, soft or firm)

Sea salt and freshly ground black pepper

Preheat the grill to high. Place the peppers on the grill rack and grill, turning often, until black and blistered all over. Put them into a bowl and cover with cling film (the trapped steam will help to lift the skins).

When the peppers are cool enough to handle, pull off the stalks and, if possible, tip out the juices into a bowl. Peel the skin from the peppers, then cut them open and remove all the seeds and membranes. Cut the flesh into broad strips, 2–3cm wide, and season with salt and pepper.

Warm the extra virgin olive oil in a small saucepan, add the garlic and rosemary, if using, and heat gently for a couple of minutes to infuse the flavours; don't let the garlic brown. Take off the heat, add the peppers, along with any juices, and turn to coat in the warm oil. Leave to cool.

Cut the crusts off the sourdough and tear each slice into rough, crouton-sized pieces. Pour 2 tablespoons of the pepper-infused oil into a frying pan and place over a medium heat. When hot, add the bread and fry, turning, until toasted and golden.

Crumble large chunks of the cheese over serving plates and add the sweet, roasted pepper strips and fried bread. Trickle over a little more of the pepper oil, sprinkle with black pepper and serve.

Toast, olive oil, honey

I realise I'm pushing my luck to call this a recipe, but I really wanted to include it because it is one of my favourite breakfast/ elevenses/teatime treats. I also like the fact that it's a bit unexpected, and a great example of three-good-things alchemy. Good sourdough bread is ideal, but a fluffy farmhouse white or nutty granary works well too.

Per person
1 thick slice of good bread
Extra virgin olive oil
Honey
Coarse sea salt (optional)

Toast the bread to your liking. Trickle it fairly generously with extra virgin olive oil and leave for a minute to soak in.

Sprinkle with a pinch of coarse salt if you like the sweet/salty collision. Trickle or spread your favourite honey generously over the oil, and eat.

SWAPS Nutty, golden rapeseed oil tastes quite different from olive oil – mild and grassy rather than pungent and bittersweet – but it is also lovely in this simple combination. Walnut oil is another fine option.

Egg, toast, anchovy

The salty pungency of anchovy works a treat with rich, creamy egg yolk, so I crush the fillets on to toast to make anchovy soldiers – a delectable, rather grown-up variation on a classic, dippy theme. Anchovies need to be carefully sourced, as they are under considerable threat in some areas. I like Fish 4 Ever's Mediterranean anchovies; you can also buy Marine Stewardship Council-certified ones from the Bay of Biscay.

Serves 2

6–8 anchovy fillets in oil, plus a little of the oil from the can or jar

4 large eggs, at room temperature

2 large slices of good bread

1 garlic clove, halved (optional)

Put the anchovy fillets into a small dish or on to a plate, keeping their oil separate. Mash the anchovies to a coarse purée, using a fork.

Bring a pan of water to the boil. Add the eggs, return to the boil and cook for exactly 4½ minutes to give you a set white and a nice runny yolk, which I prefer (but fix your boiled eggs how you like them). Remove the eggs from the pan and transfer to egg cups.

While the eggs are boiling, toast the bread. Rub each piece with the cut surface of the garlic clove (unless, of course, you're not in a garlicky mood). Trickle a little of the anchovy oil over each piece of toast, then spread roughly with the anchovy purée. Cut the toast into soldiers.

When the eggs are ready, transfer them to egg cups. Eat straight away, with the anchovy toast soldiers for dipping.

SWAPS It doesn't have to be toast that you dip into your egg: lightly cooked asparagus and purple sprouting broccoli stems are also fantastic dippers. In both cases, smear a little crushed anchovy on to the veg with a knife before you dip.

Spinach, leek, béchamel

This is the most amazing comfort food and a very appealing way to present spinach to anyone who is 'greens-shy'. Serve it as a snack with good bread or toast, or as a side dish with a piece of simply cooked white fish or chicken.

Serves 3–4

250g spinach, tough stalks removed

2–3 medium-large leeks, trimmed, washed and sliced

For the béchamel

200ml whole milk

A chunk of onion

1 bay leaf

25g butter

A dash of olive oil

25g plain flour

Sea salt and freshly ground black pepper

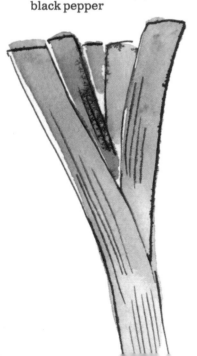

Wash the spinach and put it into a saucepan with just the water that clings to the leaves. Cover the pan and place over a medium heat for a few minutes, just until the spinach wilts. Drain in a colander. When the spinach is cool enough to handle, squeeze out all the water with your hands, then chop it coarsely.

For the béchamel, put the milk in a small pan with the onion and bay leaf and bring to just below simmering, then take off the heat and set aside to infuse. Meanwhile, heat the butter and olive oil in a large frying pan over a medium heat.

Add the leeks to the butter and oil, turn the heat down fairly low and cover the pan. Sweat gently for about 6–8 minutes until the leeks are tender and wilted. Stir in the flour, working it well into the buttery leeks. Cook, stirring often, for a couple of minutes. Strain in about a third of the hot, infused milk (reheat first, if it's cooled) and stir vigorously to incorporate smoothly. Repeat with the remaining milk.

When you have a smooth, leeky béchamel sauce, return the pan to a low heat and let it cook gently for 3–4 minutes, stirring often. Stir in the spinach and heat through, then taste and add salt and pepper as needed. Serve straight away.

PLUS ONE A good grating of Cheddar, Parmesan or any other well-flavoured hard cheese makes this dish even more rich and comforting. Either grate the cheese on top and flash the dish under the grill, or just stir it into the hot sauce before serving.

PLUS TWO For a hugely gratifying brunch or supper, poach an egg or two (for my method, see page 108), place on buttered toast and smother with the leeks and spinach in béchamel.

Potato, cheese, thyme

These scrumptious little potato cakes are good enough to enjoy
as a starter or light meal with just a crisp salad on the side.
They also make a great accompaniment to sausages or a piece
of fish. This is a good way to use up leftover potato, but it's also
worth baking some jacket spuds and leaving them to cool just
so you can do this.

Makes 6

500g cold cooked potatoes

100g mature Cheddar

1 teaspoon thyme leaves

Sunflower, rapeseed or olive
oil for frying

3 tablespoons plain flour

Sea salt and freshly ground
black pepper

Put the potatoes into a bowl and mash roughly with a fork – keep
it a little bit chunky rather than make a smooth mash. Cut the
cheese into very small cubes, about 4–5mm. Stir these into the
potato with the thyme and some salt and pepper.

Heat a thin layer of oil in a large, non-stick frying pan over a
medium heat. Scatter the flour on a plate. Take small handfuls
of the potato mixture and shape into balls, then flatten slightly
to form 6 small cakes, about 2cm deep. Dip them in the flour and
turn to coat lightly on both sides.

Place the potato cakes in the hot frying pan and cook them for
8–10 minutes until golden brown on both sides, turning them
carefully once or twice. Don't worry if some of the cheese starts
to ooze out as it melts – just encourage it back into the potato cake
with a spatula.

Transfer the potato cakes to warm plates, sprinkle with a touch
more salt, and serve.

PLUS ONE Try adding a little chopped cooked bacon to the mix,
or a couple of teaspoons of baby capers. Cold, leftover parsnips or
celeriac can also be roughly mashed and added to the potato mix.

Cauliflower, potato, curry

Taking its inspiration from timeless Coronation chicken, this very simple, lightly curried cauliflower and potato salad is perfect for a picnic or lunchbox.

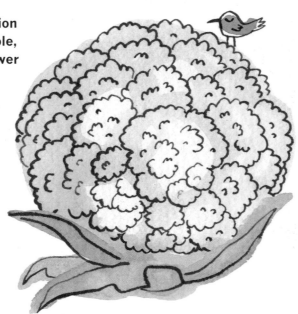

Serves 4

400g new potatoes, scrubbed

½ medium cauliflower (about 400g), trimmed

A squeeze of lemon juice

A handful of coriander or mint (optional)

Sea salt and freshly ground black pepper

For the curried mayo

3 tablespoons mayonnaise

3 tablespoons plain wholemilk yoghurt

1 heaped teaspoon curry paste

1 tablespoon mango chutney (optional)

Bring a large pan of water to the boil. Cut the new potatoes into roughly 2cm chunks and the cauliflower into small florets. When the water is boiling, add some salt, then the potatoes. Return to a simmer and cook for about 3 minutes, then add the cauliflower and cook for a further 3 minutes or until both veg are just tender but not soft. Tip the vegetables into a colander to drain and leave to cool completely.

To make the curried mayo, combine the mayonnaise, yoghurt, curry paste and mango chutney, if using, in a large bowl.

When the veg are completely cooled, add them to the curried mayo and toss to combine. Taste and add more salt and pepper if needed, and a good squeeze of lemon juice. Finish, if you like, with a generous scattering of coriander or mint.

PLUS ONE OR TWO A small handful of plump sultanas or raisins and/or a scattering of lightly toasted, roughly chopped cashew nuts or flaked almonds makes a very nice addition.

Potato, fennel, onion

I doubt I will ever tire of the delicious pairing of fried onions and fried potatoes. Adding fennel to the mix, I've found, just increases the joy. This is a very adaptable recipe – do try one of the variations below. It's also a great side dish to serve with simply cooked fish or chicken.

Serves 4

2 small-medium fennel bulbs

About 450g cooked potatoes

2–3 tablespoons sunflower, rapeseed or olive oil

1 onion, sliced from root to tip

1 garlic clove, chopped

Sea salt and freshly ground black pepper

Trim off the base and the top of the fennel, then slice the bulbs thinly, from top to bottom. Thickly slice the cooked potatoes.

Heat 2 tablespoons oil in a large, non-stick frying pan over a medium heat. Add the potato slices and cook briskly for 5 minutes or so until they start to take on a good, golden brown colour. Either remove the potatoes from the pan and set aside for a few minutes or, as I do, simply push them to the side of the pan.

Add a dash more oil to the pan, then the onion. Sauté for 5 minutes until softening. Add the fennel, stir to mix with the onion and cook for another 5 minutes or so, until the fennel starts to soften.

Now re-combine the potatoes with everything else in the pan and add a dash more oil if it is needed. Cook, stirring often, for another 5–10 minutes, until all the veg are deliciously golden brown and well caramelised in places, adding the garlic a few minutes before the end of cooking. Season with salt and pepper to taste and serve.

PLUS ONE/SWAPS Bacon is a great addition, or you can use it in place of the fennel for an equally delicious combination. Cut a few rashers into chunky strips and add to the pan before the onions.

ANOTHER TAKE Cook the onions and potatoes (fennel too, if you like) and add flakes of cooked mackerel right at the end. Scatter generously with chopped parsley before serving.

Potato, parsnip, spice

I do love a spicy roast potato and the addition of parsnips offers a little more depth and complexity. I could happily eat a plateful of this for my supper, with perhaps a dollop of yoghurt and another of mango chutney on the side, but it also makes a great addition to a spread of other spicy, pick-and-mix dishes. You can use a ready-made curry or spice blend, but it's always delicious and satisfying to grind and blend your own spices.

Serves 3–4

About 500g potatoes

3 tablespoons sunflower oil

About 500g parsnips

1 garlic clove, very finely chopped

For the curry spice mix

1 tablespoon coriander seeds

About 6 black peppercorns

½ teaspoon dried chilli flakes

1 teaspoon ground fenugreek

1 teaspoon ground turmeric

¼ teaspoon fine sea salt

Preheat the oven to 200°C/Gas 6. For the curry spice mix, put the coriander seeds and black peppercorns in a dry frying pan and toast over a gentle heat for a minute or so, until fragrant. Tip into a mortar and leave to cool. Add the chilli flakes, then crush the spices with the pestle to a coarse powder. Combine with the fenugreek, turmeric and salt.

Peel the potatoes and cut into 3–4cm chunks. Put them into a saucepan, cover with cold water and bring to a rolling boil. Boil for 1 minute, then immediately take off the heat and drain well.

Put the oil in a large roasting tray and place in the oven for 5 minutes to heat up. Meanwhile, peel the parsnips and cut them into similar-sized chunks to the potatoes.

Carefully tip the potatoes and parsnips into the hot oil, add the spice mix and toss thoroughly so that the vegetables all get a good coating of spice. Roast for about 40 minutes until the veg are golden and crisp, giving them a stir halfway through. Stir in the chopped garlic and return to the oven for 2–3 minutes.

Serve straight away, with a dish of thick, plain yoghurt (or a raita such as the one on page 148), and perhaps mango chutney.

PLUS ONE If you happen to have any celeriac to hand, this makes a great third addition to the spicy veg. Cut it into chunks and add to the potatoes along with the parsnips.

Rice, beans, coconut

Known as 'rice and peas', this traditional West Indian dish actually uses beans – usually kidney beans – not peas. These are cooked with the rice in a rich, aromatic coconut milk broth. It makes a deeply satisfying side dish, whether you serve it with spicy West Indian jerk chicken or pork, or something less authentic, such as simply grilled pork chops.

Serves 4–6

200g basmati rice

1 tablespoon rapeseed or sunflower oil

1 onion, chopped

2 garlic cloves, crushed

1 teaspoon ground allspice

1 large sprig of thyme (optional)

400ml tin coconut milk

400g tin kidney beans, drained and rinsed

Sea salt and freshly ground black pepper

Put the rice into a bowl, cover with cold water and leave to soak for about 30 minutes. Stir well to rinse off some of the starch, then tip into a sieve and rinse well under the cold tap. Drain.

Meanwhile, heat the oil in a large saucepan over a medium-low heat. Add the onion and sauté gently for about 10 minutes. Add the rice, garlic, allspice, thyme, if using, ½ teaspoon salt and some pepper. Pour in the coconut milk and 200ml water, stir well and bring to a simmer. Lower the heat, cover and cook at the gentlest possible simmer for 10 minutes. Stir in the kidney beans and simmer, covered, for a further 5 minutes.

Turn off the heat and leave to stand, covered, for 5 minutes. Now remove the thyme, if added, and give the rice a good stir. Taste before serving – to see if it needs a little more salt and pepper.

PLUS ONE OR TWO For a touch of heat, nestle a whole, fierily hot Scotch bonnet or habanero chilli into the rice during cooking. Keep the chilli whole and remove it before serving – it's too fierce to eat, but will have lent some of its fruity heat to the rice. Hot or not, rice and peas is excellent scattered generously with coarsely chopped coriander.

SWAPS Kidney beans are by no means essential: little black-eyed beans work well, as do borlotti or cannellini.

Spelt, peppers, raisins

This recipe nicely illustrates how a little time spent preparing fairly basic ingredients can really pay off. Roasting the peppers brings out all their sweet, rich flavour, while soaking the raisins in orange juice makes them a much more vibrant addition to the dish. The result is a very satisfying side salad.

Serves 3–4

100g raisins

Juice of 2 oranges, or 100ml apple juice

2 red, yellow or orange peppers (or a combination)

150g pearled spelt

3 tablespoons extra virgin olive oil

2 teaspoons cider vinegar

¼ garlic clove, crushed with a pinch of salt

Sea salt and freshly ground black pepper

Put the raisins and orange or apple juice in a small pan over a medium heat. Bring almost to the boil, then take off the heat and leave to cool and soak for at least an hour.

Meanwhile, preheat the grill to high. Place the peppers on the grill rack and grill, turning often, until black and blistered all over. Put them into a bowl and cover with cling film (the trapped steam will help to lift the skins).

When the peppers are cool enough to handle, pull off the stalks and, if possible, tip out the juices into a bowl. Peel the skin from the peppers, then cut them open and remove all the seeds and membranes. Cut the flesh into small pieces.

Rinse the spelt well, tip it into a saucepan and cover with lots of cold water. Add a pinch of salt. Bring to the boil, then reduce the heat and simmer for about 20–25 minutes, until tender.

Drain the raisins, tipping any remaining juice into a bowl. Add the extra virgin olive oil, cider vinegar, garlic and some salt and pepper to the juice to make a dressing. If you have collected any juices from the roasted peppers, add these too. Whisk or stir well to combine.

Drain the cooked spelt and toss it immediately with the dressing, raisins and red pepper pieces. Mix well and leave to cool to room temperature. Taste and add more salt and pepper if necessary before serving.

PLUS ONE A good sprinkling of flat-leaf parsley – whole or coarsely chopped leaves – adds colour and freshness to this lovely salad.

Corn-on-the-cob, butter, nuts

This is a fun way to eat a fun vegetable. Dipping bright yellow rounds of corn in warm butter is always satisfying and the added textural pleasure of a dunk in a spiced nut dip makes the dish incredibly moreish.

Serves 4

2–3 corn-on-the-cobs

About 100g butter

1 small garlic clove, very finely chopped or grated

Sea salt and freshly ground black pepper

For the spiced nuts

2–3 tablespoons flaked almonds

1 teaspoon cumin seeds

½–1 teaspoon dried chilli flakes

Strip any outer husks from the corn. Bring a very large saucepan of salted water to the boil. Add the corn-on-the-cobs and cook for 8–10 minutes, or until they are tender and the kernels come away easily from the cobs. As with many vegetables, the sooner corn is cooked after picking, the less time it needs in the pan.

For the spiced nuts, heat a small frying pan over a medium heat. Add the almonds, cumin and chilli flakes and toast gently for 2–3 minutes, keeping them moving all the time. Tip on to a plate and allow to cool. Using a pestle and mortar, bash the cooled mix roughly, keeping it fairly coarse, and season well with salt and pepper. Tip into a serving bowl.

Return the empty frying pan to a medium-low heat and add the butter. When bubbling, add the garlic and cook for just 1 minute, without colouring. This will give the butter a warm and heady depth. Pour into a bowl.

When the corn-on-the-cobs are cooked, drain and slice them into 3–4cm thick rounds. Pile into a warm, large bowl or individual bowls and serve alongside the warm garlicky butter and spicy almonds. To eat, dip the corn rounds first into the butter, then the spiced nuts. Alternatively, spoon the spiced butter over the corn and sprinkle with the nuts.

Broccoli, chilli, cashews

You can make this dish with either calabrese or purple sprouting broccoli; it works well with other greens too. Choose a medium-hot chilli and use generously, or a fierce one and be more cautious. This is a great side dish for simply cooked chicken or fish, or even for a spread of curries. It's also good served on its own as a light starter.

Serves 4

400g broccoli, trimmed

75g cashew nuts

2 tablespoons rapeseed or olive oil

¼–1 large red chilli (depending on heat), deseeded and finely chopped

1 garlic clove, chopped

A dash of soy sauce

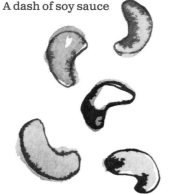

Cut the broccoli into florets and steam or boil for a few minutes until just al dente. Transfer to a colander.

Heat a wok or deep frying pan over a medium heat. Add the cashews and toast in the hot pan for a couple of minutes, tossing them often; keep a close eye on them as they can burn easily. When they are golden, tip them into a bowl.

Put the oil, chilli and garlic into the pan and heat gently for 30 seconds–1 minute, just to take the edge off the garlic. Add the toasted cashews and broccoli to the pan, turn up the heat and stir-fry for a minute or two, so the broccoli is well mingled with the nuts, oil, chilli and garlic. Season with a splash of soy sauce and serve straight away.

PLUS ONE Toss this stir-fry with rice noodles and you have yourself a hearty, zesty meal.

SWAPS Use any greens, kale or cabbage instead of the broccoli, but cook them very lightly so the veg still has plenty of crunch. You can swap peanuts or hazelnuts for cashews too.

Carrots, almonds, cumin

I like to serve this spicy dish warm with hummus and flatbreads. But it's also a great way to serve early summer carrots alongside simply grilled or barbecued lamb chops or chicken pieces.

Serves 6

500g small, finger-sized carrots, scrubbed and tops trimmed

100g blanched whole almonds

1 tablespoon cumin seeds

2 tablespoons extra virgin olive oil

Sea salt and freshly ground black pepper

Bring a large pan of salted water to the boil and add the carrots. Boil for 5–8 minutes until tender, then drain and leave to cool just a little.

Meanwhile, heat a large frying pan over a medium heat. Add the almonds and toast, tossing frequently, until they are golden with a few little brown patches. Transfer to a plate to cool. Put the cumin seeds in the same pan and toast for a few minutes until fragrant. Add to the almonds. Using a pestle and mortar, bash the almonds and cumin very lightly to break up the nuts a little.

Put the warm carrots into a large bowl. Add the almonds and cumin, extra virgin olive oil and some salt and pepper. Toss well, then transfer to a serving dish or individual plates.

PLUS ONE Let the salad cool to room temperature, then add some orange segments (prepared as for the recipe on page 18) and a squeeze of orange juice.

SWAPS The spicy almond treatment works well with other veg too: try blanched green beans, asparagus, broccoli or very fresh new potatoes.

Beetroot, mozzarella, balsamic

Deep purple beetroot and pure white mozzarella make a stunning visual combination, and a delicious one. The sweetsharp tang of balsamic vinegar, made into a dressing with the beetroot roasting juices, brings the two together beautifully.

Serves 4

500g beetroot

3–4 garlic cloves (unpeeled), lightly bashed

2 tablespoons olive oil

A couple of sprigs of thyme, plus extra thyme leaves to serve (optional)

A couple of bay leaves (optional)

3 tablespoons balsamic vinegar

2 balls of buffalo mozzarella

Sea salt and freshly ground black pepper

Preheat the oven to 190°C/Gas 5. Peel the beetroot, cut into thick wedges and put into a roasting dish in which it fits fairly snugly. Add the garlic cloves. Trickle over the olive oil and 3 tablespoons water. Season with salt and pepper, tuck in the thyme and bay, if using, and cover tightly with foil. Roast for about an hour until the beetroot is completely tender. Discard the garlic and herbs, if used.

Transfer the beetroot wedges to a bowl. Drain off the roasting juices into a small pan; if the juices are very reduced, add a splash of water to the dish first and stir to deglaze. Add the balsamic vinegar to the pan and bring to the boil. Let bubble for a few minutes until reduced by about half. Pour this syrup back over the beetroot.

Leave the beetroot to macerate in the dressing and cool to room temperature, turning occasionally. Taste and add more salt and pepper if necessary.

Arrange the beetroot on serving plates. Tear the mozzarella into small chunks and add to the plates. Finish with a sprinkling of thyme leaves, if you have them, and trickle over the remaining beetroot/balsamic syrup from the bowl.

PLUS ONE To make this lovely combination more substantial, serve it as a magnificent bruschetta. Cut the beetroot up into smaller pieces, pile it on to garlic- and thyme-rubbed toasted sourdough slices and top with the mozzarella and juices.

Avocado, lime, chilli

This is simply a take on the classic Mexican relish guacamole, but deconstructed to be a little chunkier. It's well worth having in your repertoire as it is good with so many things – grilled meats, fresh cheeses, eggs, salads etc.

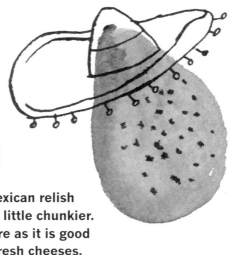

Serves 4

2 large avocados

Finely grated zest and juice of 1 lime

1 small red chilli, deseeded and finely chopped

2 tablespoons extra virgin olive oil

Sea salt and freshly ground black pepper

Halve and stone the avocados. Peel away their skins and cut the flesh into small chunks. Put into a bowl with the lime zest, half the lime juice and half of the chilli. Add the extra virgin olive oil and some salt and pepper and toss together gently. Taste and add more lime juice, chilli, salt or pepper as you like.

You can either leave the avocados in chunks, or if they are really ripe and soft, you can mash the lot roughly together with a fork – it will look less elegant this way but still taste gorgeous.

PLUS ONE Add a generous scattering of coriander leaves for an extra aromatic dimension.

PLUS TWO OR THREE The salad can be made even more colourful and substantial with various additions, including tomatoes, cut into small chunks, and spring onions, cut into 5mm slices. Don't overdo the extras though – keep the creamy avocado dominant.

SWAP You can certainly use a lemon for this recipe, if you do not have a lime. (I would say you can *almost always* use a lemon when you haven't got a lime!)

Cucumber, apple, yoghurt

Giving cucumber a light salting really improves its flavour and produces a delicate, well-seasoned juice. Combined with apple and yoghurt, it produces a sort of relish, somewhere between a raita and a salsa. Try serving it with a curry, chilli or even a kedgeree.

Serves 4

½ cucumber

2 crisp dessert apples

8 tablespoons thick, plain wholemilk yoghurt

Sea salt and freshly ground black pepper

Quarter the cucumber lengthways and scoop out the seeds with a teaspoon. Cut the cucumber into small cubes, about 5mm. Put into a bowl with a couple of good pinches of salt, toss to mix and leave for half an hour.

When the cucumber is ready, quarter and core the apples, then cut into small cubes. Add to the cucumber with the yoghurt and stir well to combine the yoghurt with the cucumber 'juice'. Sprinkle with black pepper and it's ready to serve.

PLUS ONE Mint, of course, cannot fail to enhance this trio. Scatter a few leaves, whole or chopped, over the finished dish.

ANOTHER TAKE You can make this into more of a spicy, raita-style dish by stirring in some crushed lightly toasted cumin seeds (see page 142 for preparation). The merest smidge of garlic will zip it up even further.

Vegetable Feasts

I've spent a lot of time exploring the world of meat-free cookery over the past few years. In fact, even though I wrote an entire book on the subject – *River Cottage Veg every day!* – I still can't stop experimenting with new combinations. The recipes that follow are my newest favourites, all seasoned with the principles of simplicity and culinary logic.

If you've grown up in the culinary mainstream, then abandoning meat and fish pretty much means abandoning convention. I know we don't all find that easy. But far from being scary, it's actually incredibly liberating. Once you've freed yourself from the tyranny of meat, you'll find all sorts of possibilities open up for surprising dishes that really deliver on taste and texture.

I understand the suspicion that vegetarian food somehow lacks flavour or substance. I used to have the same anxiety – but I've long since overcome it. The idea behind these dishes is to combine strong, shouty flavours with pleasing, comforting textures. And I'll always keep an eye on the vital mission of filling hungry tummies, so bready things, starchy roots and pulses with heft abound, doing stalwart service underpinning the leafy, the crunchy, the zesty, the saucy and the fresh.

Despite these unifying themes, you should expect the unexpected. You'll find recipes here for some fairly left-field treats, such as a pizza topped with puréed chestnuts and vibrant greens, tender gnocchi made with squash flesh, and an almost puddingy parsnip tarte tatin. Veg-based cookery invites this kind of bold experimentation. In fact, in my kitchen, it pretty much insists on it. I'm constantly asking myself 'What if?', as in, what if I roasted some asparagus with some spuds? Or baked some lettuce as a gratin? Or put a classic cobbler topping on a mushroom ragout? It's such a thrill when the answer comes back – 'That's what! And isn't it great?'

Using less meat – or no meat – has also brought home to me the fact that a meal doesn't have to be based around one dish. Several 'smaller' platefuls can be even more satisfying. Many of the dishes here will do great service as part of a spread of vegetable mezze – a fine way to feed your vegetarian friends and family, and surprise any carnivores. I have to say it is one of the great continuing pleasures of my cooking to hear dyed-in-the-flesh meat lovers reacting with delight to a new veg-only dish that I've placed before them. As if they had thought I was trying to spoil their fun!

Tomatoes, egg, bread

This is a very straightforward, one-dish way to enjoy the fried-breakfast partnership of egg, bread and tomato. The tomatoes are roasted until juicy, then the bread is fried in the oven so it comes out partly juice-soaked and partly crisp. A baked egg completes the meal.

Serves 4

500g tomatoes

3 tablespoons rapeseed or olive oil

200g slightly stale bread (white or wholemeal)

4 eggs

Sea salt and freshly ground black pepper

Preheat the oven to 190°C/Gas 5. Halve cherry tomatoes; cut larger tomatoes into wedges. Put them into a roasting tray or oven dish in which they fit in a single layer with just a little space in between. Trickle over 1 tablespoon oil and season with salt and pepper. Roast for 30 minutes, until soft and starting to caramelise at the edges.

Meanwhile, tear or cut the bread into bite-sized chunks. Put these into a bowl with 2 tablespoons oil and a little salt and pepper and toss to coat.

Take the dish out of the oven, add the chunks of bread and push them roughly in amongst the tomatoes. Return to the oven for 10 minutes until the bread starts to turn golden brown and crisp on top.

Remove the dish from the oven and form 4 rough hollows in amongst the tomatoes and bread. Break an egg into each hollow and return to the oven for just 4–5 minutes, until the whites are set and the yolks still a little runny. Grind over some salt and pepper and serve straight away.

PLUS ONE You can add a few roughly torn chunks of mozzarella at the same time as the eggs, letting them melt deliciously into the bread and tomatoes.

Aubergine, tomatoes, chickpeas

The aubergines and tomatoes in this dish almost melt together in the oven, forming a savoury, chunky semi-sauce for the nutty little chickpeas. Like many dishes of its kind (ratatouille, for one), this is best served warm or at room temperature, rather than piping hot or fridge cold. A bowlful of this, just as it is, makes a delicious lunch or light supper. Add rice or warm pitta breads and a green salad and you have quite a meal.

Serves 3 alone, or 4 with accompaniments

2 medium aubergines (about 650–700g in total), trimmed

4 tablespoons sunflower, rapeseed or olive oil

1 cinnamon stick (optional)

About 350g cherry tomatoes, halved

A large pinch of dried chilli flakes

400g tin chickpeas, drained and rinsed

2 garlic cloves, chopped

Finely grated zest of 1 lemon

A handful of basil or mint leaves, shredded (optional)

Sea salt and freshly ground black pepper

Preheat the oven to 200°C/Gas 6. Cut the aubergines into 2cm cubes. Heat the oil in a large oven dish or roasting tray in the oven for 5–10 minutes (this helps to prevent the aubergine absorbing too much oil during cooking).

Carefully add the aubergines to the hot oil in the dish. Season well with salt and pepper, add the cinnamon, if using, and toss together. Roast in the oven for 30 minutes, stirring once halfway through cooking.

Add the cherry tomatoes and chilli flakes to the dish. Roast for another 20 minutes, then add the drained chickpeas and garlic. Stir well and roast for a final 10 minutes.

Remove from the oven and stir in the lemon zest. Leave to cool for about 15 minutes, then stir through basil or mint, if using. Taste and adjust the seasoning and serve warm.

PLUS ONE A dollop of thick, plain yoghurt, lightly seasoned with salt, pepper and a whisper of crushed garlic, is an excellent finishing touch.

New potatoes, herbs, olive oil

For me this is the summer equivalent of 'baked potato plus topping'. You can use pretty much any herbs you like – and lots of them. Herby threesomes often work well: I like lots of chives mixed with a little thyme and tarragon; or parsley, chives and chervil. Mint and basil are good on their own, or combined with each other and parsley.

Serves 4

1kg small new or salad potatoes, scrubbed

5-6 tablespoons extra virgin olive oil

A knob of butter

At least 4 tablespoons mixed chopped herbs (as suggested above)

Sea salt and freshly ground black pepper

The potato pieces need to be roughly the same size (about the size of a golf ball), so cut up any larger ones. Put into a large saucepan, cover with water, add salt and bring to the boil. Lower the heat but cook the potatoes at a brisk simmer until very tender – they need to be soft enough to crumble and break when you 'bash' them. Depending on the variety, this will take 8–15 minutes.

Drain the cooked potatoes and let them steam off for a minute or two, then return to the hot pan. Add 3 tablespoons extra virgin olive oil, a knob of butter and plenty of salt and pepper. Put the lid on and shake the pan vigorously up and down to 'bash' the potatoes. The idea is to break them down a bit but not too much. You want some still whole, some broken up.

When the potatoes are bashed to your liking, trickle over more olive oil to taste and scatter over the herbs. Stir lightly, or give them a bit more of a 'bash' to distribute the herbs and oil, then transfer to a warm serving bowl.

SWAPS Bashed new potatoes are also delicious with tomatoes and chives. Cook and 'bash' the potatoes as above. Cut 300g cherry tomatoes into eighths and toss with 3 tablespoons chopped chives, some salt and pepper and some more oil. Toss gently, then spoon this chivey tomato salad over your bashed spuds.

ANOTHER TAKE Add peas and beans for a trio of summer veg. If fresh baby veg are not available, frozen peas or beans will do. Cook and 'bash' the potatoes as above. Meanwhile, add 150g broad beans to another pan of boiling water, return to the boil, then add 150g peas or petits pois. Cook for 2–3 minutes until both veg are tender. Drain well and toss with a knob of butter and a little salt and pepper before adding to the bashed potatoes. Finish with a scattering of chives, parsley or mint, if you like. A little fresh ricotta, crumbled over the top at the end, takes it to another level.

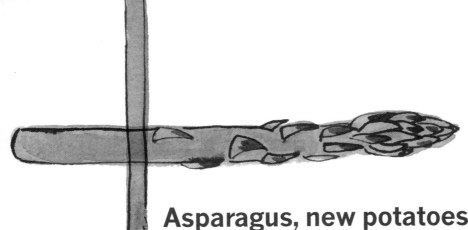

Asparagus, new potatoes, halloumi

Roasting is a surprisingly nifty cooking method for asparagus, quickly rendering this delicious vegetable tender and slightly caramelised. Mingled with earthy little new potatoes, salty halloumi cheese and a generous squeeze of lemon, it makes a fantastic early summer supper.

Serves 4

600–700g new potatoes, scrubbed or scraped

4–5 garlic cloves (unpeeled), bashed

3 tablespoons olive oil

About 400g asparagus

225g halloumi

A spritz of lemon juice

Sea salt and freshly ground black pepper

1–2 tablespoons roughly chopped flat-leaf parsley to finish (optional)

Preheat the oven to 190°C/Gas 5. Cut the potatoes into similar-sized, small chunks. Put them in a large roasting tray with the garlic, add the olive oil and some salt and pepper and toss well. Roast for 30 minutes.

Meanwhile, snap the woody ends from the asparagus and cut the spears into 3–4cm lengths. Cut the halloumi into 2cm cubes.

Take the potatoes from the oven, add the asparagus and halloumi and toss to combine. You don't want the tray to be too crowded – everything should be in a single layer. Return the tray to the oven for 15 minutes until the asparagus is tender and the cheese is starting to caramelise. Discard the garlic.

Add a generous spritz of lemon juice and toss everything again, then transfer to a serving dish. Scatter with parsley, if using, and some more black pepper. Serve straight away – with wedges of sourdough bread, if you really want to make a meal of it.

Potato, swede, egg

A warming, rooty supper dish like this is just the thing to sustain you on a cold evening. It is also an exceptionally nice way to eat swede – even if it's not usually one of your favourite veg. You can use leftover mash, but it's well worth making the dish from scratch.

Serves 4

About 500g swede

About 500g fairly floury potatoes, such as Maris Piper or King Edward

100ml whole milk

50g unsalted butter

4 large eggs, at room temperature

Sea salt and freshly ground black pepper

Preheat the oven to 200°C/Gas 6. Peel the swede and cut it into pieces, no smaller than a golf ball. Place in a saucepan, cover with water, add salt and bring to the boil. Simmer until completely tender, which will take at least 30 minutes. Drain, return to the hot pan and allow to steam for 5 minutes.

Cook the potatoes in the same way in a separate pan; they will only need 15–20 minutes. Drain, return to the hot pan and allow them to steam for 5 minutes.

Heat the milk and butter together in a medium pan until hot but not boiling. Add the drained potatoes and mash to a smooth, soft purée. Mash the swede in its own pan, then add it to the potato and mash the two together until you have a soft, fluffy, textured mash (it won't be super-smooth). Add salt and pepper as you mash, being generous with the pepper – it's delicious with swede.

You can either spread all the potato and swede mash in a large shallow oven dish, or shape it into 4 rough, shallow cakes and put them into individual baking dishes. If the mash is still hot, put it in the oven for 5–10 minutes; if you're reheating it from cold, allow about 15 minutes. It needs to be piping hot in the middle.

Remove from the oven and use the back of a spoon to create four hollows in the mash. Carefully break an egg into each hollow. Return to the oven for 8–10 minutes until the egg whites are set but the yolks still runny. Add a grinding of black pepper and serve straight away.

ANOTHER TAKE Alternatively you can fry individual mash cakes in a little oil, turning them once, until crispy, then set these aside and fry 4 eggs to serve on top.

Cabbage, onion, bread

This is an unusual way to cook greens – a sort of cabbage and stale bread gratin known as a panade. This version is inspired by a recipe from San Francisco's Zuni Café. It uses very humble ingredients to produce a rich and warming result.

Serves 6

6–8 tablespoons olive oil

5 medium or 3 large onions, finely sliced

2 garlic cloves, chopped

1 small green cabbage (600–700g), core and tough stems removed

300g slightly stale, robust bread, such as sourdough

500ml hot vegetable stock

Sea salt and freshly ground black pepper

Heat half the olive oil in a large saucepan over a medium heat. Add the onions and stir. Once they are sizzling, turn the heat right down and cover the pan. Cook gently, stirring from time to time, for about 30 minutes until the onions are very soft and golden, removing the lid for the last 10 minutes or so. Add the garlic and some salt and pepper halfway through cooking.

Meanwhile, preheat the oven to 180°C/Gas 4. Shred the cabbage into 1cm strips. Cook in a steamer for about 4 minutes, or in a pan of boiling water until tender but not soft. Drain really well.

Cut the bread into 2cm cubes and put into a large bowl. Add the remaining olive oil and some salt and pepper and toss well so the bread cubes are coated with the oil and seasoning.

Spread a third of the soft onions over the base of a large, fairly shallow oven dish, about 25cm in diameter, then scatter over one-third of the bread cubes. Spoon half the cabbage evenly over the top. Repeat these layers, then finish with the rest of the onions and bread. Make sure your stock is piping hot, then pour it over the dish, allowing it to soak into the bread cubes.

Cover the dish with foil and bake for 30 minutes, then remove the foil and bake for a further 30 minutes until golden brown and bubbling. Let the dish settle for 10–15 minutes, then serve.

PLUS ONE Adding cheese makes this dish richer and more sumptuous. Use about 175g grated mature Cheddar or Gruyère, scattering it over the layers of bread as you build up the dish.

SWAPS Both kale and Swiss chard leaves are ideal alternatives to the cabbage (use the white chard stems for another dish).

Lentils, spinach, potato

You can enjoy this easy vegetable curry as part of a spread of spicy dishes or on its own. I like to eat it with thick, plain yoghurt and a garlicky flatbread or two. A little mango chutney doesn't go amiss either, or try the lovely apple and cucumber raita on page 148.

Serves 4

250g split red lentils, rinsed

About 1 litre light vegetable stock or water

About 400g cold cooked potatoes

2 tablespoons sunflower oil

2 garlic cloves, finely chopped

1 rounded tablespoon curry powder

200–250g spinach

A good squeeze of lime or lemon juice

Sea salt and freshly ground black pepper

Lime or lemon wedges to serve

Put the lentils in a saucepan with 800ml veg stock or water. Bring to the boil, skim off any scum that rises to the surface, then add ½ teaspoon salt (less if the stock is already salted) and stir well. Simmer the lentils gently for about 15–20 minutes, stirring often with a whisk to help break them down, until you have a thick, coarse dhal (lentil purée). Add a little more stock or water if it looks a little too stiff. Remove from the heat.

Meanwhile, cut the potatoes into 5mm–1cm thick slices. Heat the oil in a large, non-stick frying pan over a medium heat. Add the potatoes and fry for about 10 minutes, tossing once or twice, until golden brown all over. Add the garlic and curry powder and stir to coat the potatoes well. Lower the heat and cook for another minute or two. Then tip the potatoes into the dhal.

Keeping the heat under the frying pan (used for the potatoes) medium-low, add the spinach in handfuls, stirring over the heat as it wilts. If you've just washed the spinach, the water clinging to the leaves will be all that's needed; if it's dry, sprinkle on a little water. When the spinach is just about all wilted, tip the dhal and potatoes back into the pan. Stir the whole lot gently together, trying not to break up the potatoes too much.

Add a good squeeze of lime or lemon juice, then taste the curry and add more salt and pepper if you think it needs it. Serve straight away, with lime or lemon wedges.

PLUS ONE Fried onions are an excellent addition. Thinly slice a couple of onions and fry in a little sunflower oil over a medium heat until golden brown and crispy, then season with salt and pepper before scattering over the curry.

Squash, coconut, chilli

This simple squash curry is the sort of thing you could rustle up quickly on a chilly weekday evening. You can make the dish as hot or mild as you like by adjusting the quantity of fresh chilli and by the curry powder or paste you choose to use. I'd go for a fairly mild variety of chilli, so you can put plenty of it in for colour and texture without blowing everyone's head off.

Serves 4

800g–1kg squash, such as Crown Prince, butternut or kabocha

2 tablespoons sunflower oil

1 onion, thinly sliced

2 garlic cloves, thinly sliced

2–4 mild or medium red chillies, deseeded and sliced

1 good tablespoon of your favourite curry powder or paste, or to taste

400ml tin coconut milk

A squeeze of lime or lemon juice

Sea salt and freshly ground black pepper

Peel and deseed the squash, then cut it into bite-sized chunks. Heat the oil in a large saucepan over a medium-low heat. Add the onion and cook gently for about 10 minutes. Add the garlic and chillies and cook for another couple of minutes. Stir in the curry powder or paste and cook for a minute or two. Now add the squash, with some salt and pepper, and stir well to coat it in the spicy, oniony mixture. Cook for a further 2 minutes or so.

Pour in the coconut milk, stir well and bring to a simmer. Cover and cook gently for 20–25 minutes, stirring carefully every now and then. You want the squash to be perfectly tender and yielding, but not mushy or falling apart. The cooking time will depend on the squash variety.

When the squash is cooked to your liking, taste the curry and add more salt and pepper if needed. Finish with a good spritz of lime or lemon juice. Ladle into bowls and serve with rice and/or naan or flatbreads.

PLUS ONE OR TWO Green beans, whole or cut into 4–5 cm lengths, added to the curry about 8–10 minutes before the end of cooking, will add colour and texture. And, of course, a generous scattering of chopped coriander leaves is a nice way to finish the dish.

Mushrooms, scone, soured cream

Pretty much a classic savoury 'cobbler', this hearty vegetarian main course looks fabulous as you bring it bubbling to the table. You can boost the flavour if you like by adding some wild mushrooms or a handful of pre-soaked dried mushrooms. Steamed greens or leeks make a good accompaniment.

Serves 6

3 tablespoons olive or rapeseed oil

1 onion, finely diced

1 medium carrot, finely diced

1 celery stalk, finely diced

A large knob of butter

700–750g mushrooms, thickly sliced

1 large garlic clove, finely chopped

1 teaspoon roughly chopped thyme (optional)

150ml red wine

250ml vegetable stock

Sea salt and freshly ground black pepper

For the scone topping

175g self-raising flour

½ teaspoon salt

75g chilled butter, diced

1 teaspoon English mustard powder

75g mature Cheddar or other well-flavoured hard cheese, grated

1 large egg

125ml milk

To serve

Soured cream (or plain wholemilk yoghurt)

Preheat the oven to 190°C/Gas 5. Heat 1 tablespoon oil in a large, wide flameproof casserole or heavy-based saucepan and add the onion, carrot and celery. Cover and sweat over a low heat for 15 minutes, stirring occasionally, until tender.

Meanwhile, cook the mushrooms in 2 or 3 batches. To do so, heat 1 tablespoon oil and a knob of butter in a large, wide frying pan over a medium heat. Add a batch of mushrooms, turn the heat up high and cook, stirring often, to encourage them to release their juices. Continue to cook until most of the juices have evaporated and the mushrooms are starting to caramelise. Add them to the sweated vegetables. Repeat with the remaining mushrooms, adding the garlic and thyme, if using, to the last batch towards the end of cooking.

Pour the wine into the frying pan and let it bubble for a couple of minutes, stirring to release the tasty bits stuck to the bottom of the pan. Pour over the mushrooms, then add the stock. Bring to a simmer and leave to cook gently while you make the topping.

Sift the flour and salt into a bowl, add the butter and rub in with your fingertips until it resembles coarse breadcrumbs. Stir in the mustard powder and cheese. Beat the egg with the milk, then stir lightly into the flour mix, bringing it together into a very soft, sticky dough (much looser than a conventional scone dough).

Taste the mushroom stew and add more salt and pepper if needed. If you've used a saucepan, transfer the stew to a wide oven dish. Drop large spoonfuls of the scone dough on to the mushroom mixture. Bake for about 30 minutes, until the scone topping is well risen and golden. Poke a skewer into one of the 'cobbles' to check that it is cooked right through.

Serve the 'cobbler' without further ado, with a bowl of soured cream (or yoghurt) for dolloping on top.

Squash, gnocchi, cheese

This variation on simple potato gnocchi has a lovely sweet note from the squash. It works best with a reasonably dry-fleshed variety such as Crown Prince or Sweet Dumpling. A butternut squash will work too, though you might need an extra shake of flour to bring the gnocchi together.

Serves 4

For the gnocchi

500g peeled, deseeded squash

1 tablespoon olive oil

3–4 garlic cloves (unpeeled), lightly bashed

About 6 sage leaves, roughly chopped (optional)

100g soft goat's cheese, crumbled

200–250g plain flour

1 egg, lightly beaten

Sea salt and freshly ground black pepper

To finish

Butter

Plenty of freshly grated hard goat's or sheep's cheese, or Parmesan

Preheat the oven to 190°C/Gas 5. Cut the squash into 3–4cm chunks. Put into an oven dish and toss with the olive oil, garlic and some salt and pepper. Roast for about 45 minutes until the squash is completely tender, stirring well and adding the sage, if using, halfway through. Discard the garlic at the end of cooking.

Tip the squash into a bowl. Break it up a little with a fork, but don't mash it completely – you want the gnocchi to have some texture. When the squash has cooled but is still just warm, add the goat's cheese, 200g flour, the egg and some salt and pepper. Using a wooden spoon or your hands, bring the ingredients together to make a firm dough. If it seems very soft and sticky, add a little more flour. Knead the dough gently for a minute; don't overwork it. Divide it into 3 or 4 pieces and roll each into a sausage, 1.5–2cm in diameter. Cut into 3cm lengths.

Bring a large pan of water to a gentle simmer. Cook the gnocchi in the simmering water, in batches, for 2–3 minutes, until they rise to the surface. Scoop them out with a slotted spoon and transfer to a lightly buttered warm dish. Toss with more butter, plenty of cheese and some salt and pepper. Serve at once, with a bowl of grated cheese on the table.

PLUS ONE Wilted shredded kale, greens or spinach are a delicious addition. Put them under or on top of the gnocchi, along with the butter and cheese.

Nettles, cheese, puff pastry

I love nettles – they are one of the first wild greens available in the spring, easy to find, bursting with goodness and absolutely delicious. March and April are the best months to pick them, while the nettles are still very young and tender. Take only the top four or six leaves of each plant. You'll need stout gloves for picking and washing them but their sting disappears as soon as they hit hot water. This simple tart is a great way to enjoy them.

Serves 3–4

About 175g nettle tops (1 heaped colander full)

A little polenta or cornmeal for dusting (optional)

2 tablespoons extra virgin olive oil, plus extra to finish

1 garlic clove, finely chopped

Freshly grated nutmeg (optional)

1 ready-rolled puff pastry sheet (about 200g), or roughly the same weight of block puff pastry

50g semi-soft sheep's or goat's cheese

Sea salt and freshly ground black pepper

Put the nettle tops in a sink full of cold water and wash thoroughly, picking them over to remove any unwanted plant matter or insect life. Transfer to a colander. Bring a large pan of salted water to the boil. Add the nettle tops, prodding them down with a wooden spoon. Once simmering again, cook for 4–5 minutes, or until tender. Drain in a colander and leave to cool.

Preheat the oven to 200°C/Gas 6. Scatter a baking sheet with polenta, or grease it lightly with oil if you prefer.

Use your hand to squeeze all the liquid out of the drained nettles. Put them on a board and chop coarsely, then transfer to a bowl. Add the 2 tablespoons olive oil, garlic, a light grating of nutmeg if you like, and some salt and pepper. Mix well with a fork, working the seasoning into the nettles.

Lay your ready-rolled pastry sheet on the prepared baking tray. If using a block of pastry, roll it out on a lightly floured surface until about 5mm thick, trim the edges to straighten, then transfer to the tray. Spread the nettle mixture over the pastry, leaving a 1–2cm clear border at the edge. Crumble over the cheese. Bake for 20–25 minutes until the pastry edges are puffed and golden.

Trickle the tart generously with extra virgin olive oil, sprinkle with salt and pepper, then serve.

PLUS ONE/SWAP You can have this topping on a pizza base, instead of puff pastry. Make the pizza dough (on page 183) and prepare it for topping as described. Sweat a couple of onions in olive oil, cool, then spread over the pizza base. Top as above with nettles and cheese and bake as for the pizza.

Parsnips, shallots, puff pastry

The idea of creating a savoury tarte tatin is not a new one – indeed I've been championing a beetroot version for a while now. However, this particular incarnation, using tender parsnips and caramelised shallots, is my latest favourite.

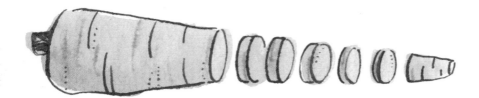

Serves 4–6

1 ready-rolled puff pastry sheet (about 200g), or roughly the same weight of block puff pastry

1 tablespoon olive, sunflower or rapeseed oil

3–4 small-medium parsnips, peeled and cut into 2cm thick rounds (about 250g prepared weight)

150g shallots, peeled but left whole

30g soft brown sugar

30ml cider vinegar

15g butter

Sea salt and freshly ground black pepper

Preheat the oven to 180°C/Gas 4. Take a non-stick, ovenproof frying pan or tatin dish, 20–25cm in diameter. If your pastry is not ready-rolled, roll it out to about a 5mm thickness. Using the pan or tatin dish as a template, cut a disc of pastry the diameter of the top of the pan. Chill in the fridge while you prepare the filling.

Heat the oil in the frying pan or tatin dish over a medium heat. Add the parsnips and shallots and fry gently for 3–4 minutes. Turn them over and cook for few more minutes so both sides take on a nice caramel colour.

Combine the brown sugar and cider vinegar with 30ml water, then add to the pan along with the butter and plenty of salt and pepper. Cover the pan tightly with foil and place in the oven. Roast for about 40 minutes until the parsnips and shallots are tender. Remove from the oven. If, at this stage, the sugar-vinegar syrup is looking a little dry, add 1–2 tablespoons water and give the pan a good shake to release any veg that are sticking.

Lay the pastry disc over the parsnips and shallots, patting it down and tucking the edges down the side of the pan. Turn the oven setting up to 190°C/Gas 5 and return the pan to the oven. Bake for 20–25 minutes until the pastry is puffed up and golden brown.

Leave the tart to cool in its dish for about 15 minutes. Then, to turn it out, put a large plate over the top and invert the plate and pan to unmould the tart. Scrape any juices left in the pan back over the tart, and it's ready to serve. I like to eat this with a crisp green salad trickled with a mustardy dressing.

Potato, onion, chestnut

Filling, comforting and so easy, it's hard to beat the good old jacket spud. It's also a blank canvas on to which you can project all manner of other tasty ingredients. I wouldn't say no to a supper of jacket potato, cheese and baked beans, but as you will know how to knock that one up yourself, here are some less familiar toppers, starting with a lovely chestnutty number.

Serves 4

4 baking potatoes, 250–300g each

2 tablespoons olive oil

2 medium-large red onions, finely sliced

1 garlic clove, finely chopped

200g cooked, peeled chestnuts, roughly chopped or crumbled

4 generous knobs of butter, plus extra to serve

Sea salt and freshly ground black pepper

Preheat the oven to 200°C/Gas 6. Scrub the potatoes and prick the skin of each one a few times with a fork (this stops the occasional spud explosion, which can make a real mess of your oven). Bake the potatoes, either on a baking tray or directly on the shelf of the oven, for about 1 hour, or until they feel completely tender when pierced with a small, sharp knife.

Meanwhile, heat the olive oil in a large frying pan over a medium-low heat. Add the onions and fry gently for 10–15 minutes until soft and lightly coloured. Add the garlic and chestnuts and cook, stirring, for a few more minutes. Take off the heat and season with salt and pepper. Keep warm, or reheat gently before serving.

When the potatoes are cooked, transfer them to warm bowls. Cut a deep cross in the top of each one. Covering your hands with a tea towel to protect them from the heat, firmly pinch each side of the potato to open up the cross and expose the fluffy, steaming flesh inside. Add a generous knob of butter to each potato, then pile the oniony, chestnut mixture on top. Grind over some salt and pepper, then serve, with more butter on the table.

PLUS ONE To finish, a crumbling of blue cheese, such as Dorset Blue Vinney, enriches the onions and chestnuts beautifully.

SWAPS Another great topper is the celeriac and cabbage slaw on page 32. You can use a plain mayonnaise if you like, or just olive oil and a few drops of cider vinegar. A handful of raisins, pre-soaked in warm apple juice to plump up, is a great 'plus-one'. Another favourite topper of mine is apple and Cheddar. Use one cored and finely diced medium dessert apple tossed with about 50g diced Cheddar per potato. A little diced celery (use a tender inner stem) is a nice addition to this combination.

Potato, mushrooms, curry

Scooping out the fluffy middle of a just-baked potato and mashing it up with a little butter and a couple of tasty extras before popping it back in the oven is a great way to make a jacket spud extra appealing. This spicy, mushroomy filling is delicious; I've given a couple of alternatives too.

Serves 4

4 baking potatoes, 250–300g each

2 tablespoons sunflower, rapeseed or olive oil

400g mushrooms, thickly sliced

1 fat garlic clove, chopped

2 tablespoons curry paste

A large knob of butter (30–50g)

Sea salt and freshly ground black pepper

Preheat the oven to 200°C/Gas 6. Scrub the potatoes and prick the skin of each a few times with a fork. Bake the potatoes, either on a baking tray or directly on the shelf of the oven, for about 1 hour, or until they feel completely tender when pierced with a knife.

Meanwhile, heat half the oil in a large frying pan over a medium heat. Add half the mushrooms and fry fairly briskly for about 5 minutes until tender and starting to colour, keeping the heat fairly high to drive off the moisture the mushrooms release. Transfer to a dish. Repeat with the remaining oil and mushrooms, then return the first lot back to the pan, adding the garlic and curry paste. Stir over the heat for about a minute, then remove.

Halve the baked potatoes lengthways, holding them in a tea towel so you don't scald your fingers. Scoop out most of the baked flesh into a bowl, leaving each potato skin with a 5mm thick shell of flesh. Return the potato shells to the oven to keep hot while you make the filling (for no longer than 10 minutes).

Mash the scooped-out potato with the butter and some salt and pepper, then lightly stir in the curried mushrooms. Spoon the mixture back into the potato shells and heat through in the oven for 10–15 minutes.

Leave to stand for about 5 minutes to cool slightly, then grind over some salt and pepper before serving. A dollop of mango chutney on the side goes well here.

SWAPS Puy lentils, cooked as for the recipe on page 27, and a couple of leeks, sliced and sweated down gently in butter, are delicious folded into the potato flesh instead of the mushrooms. Or try replacing the mushrooms with crumbled goat's cheese and finely sliced spring onions or chopped chives.

Kale, onions, chestnuts

Coming up with unusual pizza toppings has become a bit of an obsession for me – this is a current favourite. It's not worth making the dough in smaller quantities than this, but if you're only feeding a few, you can freeze some of the dough (in pizza-sized portions) and scale down the topping accordingly.

Makes 3 pizzas, each serving 2–3

For the pizza dough

250g plain white flour

250g strong white flour

1½ level teaspoons fine sea salt

1 teaspoon easy blend (instant) yeast

1 tablespoon rapeseed or olive oil, plus a little extra

For the topping

About 300g kale or cavolo nero, leaves stripped from stalks and cut into ribbons

A dash of extra virgin olive oil, plus extra to trickle

25g butter

3 onions, finely sliced

3 garlic cloves, sliced

200g cooked peeled chestnuts (vacuum-packed are fine)

Sea salt and freshly ground black pepper

To make the pizza dough, put the flours in a large bowl with the salt and yeast. Mix well. Add the 1 tablespoon oil and 325ml warm water and mix to a rough dough. Flour your hands a little. Tip the dough out on to a work surface and knead for 5–10 minutes until smooth. This is quite a loose, sticky dough – as it should be – so try not to add too much flour. It will become less sticky as you knead.

Trickle a little oil into a bowl, add the dough and turn it. Cover with a tea towel and leave in a warm place to rise until doubled in size, 1–2 hours. Preheat the oven to 250°C/Gas 9, if it goes that high, or at least 220°C/Gas 7. Put a baking sheet in to warm up.

Meanwhile, add the kale or cavolo to a pan of boiling salted water and cook for about 3 minutes until tender. Drain in a colander and refresh under cold water. Drain, then squeeze out excess water.

Return the pan to a medium heat. Add a dash of extra virgin olive oil and the butter. Add the onions and sweat for about 10 minutes until soft and golden. Take out half the onions and combine with the kale. Add the garlic and chestnuts to the onions in the pan and cook for 5 minutes. Add 200ml water and simmer for 2–3 minutes. Blitz to a rough purée with a handheld stick blender. Season.

Tip the dough out on to a lightly floured surface and deflate with your fingers. Rest it for a few minutes, then cut into three. Roll out one piece as thinly as you can. Scatter a peel (pizza shovel) or another baking sheet with a little flour (or polenta) and place the dough base on it. Spread one-third of the chestnut purée over the base, then scatter over one-third of the kale and fried onion. Give the whole lot a generous trickle of olive oil and a sprinkle of salt.

Slide the pizza on to the hot baking sheet in the oven (for a really crisp crust). Or, simply lay the baking sheet on the hot one in the oven (to avoid the tricky pizza transfer). Bake the pizza for 10–12 minutes until crisp and golden brown at the edges – even a little burnt in places. Repeat with the remaining dough and topping.

Beans, olives, mozzarella

This is a very unusual pizza. There are no tomatoes forming a moist 'under-layer'; there aren't even any onions. Instead, the dough is topped with a garlicky purée of white beans, piquant olives and melting, milky mozzarella. The results are deeply savoury, moreish and comforting.

Makes 3 pizzas, each serving 2–3

1 quantity pizza dough (see page 183)

3 tablespoons extra virgin olive oil, plus extra to trickle

3 garlic cloves, chopped

2 x 400g tins white beans, such as cannellini, drained and rinsed

3 balls of buffalo mozzarella (about 125g each)

150g stoned black olives, very roughly chopped or torn

Sea salt and freshly ground black pepper

Make the pizza dough and leave to rise as described on page 183. Preheat the oven to 250°C/Gas 9, if it goes that high, or at least 220°C/Gas 7. Put a baking sheet in to warm up.

Meanwhile, heat the 3 tablespoons extra virgin olive oil in a large frying pan over a low heat. Add the garlic and cook gently for 30 seconds or so, just until it starts to fizz. Add the beans with 200ml water and increase the heat. Simmer for a minute or two. Then use a handheld stick blender to blitz the beans and their liquid to a purée. Season with salt and pepper. The purée should be a spreadable consistency; if too thick, stir in a splash of water.

Knock the air out of the risen pizza dough, leave it to rest for a few minutes on a lightly floured surface, then cut it into three. Roll out one piece as thinly as you can. Scatter a peel (pizza shovel) if you have one, or another flat baking sheet, with a little flour (or polenta) and place the dough base on it.

Spread one-third of the bean purée over the dough. Tear up one ball of mozzarella and distribute it over the dough, followed by one-third of the olives. Trickle with a little more olive oil and sprinkle with salt and pepper.

Slide the pizza on to the hot baking sheet in the oven (for a really crisp crust). Alternatively, simply lay the baking sheet on the hot one in the oven (to avoid the tricky pizza transfer). Cook the pizza in the hot oven for 10–12 minutes until crisp and golden brown at the edges. Repeat with the remaining dough and topping. Serve hot, in slices or wedges.

Fish
and Friends

I love my fish.

Fresh, well-seasoned, well-cooked fish flesh never bores me, and I always delight in serving this wonderful food to my family. For me the key to piscatorial pleasure (besides sustainability, of course) is simplicity. My favourite dishes are those that let the fish speak for itself, with perhaps a couple of agreeable companions to further talk up its qualities.

You really need do very little to a lovely piece of fish to make it great to eat. Bread and butter on one side, a wedge of lemon on the other. But it's fun to play too. And fish (particularly the fuller-flavoured ones) kick off very nicely against partners that are small in terms of stature but massive in terms of taste, such as a dollop of intense tapenade, or a blob of horseradish relish.

I like mucking around with the starchy element too. Sometimes I'll turn trad mash into an almost-sauce, with lashings of lemon juice (page 216); or I'll set sweet earthy beetroot against the richness of smoked oily fish (pages 228 and 230); or, when the fish is going to be saucy, I'll deploy couscous (page 220) or spelt (page 204) as a change from rice or mash. These uncluttered assemblies usually look pretty elegant too.

I mentioned sustainability. It's more important than ever to choose your fish carefully. It's not just about the species itself, but about how and where it was caught. The situation is constantly shifting, so I'd suggest checking a resource such as the Marine Conservation Society's goodfishguide.org for the latest info.

The fish I turn to most often are south-west mackerel, sardines, gurnard, bream and hake – caught by line or nets from smaller boats rather than by big trawlers dragging heavy gear along the bottom. If I want a nice chunky piece of white fish, then it's usually coley, which is a great sustainable choice, or locally line-caught pollack. If you hanker for the curdy white flesh of cod or haddock, choose sustainably caught examples – look out for the Marine Stewardship Council's blue eco-label. Bivalves and crustacea are often a smart alternative to fin fish, and rope-grown mussels and creel-caught crabs are my first-stop shellfish of choice.

Occasionally I pare my fish cookery down to the simplest level: fish plus one can be so good. I'm thinking of a lightly floured, crisply fried fillet of dab with tartare sauce, or a big bowlful of steamed mussels with chips, or a just-caught mackerel, cooked on a grill over a driftwood fire with... well... fingers, frankly.

Clams, tomatoes, garlic

This is the most fantastic, simple way to cook clams alongside two of their finest companions, tomatoes and garlic. All you need in addition is some good bread for soaking up those delicious, salty-savoury pan juices. Alternatively, just pile the lot on to a heap of freshly cooked spaghetti or linguine for a quick and delicious interpretation of pasta alle vongole.

Serves 6

About 500g mixed tomatoes

3 garlic cloves, thinly sliced

3 tablespoons extra virgin olive oil

1.5kg fresh live clams (the palourde variety is best)

A glass of white wine

30g butter

Sea salt and freshly ground black pepper

A handful of flat-leaf parsley, leaves only, finely chopped, to finish (optional)

Preheat the oven to 200°C/Gas 6. Halve the tomatoes and place them in a large, deep-sided roasting tin. Scatter the garlic over the tomatoes, season well with salt and pepper and trickle over the extra virgin olive oil. Roast for 15–20 minutes or until the tomatoes are soft and blistering around the edges.

Meanwhile, scrub the clams well under cold running water. Discard any with broken shells and any that are open and do not close if you tap them sharply against the side of the sink. (Open clams are dead, and since you don't know how long they've been dead, it's best not to eat them.)

Take the roasting tin from the oven and add the clams, settling them in among the tomatoes so you have as shallow a layer as possible. Sprinkle over the wine and dot with the butter. Add a little more salt and pepper. Give the tin a good shake, then return it to the oven for a further 8–12 minutes or until all, or almost all, the clams are open. Discard any that have not opened.

Remove from the oven and scatter with chopped parsley, if you like. Serve in warm bowls, with lots of warm, crusty bread.

Mussels, leeks, cider

I love cooking mussels in cider, and often use a leek or two rather than an onion for the base. This version makes a bit more of the leeks. It's really a mussely version of classic leeks vinaigrette and makes a great starter or light lunch.

Serves 2

300g fresh live mussels

About 4–6 small leeks or 10 baby ones, trimmed and washed thoroughly

300ml medium dry cider

2 tablespoons olive oil

1–2 teaspoons cider vinegar

½ teaspoon thyme leaves (optional)

Sea salt and freshly ground black pepper

To prepare your mussels, scrub them thoroughly with a stiff brush under cold running water. Rope-grown farmed mussels are usually very clean, but if you've gathered them, you'll need to use a small, stout knife to prise off any little barnacles clinging to the shells. Pull away the wiry little 'beard' – a bunch of fibres attached to one side of the shell. Discard any mussels with broken shells and any that are open and do not close if you tap them sharply against the side of the sink, as these will be dead.

Put the leeks into a large, heavy-based pan (that is big enough to take them pretty much in a single layer and has a tight-fitting lid). Season with salt and pepper and pour over the cider. Bring to a simmer, then cover and cook gently over a medium-low heat for about 6–8 minutes until the leeks are tender. Remove the leeks with a slotted spoon and set aside to cool.

Turn the heat up under the pan so the cider is boiling steadily, then add the mussels. Replace the lid and cook the mussels for about 2 minutes, or until all, or almost all, the shells have opened. Discard any that do not open. Tip the mussels into a colander set over a bowl to catch all that lovely, well-flavoured cooking liquor. When the mussels are cool, pick the meat from the shells.

In a large bowl, whisk 100ml of the mussel liquor with the olive oil, 1 teaspoon cider vinegar and the thyme, if using. Taste and add more vinegar, salt and pepper if needed. Add the mussels.

Arrange the mussels and leeks on warm plates and spoon over as much of the dressing as you fancy. Serve with warm brown bread.

SWAP If you are unable to find small or baby leeks, use about 20 spring onions instead.

Crab, mayonnaise, bread

Fresh crab needs only good mayo and great bread to become a sumptuous feast. Cook your own crab for the tastiest meat, or buy a very fresh ready-cooked crab from a good fishmonger.

Serves 2

1 large brown cock crab (800g–1kg)

2 generous slices of brown bread

Butter for spreading

Lemon juice

Sea salt and freshly ground black pepper

For the mayonnaise

½ small garlic clove

2 large egg yolks

½ teaspoon English mustard

1 teaspoon white wine vinegar

About 250ml light olive oil, or 100ml extra virgin olive oil blended with 150ml sunflower oil

For the mayonnaise, crush the garlic with a good pinch of salt. Mix with the egg yolks, mustard, wine vinegar and some pepper in a bowl. Whisk in the oil, a few drops at a time to start with, then in small dashes. Stop when you have a glossy, wobbly mayo. Taste for seasoning, adding salt, pepper and vinegar as needed. Chill.

Bring a large pan of well-salted water (about 10g salt per litre) to the boil ready to cook your crab. First, to kill it, lay it on its back and lift the tail flap to reveal a cone-shaped indentation in the shell. Drive a sharp spike (an awl or small pointed screwdriver) into this and twist a couple of times to sever tissues in the ventral nerve centre. Then immediately drive the spike into the crab's head, through the mouth, between and below the eyes, and lever it back and forth a few times to destroy the nerve tissues here. Lower the crab into the boiling water. When it returns to the boil, cook for 10–12 minutes. For crabs over 1kg, add 3–4 minutes for every extra 500g. Take the crab out of the pan and leave to cool.

To pick the meat from your crab, first twist off the legs and claws. Then open up the body by pulling the undercarriage (body) away from the hard-topped carapace. From the carapace, discard the spiny, plastic-looking mandibles behind the eyes and around the mouthparts. Also discard the small, yellow–white papery stomach sac attached to them. What remains is the rich, brown meat – some of it firm and some very soft and creamy. Dig right into the edges of the carapace with a teaspoon to get it out. It's all good.

From the body, discard the grey feathery gills or 'dead man's fingers'. Break off the legs. Cut the body in half down the middle and pick out the white meat, getting into every recess – use the handle of a teaspoon or a tailor-made crab pick. Lightly crack the legs and claws using a wooden spoon or a small mallet. Pull the shell carefully away and retrieve every last scrap of white meat.

Lightly toast the bread if you like. Butter it and spread with the soft brown meat, then top with flakes of white meat. Season with salt, pepper and a squeeze of lemon, then serve with the mayo.

Crab, peas, chorizo

I like this flavourful combination stirred through pasta or noodles – the soft crab meat clings to the strands like a sauce. However, you can also serve it on its own, perhaps with some warm flatbreads and a salad, or even on toast.

Serves 2, with pasta or noodles

150g peas (freshly podded or frozen)

75g cooking chorizo

1 tablespoon olive oil

About 150g mixed white and brown crab meat (the yield from a medium brown crab)

A good spritz of lemon juice

A knob of butter (optional)

Sea salt and freshly ground black pepper

If using frozen peas, put them in a pan, add boiling water to cover and a shake of salt, then bring back to the boil and simmer for 2–3 minutes until tender. For fresh peas, bring a pan of salted water to the boil, add the peas and bring back to the boil. Simmer for 2–5 minutes until tender (older, fatter peas will take longer than baby ones).

Remove the skin from the chorizo and cut into thick matchsticks. Heat the olive oil in a frying pan over a medium heat. Add the chorizo and fry for a couple of minutes until the fat runs and the chorizo takes on some colour. Add the cooked peas and crush a few of them roughly with a fork so they mingle with the chorizo and oil. Add the crab meat and stir to combine, taking the pan off the heat as soon as the crab is heated through. Season with salt, pepper and plenty of lemon juice.

If you are tossing the crab mixture into hot pasta or noodles, add a knob of butter to lubricate everything. Otherwise, pile on to toast, or on to warm plates with flatbreads or bread on the side.

Lobster, cucumber, apple

Lobster is a true delicacy and a pretty sustainable choice too, as it's almost always pot-caught. A good fishmonger will boil one to order for you, and may even dress it (extract the meat), but it's quite straightforward and very satisfying to do this yourself.

Serves 4

1 live lobster, about 750g (or a freshly cooked one from your fishmonger)

200g cucumber

5g fine sea salt

10g caster sugar

20ml cider vinegar

2 small dessert apples

For the dressing

1½ tablespoons mayonnaise, preferably homemade (see page 194)

1 tablespoon plain wholemilk yoghurt

Juice of ½ lemon

2 teaspoons extra virgin olive oil

A few mint leaves, finely chopped (optional)

If you're cooking the lobster yourself, first put it in the freezer for 1 hour to render it unconscious. Meanwhile, peel and thinly slice the cucumber into rounds. Put into a bowl with the salt, sugar and cider vinegar and mix well. Leave for 2–3 hours in the fridge.

Bring a very large pan of well-salted water (about 10g salt per litre) to the boil. Add the dormant lobster, put a lid on the pan and bring back to the boil as quickly as possible. Boil the lobster for 15 minutes, then remove from the pan and allow to cool.

To extract the meat from your cooked lobster, first twist the big front claws away from the body. Using a small hammer or the back of a heavy knife, crack the claws in several places so you can pull the shell away from the meat. Be careful to remove all fragments of shell. Roughly chop the claw meat and set aside.

Now grasp the long tail section of the lobster and twist: it will come away from the head. Using kitchen scissors, cut along the thinner shell down the underside of the tail. Pull the shell apart, releasing the tail meat. Turn the tail meat over, so the back is uppermost, and make a cut along the length of the tail to reveal the dark intestinal vein. Ease it out with the tip of your knife and discard. Slice the tail meat into thin rounds. If there is any soft, pinky-brown tomalley in the head or tail and/or any firmer red roe, save it – it's all good stuff. And keep the shell to make stock.

For the dressing, combine the mayonnaise with the yoghurt, lemon juice, extra virgin olive oil and mint, if using.

Drain the cucumber in a colander, rinse quickly under the cold tap, then drain thoroughly. Peel, quarter and core the apples. Cut each apple quarter into 3 or 4 wedges.

Gently toss the lobster meat (including any roe and tomalley), cucumber and apple with the dressing. Season with salt and pepper. Divide the salad between plates and serve with brown bread and butter. Rye bread is especially good.

Squid, potato, chilli

Roasting is such an easy way to cook squid. Protected by a light flour coating, it becomes tender, yielding and softly caramelised around the edges – a touch more chewy than deep-fried squid, but in a good way. Chilli brings the dish alive: choose a variety that is pleasantly hot but not too fierce, as you'll be encountering whole strips in the finished dish.

Serves 2

4 tablespoons rapeseed or olive oil

500g potatoes (unpeeled)

3–4 garlic cloves (unpeeled), lightly bashed

3 tablespoons plain flour

250g cleaned squid, with tentacles if you like

1–2 fairly large, not-too-hot red chillies, deseeded and sliced into fine strips

Sea salt and freshly ground black pepper

Lemon wedges to serve

Preheat the oven to 200°C/Gas 6. Put the oil in a large roasting tin and place in the oven for 5 minutes until very hot. Meanwhile, cut the potatoes into roughly 3cm chunks. Add to the roasting tin with the bashed garlic and plenty of salt and pepper, toss in the oil and then roast in the oven for 30 minutes.

In the meantime, put the flour in a dish and season well with salt and pepper. Slice the squid bodies into 1cm thick rings, then turn them inside out, which helps them stay 'open' during cooking. Toss the rings and any tentacles in the seasoned flour.

After their 30 minutes, take the potatoes out of the oven and turn the setting up to 240°C/Gas 9. Stir the potatoes well. Push them to one side of the tray to create space for the squid. Put the squid pieces into the tray and stir gently to coat them in the hot oil. Return to the oven for 5–7 minutes until the squid is starting to colour on the base, then stir in the chilli slices and roast for another 5 minutes. Discard the garlic.

Using a slotted spoon, transfer the potatoes, squid and chilli to warm serving bowls. Serve straight away, with lemon wedges for squeezing.

Squid, hummus, almonds

This clever combination from Gill Meller, River Cottage head chef, makes an elegant starter or light main course – and it's a great recipe to try if you're new to cooking squid. If you don't fancy prepping the squid yourself, you can buy it ready-cleaned or ask your fishmonger to do it for you. You can use a good-quality shop-bought hummus here if you like, but I'd advise you to loosen it with extra lemon juice and good olive oil. Better still, make your own – it doesn't take long in a processor.

Serves 4

About 300g cleaned squid, with tentacles if you like

4 tablespoons flaked almonds

1 tablespoon olive oil

A little sweet or smoked paprika (optional)

Sea salt and freshly ground black pepper

For the hummus

400g tin chickpeas, drained and rinsed

Juice of 1 lemon

1 garlic clove, crushed

2 pinches of ground cumin

2 tablespoons tahini (sesame seed paste)

3–4 tablespoons extra virgin olive oil, plus extra to serve

To make the hummus, put the chickpeas, half the lemon juice, half the garlic, a good pinch of cumin and the tahini in a food processor with a pinch of salt and 4 tablespoons water. Pulse to a coarse mixture, then keep blending as you add 3 tablespoons extra virgin olive oil. You might need to stop and scrape down the sides once or twice. Add more lemon juice, garlic, cumin, salt or pepper to taste. Scrape the hummus into a small pan.

Cut the squid pouches open along their length. Score the inside of the flesh in a diamond pattern with a knife, being careful not to go all the way through the flesh. Cut each one into a few pieces. Cut the rings of tentacles in half at the base.

Warm the hummus very gently, adding a little more oil and/or water, if necessary, to keep it a thick purée consistency. Keep warm in the pan.

Place a medium, non-stick frying pan over a medium heat, add the almonds and toast them for 1–2 minutes, tossing frequently, until starting to colour. Remove the almonds and set aside.

Return the pan to a high heat and add the olive oil. When smoking hot, add the squid and some salt and pepper. Cook for 2 minutes maximum, tossing the squid around in the pan, until it is opaque and has patches of golden-brown colour. It will curl up in the heat – don't worry about this, just try to ensure most of the surface makes contact with the pan at some point.

Spoon the warm hummus into mounds on warm plates, top with the squid and scatter over the toasted almonds. Sprinkle, if you like, with a pinch or two of sweet or smoked paprika. Trickle a little more olive oil over and around the whole thing, and serve.

Trout, watercress, spelt

I've always loved the clean, fresh pairing of watercress and trout. Here I've added nutty grains of pearled spelt to the mix to create a smart but simple salad starter. If I can't catch my own, I always buy organically farmed trout.

Serves 4

1 organic rainbow trout (about 500g), or 2 smaller fish, scaled and gutted

½ onion, sliced

½ teaspoon black peppercorns

2 bay leaves

A few parsley stalks (optional)

100g pearled spelt

2 handfuls of young, tender watercress

Sea salt and freshly ground black pepper

For the dressing

50g plain wholemilk yoghurt

½ teaspoon English mustard

Juice of ½ lemon

A pinch of sugar

To poach the trout, gently wash the fish under cold running water, then lay it in a suitably sized saucepan and pour on enough fresh cold water to just cover. Add the onion, peppercorns, bay leaves and parsley stalks, if using. Bring to a very gentle simmer and cook for 8–10 minutes, no longer. Lift out the fish on to a board and allow it to cool completely. Strain the liquid (now a fish stock) into a clean pan and return to the heat.

Wash the spelt well, then add to the fish stock. Add 1 teaspoon salt, bring to a simmer and cook for 25–30 minutes, until tender. Drain and allow to cool.

Peel the skin from the trout, then carefully lift the flesh from the bones, removing any small pin bones as you go. You should get around 250g cooked trout flesh.

For the dressing, put the ingredients into a bowl and whisk well to combine. Season with salt and pepper to taste.

Gently combine the fish with the cooled spelt, being careful not to break up the pieces too much. Divide the fish and spelt between serving plates, scatter over the watercress and trickle over the dressing. Give a final seasoning of salt and pepper before serving, with brown bread and butter, and a glass of crisp white wine.

SWAP You can make a nice version of this salad using small, waxy new potatoes instead of spelt. Scrub the potatoes and simmer in lightly salted boiling water until just cooked. Drain and leave to cool completely. Peel only if the skin looks coarse after cooking. Cut the potatoes into quarters or smallish chunks and toss with the flaked fish and dressing. Scatter over the watercress.

Sardines, garlic, leaves

The trick with this recipe is to get your oven as hot as you can so the skin of the sardines can blister and crackle in the short time it takes for the rich, oily flesh to cook through. Pairing that delicious garlic-infused flesh with some crisp leaves creates an irresistible plateful. You can use any leaves you fancy here but I particularly like those with a delicate bitterness such as frisée or white chicory. Crisp-leaved romaine lettuce is good too. Add a few herbs to the mix if you can – chervil, parsley, chives and sorrel all work well.

Serves 4

3 garlic cloves, cut into 1–2mm thick slices

A stem of rosemary, leaves only, roughly chopped (optional)

2 tablespoons extra virgin olive oil

12 sardines, scaled and gutted

4 large handfuls of crisp salad leaves

Juice of ½ lemon

Sea salt and freshly ground black pepper

Preheat the oven to 250°C/Gas 9 or its hottest possible setting. Place a large roasting tin in the oven to get really hot.

In a bowl, mix the garlic and chopped rosemary, if using, together with the extra virgin olive oil.

Take the roasting tin from the oven, spoon a little of this pungent mix over the base, then quickly but carefully arrange the sardines in the tin. Spoon the remaining garlic, rosemary and oil over the fish and season well with salt and pepper. Roast in the oven for 8–10 minutes until the sardines are cooked through and fragrant.

Transfer the sardines to plates and pile the crisp salad leaves to one side. Add the lemon juice to the pan, mix with the oily pan juices, then spoon over both fish and leaves. Serve with bread.

Mackerel, celery, orange

This unexpected but excellent blend of flavours is a perfect example of three-good-things alchemy: full-flavoured oily fish, cut with the crunch of celery and the aromatic sweet-sharp tang of orange flesh. It's an all-round winner.

Serves 4

1 tablespoon rapeseed, sunflower or olive oil

2 garlic cloves (unpeeled), lightly bashed

2 bay leaves (optional)

8 mackerel fillets from 4 medium fish

Sea salt and freshly ground black pepper

For the orange and celery salad

2 large or 3 medium oranges

4 inner celery stalks, plus a few of the leaves

A dash of extra virgin rapeseed or olive oil

A few drops of cider vinegar

Sea salt and freshly ground black pepper

For the salad, using a fine grater, lightly grate the zest from one of the oranges and set aside. Now slice all the peel and pith away from both oranges. To do this, cut a slice off the base of each and stand the orange on a board. Then use a sharp knife to cut down through the peel and pith, slicing it away completely, in sections. Now, working over a bowl to catch any juice, slice the segments of orange out from between the membranes, dropping them into the bowl. Remove any pips as you go. Squeeze out the remaining juice from the orange membrane into the bowl and add the zest.

Strip off any obvious fibres from the outside of the celery stalks, then slice on the diagonal into roughly 1cm pieces. Add to the oranges, along with a little extra virgin oil, a few drops of cider vinegar and some salt and pepper. Arrange on serving plates with a few little roughly torn celery leaves.

You will need to cook the mackerel in two batches if you haven't a large enough pan to take all the fillets comfortably. Heat the oil in a large, non-stick frying pan over a medium heat. Add the garlic and bay, if using, and let sizzle for a minute. Season the mackerel fillets well with salt and pepper, then place in the pan, skin side down. Cook for about 2 minutes, until the skin is crisp, then carefully turn the fillets and finish cooking for a minute or so.

Place the mackerel on top of the salad and serve straight away, with brown bread if you like.

SWAPS Replace the celery with thinly sliced, raw fennel for an equally delicious result. You could also swap the orange with grapefruit, choosing a relatively sweet ruby or pink variety.

Mackerel, oatmeal, rhubarb

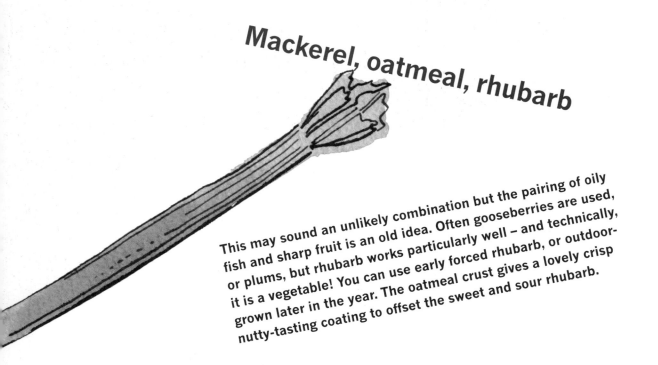

This may sound an unlikely combination but the pairing of oily fish and sharp fruit is an old idea. Often gooseberries are used, or plums, but rhubarb works particularly well – and technically, it is a vegetable! You can use early forced rhubarb, or outdoor-grown later in the year. The oatmeal crust gives a lovely crisp nutty-tasting coating to offset the sweet and sour rhubarb.

Serves 2

2 medium-thick rhubarb stems or 3–4 smaller, thinner ones (about 150g)

20g caster sugar

A pinch of thyme leaves (optional)

4 mackerel fillets from 2 medium fish

100g medium oatmeal

Rapeseed or sunflower oil for frying

Sea salt and freshly ground black pepper

Trim the rhubarb, then cut into 2–3cm pieces. Place in a pan with the sugar, thyme leaves, if using, and 1 tablespoon water. Partially cover with a lid and cook gently, at a bare simmer, for 5–7 minutes. Don't stir the rhubarb or it will lose its shape. When it is tender, remove the pan from the heat.

Season the mackerel fillets all over with salt and pepper. Spread out the oatmeal on a plate. Coat the fillets on both sides, pressing the oatmeal on well and gently shaking off any loose bits. (For a decent coating, the mackerel should be 'tacky'. If the oatmeal doesn't stick, brush the fillets with just a little milk, and try again.)

Heat about 2 tablespoons oil in a large frying pan over a medium heat. Add the mackerel fillets, flesh side down, and cook for 3 minutes, until the oatmeal coating is crispy and golden brown. Then carefully flip them over and cook for 2 minutes on the skin side, until cooked through. Transfer the fish to warm plates and accompany with a spoonful of the warm rhubarb compote. Serve with bread and/or a green salad.

SWAPS You can use herring or sardine fillets, instead of mackerel, allowing 3 or 4 per person. A tart compote of gooseberries or plums makes a good seasonal change from the rhubarb.

Mackerel, new potatoes, shallots

I absolutely love cooking mackerel like this – it's such a neat one-tray dish and the blend of mingled flavours is wonderful. It also works well with other fish.

Serves 4

500–750g small new potatoes

300g shallots

3 tablespoons olive oil, plus extra for brushing

About 6 bay leaves, each twisted or torn

8 mackerel fillets from 4 small-medium fish

Sea salt and freshly ground black pepper

Lemon wedges to serve

Preheat the oven to 190°C/Gas 5. Scrub or scrape the new potatoes and cut into quarters or smallish chunks, roughly walnut-sized. Peel the shallots and halve them.

Put the potatoes and shallots into a large roasting dish. Add the 3 tablespoons olive oil, plenty of salt and pepper and the bay leaves and toss the lot together. Roast for about 40 minutes until the potatoes are golden brown and the shallots are starting to caramelise, giving them a good stir halfway through cooking.

Brush the mackerel fillets with a little olive oil and season well with salt and pepper. Lay them, skin side up, on the potatoes and shallots, nestling them down into the veg a little, but not burying them completely. Turn the oven setting up to 200°C/Gas 6. Roast the fish and veg together for about 8 minutes until the mackerel is cooked through.

Serve straight away, with lemon wedges for squeezing. You don't really need an accompaniment, but I do sometimes like a green salad before or alongside this lovely dish.

SWAPS You can replace the mackerel with pretty much any other fish, from whole sardines to a slab of white fish such as pollack, or fillets of gurnard or bass.

Fish, bread, capers

This might sound an unusual dish but it's really a variation on good old chip-shop battered fish. You have the crisp outer layer (bread rather than batter in this case), the tender white fish and the vinegary, salty capers. A fairly open-textured bread works best. The edges and base get nice and crispy with the oil, while the middle gets a little soggy with fishy, capery buttery juices.

Serves 2

2 thick slices of bread

1 garlic clove, halved

Soft butter for spreading

2 pollack, whiting or sustainably caught cod fillets (about 150g each)

2 tablespoons olive oil

2–4 bay leaves (optional)

A few sprigs of thyme (optional)

2 tablespoons small capers, rinsed

Sea salt and freshly ground black pepper

Preheat the oven to 220°C/Gas 7. Rub the bread slices with the cut garlic clove, then spread with the butter. Season with salt and pepper and place, butter side up, in a small roasting tin.

Rub the fish all over with a little of the olive oil and season well. Place, skin side up, on top of the bread. Tuck the bay leaves and thyme, if using, under the pieces of fish. Scatter the capers over the fish and tuck a few underneath too. Trickle over the rest of the olive oil.

Roast in the oven for about 8–10 minutes or until the bread is toasted and golden around the edges and the fish is just cooked through. Serve at once with a green salad.

PLUS ONE OR TWO You can amplify the piquant character of this dish by scattering some roughly chopped stoned black olives over the fish as soon as it comes out of the oven. A few deseeded and chopped tomatoes – seasoned and bound with a little more olive oil, then spooned around the fish – make a further lovely addition.

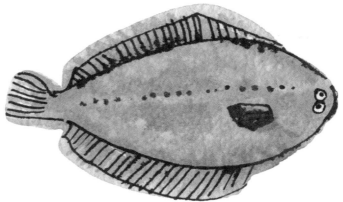

Sole, lemon, potato

This is simply fried fish with mash, but the potato is laced with lemon juice and peppery olive oil, making it almost a lemony sauce. It's a great illustration of the fact that a sophisticated dish needn't have an ingredients list as long as your arm.

Serves 4

500g floury potatoes, such as Maris Piper, peeled and cubed

1 garlic clove, peeled

100ml extra virgin olive oil, plus extra for frying

Finely grated zest and juice of 1–2 lemons, plus an extra 1 or 2 lemons to serve

2 lemon sole, filleted to give 8 fillets (about 600g in total)

A knob of butter

1 teaspoon thyme or lemon thyme leaves (optional)

Sea salt and freshly ground black pepper

Put the potatoes and whole garlic clove in a pan, cover with water and add some salt. Bring to the boil, then lower the heat and simmer until tender, 15–20 minutes. Drain, reserving the cooking water, and allow to steam-dry in a colander for 5–10 minutes.

Pass the potatoes and the soft garlic clove through a potato ricer or press through a fine sieve into a bowl or pan. Use a wooden spoon to combine this hot mash with the extra virgin olive oil and some salt and pepper, then add the juice of 1 lemon. Taste and add more lemon juice if you like. Add enough of the potato cooking water to give the mash a loose, creamy consistency. Keep warm.

Season the sole fillets with salt and pepper. Place a non-stick frying pan over a medium heat and add 1 tablespoon extra virgin olive oil. Lay the fillets, skin side down, in the pan and fry gently for 2 minutes, then turn them. Fry for another minute or two until just cooked through, adding the butter, lemon zest and thyme leaves, if using, for the last 30 seconds and spooning them over the fish as the butter melts. Remove from the heat.

Spoon the lemony potato on to warm plates, add the fish fillets and grind over some pepper. Serve with lemon(s) for squeezing and a side salad.

SWAPS This will work very well with other flat fish fillets, such as megrim, dab or plaice.

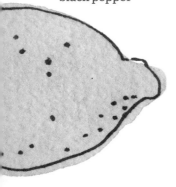

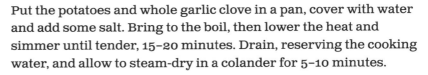

Fish, coconut, coriander

This pretty dish is simple and well balanced. It's also very quick and easy: pick up a fillet of super-fresh fish on your way home and you can have this lovely, fragrant supper on the table in next to no time. I've chosen inexpensive white fish here, but pretty much any fish fillet will work.

Serves 2

250g skinless pollack, coley or whiting fillet

1 garlic clove, finely chopped or grated

½ thumb-sized piece of ginger, peeled and grated (optional)

1 tablespoon olive oil

A knob of butter

165ml tin coconut milk

A bunch of coriander, leaves only

A good squeeze of lime juice

Sea salt and freshly ground black pepper

Cut the fish into finger-sized pieces, carefully removing any bones or scraps of skin or scale as you go. Combine the fish in a bowl with the garlic, ginger, if using, the olive oil and some salt and pepper. Leave to marinate for 15–20 minutes.

Place a small frying pan over a medium-high heat. Add the butter and, when foaming, put the fish in the pan with the marinade. Cook for barely a minute, turning the fish pieces a few times, then pour in the coconut milk. Bring to a simmer and cook for a further 1–2 minutes or until the fish is cooked through.

Throw in the coriander and squeeze over some lime. Taste and add more salt and pepper if needed, then bring to the table. Serve with plain boiled rice, or over rice noodles.

Bream, olives, couscous

I like my fish cooked simply – just whacked in the pan for a few minutes suits me fine – but I then like to pair it with strong, piquant flavours. Tapenade, a coarse purée of black olives, garlic, anchovies and olive oil, is just the thing to accentuate the subtle qualities of a good piece of fish.

Serves 4

200g couscous

2 tablespoons olive oil

A sprig of thyme or 2 bay leaves (optional)

4 fillets from 2 medium (500–600g) bream

A squeeze of lemon juice

Sea salt and freshly ground black pepper

For the tapenade

200g stoned black olives

1 tablespoon capers, rinsed

1 teaspoon thyme leaves

1 large garlic clove, chopped

4 anchovy fillets (or use more if you're a real anchovy fan)

4 tablespoons olive oil

A squeeze of lemon juice, or more to taste

To serve

Lemon wedges

For the tapenade, put all the ingredients in a food processor and whiz to a coarse purée. Add pepper and more lemon juice to taste, but you are unlikely to need salt (the olives, capers and anchovies add plenty). Scrape the tapenade out of the processor into a bowl and set aside.

Prepare the couscous according to the packet instructions. When cooked, fluff it up with a fork to separate the grains, then trickle over 1 tablespoon olive oil, season with salt and pepper and fork through. Keep the couscous warm.

Heat the remaining 1 tablespoon olive oil in a large frying pan over a medium heat. Add the thyme or bay leaves, if using. Season the fish all over and add to the pan, skin side down. Cook for about 3 minutes until the skin is golden, then flip the fillets over and cook for another 1–2 minutes until the fish is just cooked through.

Heap the couscous on to warm plates, place a fish fillet alongside and spoon a generous portion of tapenade between the two. Put any remaining tapenade in a dish on the table for people to help themselves. Serve with lemon wedges and a simply cooked green vegetable such as French or broad beans, or a crisp green salad.

SWAPS Bream is my favourite for this dish, but sea bass, mackerel, grey mullet and gurnard all work very well too.

Fish, onion, olives

The strong, aromatic presence of onions and black olives works a treat with well-flavoured fish and they give this dish a lovely Mediterranean feel. I often make this with mackerel fillets, but the suggested swaps are all good choices – from a sustainability angle too.

Serves 2

3 tablespoons olive oil

2–3 large onions, finely sliced

3–4 bay leaves (optional)

A sprig of thyme (optional)

75g stoned black olives, roughly chopped

50ml white wine

Fillets from 2 medium mackerel or gurnard, or 1 small sea bass

Heat the olive oil in a large frying pan over a medium heat. Add the onions, with the bay leaves and thyme, if using, and stir well to break up the onion slices. Once they are sizzling, turn the heat down low. Cook very gently, stirring from time to time, for 20–25 minutes, until the onions are very soft and golden. You can cover the pan if you like, for part of the cooking time, to help them sweat rather than brown.

Add the olives and wine to the pan. Turn up the heat to medium and cook for about 10 minutes until the wine has evaporated. Season with salt and pepper. Push the onions to the edges of the pan to make space for the fish in the middle.

Lay the fish fillets in the pan, flesh side down. Turn them over after a few minutes to cook the skin side, spreading the onions over the fish to help the heat penetrate. They should be cooked through in about 8 minutes.

Grind some pepper over the fish and serve hot, straight from the pan, or at room temperature, with new potatoes or couscous.

SWAP Fillets of red mullet are also delicious cooked this way.

Smoked fish, sweetcorn, batter

Crisp on the outside and tender in the centre, with just the right amount of bite from the sweetcorn and a salty tang from the smoked fish, these little fritters make incredibly tasty – and pleasingly untidy – alternatives to the ubiquitous neat fishcake.

Serves 4

200g smoked pollack or haddock fillet

About 500ml whole milk

1 bay leaf

A chunk of onion

2 corn-on-the-cobs

Sunflower oil for frying

Sea salt and freshly ground black pepper

For the batter

50g plain flour

25g cornflour

½ teaspoon baking powder

To serve

Lemon wedges

Put the fish in a saucepan and pour on enough milk to barely cover it. Add the bay leaf, onion and a grinding of pepper. Bring slowly to the boil, then take off the heat and flip the fish over in the pan. Cover and leave to cook in the residual heat for 3 minutes. Turn the fish over and check that it is cooked – the flesh should be opaque and flake easily from the skin. If it's not quite done, leave it in the covered pan for a couple of minutes longer. Slightly undercooked is fine, however, as the fish will be cooked further in the cakes. Once cooked, remove the fish with a slotted spoon and set aside to cool. Strain the milk and leave to cool.

For the batter, sift the flour with the cornflour and baking powder into a large bowl. Measure 125ml of the cooled milk and gradually whisk it into the flour. You want a smooth, thin batter, about the consistency of single cream, so add a little more or less milk as needed, erring on the side of thinness. Taste the batter, adding a little salt only if required (the fish-infused milk contributes salt).

Using a sharp knife, cut the kernels from the corn cobs. Take the cooled fish off its skin in large flakes, removing any bones as you go. Add to the batter, with the corn. Turn gently together with a spoon. Tip out any excess batter, to ensure just a light coating.

Heat about a 1cm depth of oil in a heavy-based frying pan over a medium-high heat. To check it is hot enough, drop in a cube of white bread – it should turn light golden brown in 30–40 seconds. Place heaped tablespoonfuls of the mixture in the pan, flattening them slightly with the spoon. Cook for a minute or so until golden brown underneath, then flip over and cook for another minute or two. Remove and drain on kitchen paper for a minute. Serve piping hot, with a sprinkling of salt and lemon wedges on the side.

PLUS ONE A dollop of tartare sauce is a lovely extra – just stir some chopped spring onion, capers, gherkins and parsley into mayonnaise, preferably homemade (see page 194).

Smoked fish, spinach, béchamel

Creamed spinach – wilted, chopped and stirred into a thick, well-seasoned béchamel sauce – has long been one of my favourite kinds of comfort food. Adding some flaked smoked fish turns it into the sort of supper that will rescue anyone from the doldrums – especially if you top it with a poached egg.

Serves 2

250g spinach, any tough stalks removed

250g smoked pollack or haddock fillet

For the béchamel

350ml whole milk

1 bay leaf

A wedge of onion

25g butter

25g plain flour

Sea salt and freshly ground black pepper

Wash the spinach and put it into a pan with just the water clinging to the leaves. Cover the pan and place over a medium heat for a few minutes, just until the spinach wilts. Drain in a colander, cool, then squeeze out the water and chop the spinach coarsely.

Put the fish in a saucepan and pour on the milk for the béchamel. Add the bay leaf, onion and a grinding of black pepper. Bring slowly to the boil, take off the heat and flip the fish over. Cover and leave to cook in the residual heat for 3 minutes. Turn the fish over and check that it is cooked – the flesh should be opaque and flake easily from the skin. If it's not quite done, leave it in the covered pan for a couple of minutes longer. Remove the fish with a slotted spoon. Strain the milk.

Heat the butter in a medium saucepan over a medium heat until melted and bubbling. Stir in the flour to make a smooth roux and cook gently for 2–3 minutes. Remove from the heat and add about a quarter of the warm, fishy milk. Beat vigorously to form a smooth paste. Add another quarter of the milk and beat again until smooth. Repeat with the remaining milk. When you have a smooth, fishy béchamel sauce, return it to the heat and let it simmer gently, stirring often, for 4–5 minutes. Take off the heat.

Stir the chopped spinach into the sauce. Flake the smoked fish off the skin in reasonably large chunks, removing any bones as you go, and add it straight to the sauce. Stir the fish in very gently so as not to break up the flakes too much. Taste and add pepper, and salt only if necessary – the fish will have contributed salt.

PLUS ONE I love to serve this dish topped off with a poached egg or two. (See page 108 for egg poaching instructions.)

ANOTHER TAKE This is also lovely as a gratin: spread the spinach and fish mixture in a shallow gratin dish, scatter breadcrumbs on top and dot with butter. Flash under the grill until golden brown.

Smoked mackerel, beetroot, horseradish

This is a fantastic, substantial salad, bursting with good things.
If you can roast the beetroot ahead of time – or if you have
some left over from another dish – then the whole ensemble
takes just minutes to put together.

*Serves 4–5 as a starter,
2–3 as a main course*

About 400g smallish
beetroot

2–3 garlic cloves (unpeeled),
bashed

A sprig of thyme (optional)

3 tablespoons sunflower,
rapeseed or olive oil

3 smoked mackerel fillets
(about 200g in total), skin
removed

Sea salt and freshly ground
black pepper

For the horseradish dressing

3 tablespoons plain
wholemilk yoghurt
or soured cream

1 tablespoon rapeseed
or olive oil

3 teaspoons grated
fresh horseradish, or
2 tablespoons creamed
horseradish from a jar

½ teaspoon caster sugar

A squeeze of lemon juice

Preheat the oven to 190°C/Gas 5. Scrub the beetroot and cut any
larger ones into chunks, so they are all roughly the same size. Put
in a roasting tray with the garlic, thyme, if using, 2 tablespoons oil
and some salt and pepper. Shake the tray to toss the ingredients
together. Cover with foil and bake until the beetroot are tender,
about 1 hour but possibly longer. Discard the garlic. Leave the
beetroot to cool completely, then peel and cut into thick slices.

To make the dressing, whisk all the ingredients together with
some salt and pepper to combine. Set aside.

Break the smoked mackerel into bite-sized chunks, checking
for any small bones. Divide the mackerel and beetroot between
serving bowls. Spoon some of the horseradish dressing over the
salad and put the rest into a small bowl on the table so people can
help themselves to more. Serve with bread on the side.

PLUS ONE A couple of handfuls of flat-leaf parsley or watercress
add colour and even more flavour to this salad. Toss lightly with
the beetroot and fish before adding the dressing.

SWAPS Kipper fillets work as well as smoked mackerel. Grill or
poach lightly, let cool, then break up and use as the mackerel.

Smoked mackerel, beetroot, horseradish

No holds should be barred and no stone left unturned when it comes to searching out delicious and unexpected new pizza toppings. For this one, I simply took the ingredients from the lovely salad on the previous page and reinterpreted them in pizza form. It's a winner.

Makes 3 pizzas, each serving 2–3

1 quantity pizza dough (see page 183)

3 smoked mackerel fillets (about 200g in total), skin removed

About 200g cooked, peeled beetroot (see page 228, or use vacuum-packed, but not pickled!)

3–4 shallots, very thinly sliced into rings

Extra virgin olive oil to trickle

Sea salt and freshly ground black pepper

For the horseradish dressing

1½ tablespoons horseradish sauce

3 tablespoons plain wholemilk yoghurt

A squeeze of lemon juice

Prepare the dough and leave to rise as described on page 183. Preheat the oven to 250°C/Gas 9, if it goes that high, or at least 220°C/Gas 7. Put a baking sheet in to warm up.

Tip the risen dough out on to a lightly floured surface and deflate with your fingers. Leave it to rest for a few minutes, then cut it into three. Roll out one piece as thinly as you can. Scatter a peel (pizza shovel), if you have one, or another flat baking sheet with a little flour (or polenta) and place the dough base on it.

Flake the smoked mackerel into large pieces, checking for any small bones. Slice the beetroot thickly. Toss the shallot rings with a little extra virgin olive oil, salt and pepper. Arrange a third of the mackerel and beetroot over the pizza base and scatter a third of the shallot rings on top.

Slide the pizza on to the hot baking sheet in the oven (for a really crisp crust). Alternatively, simply lay the baking sheet on the hot one in the oven (to avoid the tricky pizza transfer). Cook the pizza in the hot oven for 10–12 minutes until crisp and golden. Repeat with the remaining dough and topping.

Meanwhile, for the dressing, whisk the horseradish and yoghurt together with a squeeze of lemon juice. Season to taste with salt and pepper. Trickle the sauce over the pizzas, then trickle over a little more extra virgin olive oil. Serve straight away, with a crisp green salad.

Meat and Two Veg

'Meat and two veg'

'Meat and two veg' – that workaday phrase – doesn't sound like a meal worth writing home about, does it? It's hardly going to blow you away with an awesomely original combination of ingredients, is it? But hang on, before we dismiss it out of hand, what about a glistening, juicy Sunday roast with proper crisp spuds and fresh greens; top-drawer butcher's bangers with creamy mash and peas; or the lamb chop, onions and potatoes of a classic Lancashire hotpot? Any of these classic threesomes can provide satisfaction off the scale.

Still, the real fun starts when you pull apart the notion of meat and two veg and reassemble it in unexpected ways. The result is some frankly barn-storming dishes that tear up the rule book. The key is to be open-minded about what qualifies as a 'veg'. In my book – which this is! – it can certainly be a fruit, for instance (try the delicious lamb, kale and quince on page 252, or the pork, potatoes and apples on page 267); it may well be a fresh herb used boldly (as in the chicken, tomatoes and tarragon, page 237), a pulse (pigeon, sorrel, lentils, page 244) or even, in extremis, a jar of marmalade (ham, squash, marmalade, page 270) or a liquid from a bottle (lamb, lettuce, vinegar, page 250).

The traditional proportioning of the meat and two veg need not apply either – there is no reason the meat should dominate. Not for me the anonymous 'seasonal veg' or the limp 'salad garnish' that you so often find on the side of the plate. I want my veg – in the most inclusive sense of the word – to be as exciting as the meat to which it's cosying up. Often the different elements will be fully integrated and equally weighted. In the casually tumbled salad of ham, potatoes and parsley (page 269) or the sumptuously stewed bacon, beans and tomatoes (page 272), the elements are indivisible, the sum greater than the parts – and meat by no means trumps veg.

Indeed, meat can be the finishing touch, rather than the backbone of the meal: a few shards of salt beef and some leftover mash and onion make for delicious, hearty potato cakes (page 262); snippets of streaky bacon scattered over a roasting dish of radicchio and shallots give a lovely salty-crisp contrast to these bittersweet veg (page 275).

Sometimes, you see, meat is the seasoning for a cracking plate of vegetables. And when you turn convention on its head like this, you're well on the way to a daringly different and deliciously new definition of modest old 'meat and two veg'.

Chicken, tomatoes, tarragon

As it cooks, this very easy dish makes its own delicious sauce – a combination of the roast chicken juices and the deeply savoury tomato liquor. The tarragon is much more than just a background herb here. Its distinctive aniseed flavour is quite dominant, holding its own with the chicken and tomatoes, and rounding out the dish perfectly.

Serves 6–8

1 free-range chicken (about 1.8kg), jointed into 8 pieces (or a similar weight of bone-in, skin-on chicken pieces)

2 tablespoons olive oil

½ glass of white wine (or use water if you prefer)

Juice of ½ lemon

About 500g ripe tomatoes (any shape or size), halved or quartered

A bunch of tarragon, leaves only, coarsely chopped

Sea salt and freshly ground black pepper

Preheat the oven to 190°C/Gas 5. Season the chicken pieces well all over with salt and pepper. You'll probably need to sear them in two batches. Heat the olive oil in large non-stick frying pan over a medium-high heat, add the chicken and sear, turning the pieces several times, until they are golden brown all over. Transfer, skin side up, to an oven dish or roasting tin.

Now, to deglaze the frying pan, pour in the wine and let it bubble over the heat, stirring well to scrape up any bits of caramelised chicken from the bottom. Pour the liquid from the pan into the oven dish (but not directly over the chicken). Add the lemon juice and give the chicken skin an extra scattering of salt and pepper. Cover the dish with foil and bake for 30 minutes.

Take the dish from the oven, uncover and add the tomatoes, nestling them, cut side up as far as possible, among the chicken pieces. Roast, uncovered, for a further 20–25 minutes, or until the chicken pieces are cooked through and the tomatoes are soft and blistered. Scatter over most of the tarragon and toss to mix. Rest for a few minutes so the tarragon flavour infuses the juices.

Sprinkle over the remaining chopped tarragon and the dish is ready to serve. It's good with new potatoes, mash, rice or bread.

SWAPS If you can't lay your hands on fresh tarragon, try this with flat-leaf parsley – using about three times as much. Or try roughly shredded sorrel leaves. In each case, the effect is quite different, but still delicious.

ANOTHER TAKE The dish also works really well with pheasant in place of chicken.

Chicken, rocket, redcurrants

Redcurrants look incredibly pretty in a salad and add a lovely, fruity-sharp tang. This is a particularly nice way to use up the leftovers from a roast chicken.

Serves 4

4 handfuls of rocket leaves

About 300g cold, cooked chicken, in bite-sized pieces

100g redcurrants

For the dressing

½ teaspoon English mustard

1 teaspoon honey

1 teaspoon cider vinegar

3 tablespoons olive oil

Sea salt and freshly ground black pepper

For the dressing, put the mustard, honey and cider vinegar in a small jam jar with a good pinch each of salt and pepper and stir until smooth. Add the olive oil, screw the lid on the jar and shake vigorously to emulsify.

Put the rocket in a large bowl, trickle over about half the dressing and toss gently. Arrange the rocket and chicken on individual plates, or in a large serving bowl.

Put the redcurrants in a small bowl and give them a quick press or two with the end of a rolling pin or with a pestle, just to crush a few of them and create a bit of juice – you still want plenty of the redcurrants to stay whole.

Scatter the redcurrants and juice over the salad. Trickle over the remaining dressing, sprinkle with salt and pepper and serve, with bread or new potatoes on the side.

SWAPS Try using raspberries instead of redcurrants. Tart little dried cranberries are another alternative: soak them in hot apple or orange juice for a couple of hours, then drain and scatter over the dressed rocket and chicken.

ANOTHER TAKE The recipe also works well with leftover pheasant or roast pork instead of chicken.

Chicken, plums, soy

Sweet plums and salty-tangy soy sauce are brilliant paired with tender chicken. Chilli and ginger are desirable but optional. I would say the garlic is a must though.

Serves 4

8 bone-in, skin-on, free-range chicken thighs (or 1 small free-range chicken, jointed into 8 pieces)

1 tablespoon sunflower oil

1–4 red, mild-to-medium-hot, fleshy chillies, to taste (optional)

4 garlic cloves, sliced

A thumb-sized piece of ginger, peeled and coarsely grated or thinly sliced (optional)

8 plums, halved and stoned

3 tablespoons soy sauce

A small bunch of coriander, leaves only, chopped (optional)

Sea salt and freshly ground black pepper

Preheat the oven to 200°C/Gas 6. Put the chicken thighs in a roasting tray, trickle with the oil and season well with salt and pepper. Roast for 30 minutes, turning once or twice.

Meanwhile, halve and deseed the chillies, if using, then cut each into 1cm strips. After its 30 minutes, take the chicken out of the oven and add the sliced chillies, garlic and ginger, if using, to the roasting tray. Turn the chicken again to make sure the aromatics are evenly distributed around and under the pieces. Roast for a further 10 minutes.

Tuck the plum halves around the chicken pieces and trickle over the soy. If there doesn't seem to be much liquid in the tray, add a few tablespoons of water. Return to the oven for 10–15 minutes until the plums are soft and yielding their juices.

Baste the chicken and plums with the pan juices, then leave to rest in a warm place for 10 minutes. Finish with a scattering of chopped coriander, if you like. Serve with noodles or plain rice.

SWAPS For a storecupboard version of this dish, you could use prunes or dried apricots (ideally the plump, ready-to eat ones) instead of fresh plums.

Duck, blackberries, greens

Serving roast duck with some form of tart fruit is a time-honoured tradition. This recipe plays on that theme, with a particular nod to Chinese-style duck and plum sauce.

Serves 5–6

1 large free-range duck (about 2.2–2.5kg)

A small thumb-sized piece of ginger, peeled and roughly chopped

2 garlic cloves, finely sliced

A pinch of dried chilli flakes

2 tablespoons soy sauce

250g ripe blackberries (fresh or frozen)

1 teaspoon redcurrant or crab apple jelly (optional)

500g pak choi (or other tender greens such as choi sum or young spring greens), trimmed and washed

A knob of butter

Sea salt and freshly ground black pepper

Preheat the oven to 220°C/Gas 7. If the duck is tied, untruss it and gently pull the legs away from the body (to encourage the heat to penetrate). Season the skin well with salt and pepper. Put the duck in a roasting tin and roast for 20 minutes, so the fat starts to run.

Baste the bird with the pan juices and cover tightly with foil. Return to the oven, lowering the setting to 150°C/Gas 2. Cook for 2–3 hours until the meat is very tender and easily comes away from the bone. Tip the bird so any juices in the cavity run into the tin. Transfer the duck to a warm plate to rest.

Carefully pour off most of the fat from the roasting tin (save for roasting potatoes), leaving the dark juices in the tin. Put the tin over a low heat, add the ginger, garlic and chilli flakes and cook for 2–3 minutes. Add 4–5 tablespoons water and the soy sauce, followed by all but a few of the blackberries. Simmer, stirring occasionally, for 4–5 minutes until the berries are tender. Now press through a sieve to remove the blackberry seeds, ginger and garlic. Return to a clean pan, bring to the boil and simmer for a minute or two. Taste and tweak – you can whisk in a blob of redcurrant or crab apple jelly to sweeten it, and another dash of soy if you want it saltier. When you're happy, add the remaining whole blackberries. Keep warm.

Bring a large pan of salted water to the boil. Separate the pak choi leaves, add to the pan and cook for 3–4 minutes. Drain, add a knob of butter and season with salt and pepper. Keep warm.

To serve, take the meat from the duck – it should be forkably tender. Divide between warm plates and add a portion of pak choi to each. Spoon the blackberry sauce over and around the meat and serve. Noodles are the perfect accompaniment.

SWAP Use 250g plums instead of the blackberries. Halve, stone and roast in a small dish, in the oven with the roasting duck, for 30 minutes. Then give them a second cooking with the meat juices, as above.

Pigeon, sorrel, lentils

There's a lovely, sophisticated interplay of flavours and textures here – pigeon is gamey and lean, Puy lentils nutty and earthy, the sorrel sauce sharp but silky and rich. Together, they make an elegant trio, ideal for a special dinner.

Serves 4

For the lentils

100g Puy lentils

1 garlic clove (unpeeled), bashed

1 bay leaf (optional)

A few parsley stalks (optional)

1 tablespoon olive oil

For the pigeon and sorrel

8 pigeon breasts

1 tablespoon olive oil

50g butter

300g fresh sorrel, larger leaves stripped from the stalks, roughly shredded

1 tablespoon double cream

Sea salt and freshly ground black pepper

Put the lentils into a saucepan and cover with cold water. Bring to the boil and boil for 1 minute only, then drain. Return the lentils to the pan and cover with fresh water. Add the garlic, and bay leaf and parsley stalks, if using. Bring back to a very gentle simmer and cook slowly for about half an hour, topping up with boiling water if necessary, until tender but not mushy.

Drain the lentils and discard the herbs and garlic, then toss with the olive oil and some salt and pepper. Set aside in a warm place.

Season the pigeon breasts with salt and pepper. Place a medium frying pan over a medium heat and add 1 tablespoon olive oil. When hot, add the pigeon breasts and fry for 2–3 minutes on each side. Remove from the pan to a warmed plate to rest; keep warm.

Turn the heat down under the frying pan and add the butter. Add the shredded sorrel and cook, turning in the butter, until the leaves begin to wilt and darken – this will happen pretty quickly. Add the cream and any juices that have seeped from the resting pigeon. Cook for a minute or two to reduce the juices a little, then season with salt and pepper. If the sorrel sauce seems too thick, thin it down slightly with a spoonful or two of water or stock.

Spoon the sorrel sauce on to warm plates. Slice the pigeon breasts and arrange on the plates, with a good scattering of lentils around and about.

PLUS ONE For a richer, meatier dish – and a crispy, salty tang – I sometimes fry a handful of bacon or pancetta lardons in the frying pan before cooking the pigeon and sorrel, then take them out and set aside to add before serving.

Pheasant, bacon, prunes

Pheasant is a delicious game bird if carefully cooked, but it often ends up a little on the dry side. Combining it with some fatty bacon is a great way to remedy that. The luscious prunes add a third enriching element.

Serves 4

A knob of butter

3 tablespoons olive oil

2 onions, finely sliced

4 garlic cloves, finely sliced

4 sprigs of thyme (optional)

2 bay leaves (optional)

300g thickly sliced streaky bacon, or pancetta, cut into thick strips

2 oven-ready pheasants

1 small glass of Calvados or brandy (optional)

400ml white wine

200g prunes

Sea salt and freshly ground black pepper

Preheat the oven to 150°C/Gas 2. Place a flameproof casserole dish, large enough to take both pheasants, over a medium heat. Add the butter and 1 tablespoon olive oil. Then add the onions, garlic, and thyme and bay leaves, if using, and cook for about 10 minutes until the onions are soft and slightly golden.

While the onions are cooking, place a large frying pan over a medium-high heat and add the remaining 2 tablespoons olive oil. When hot, add the bacon and fry for about 5 minutes until it takes on some colour, then tip into the casserole with the onions. Turn up the heat a little under the frying pan. Season the pheasants all over with salt and pepper, add to the frying pan and cook for about 5 minutes, turning often, until well browned on all sides.

If you're using the brandy (which gives a lovely richness), you must be extremely careful, as you need to flambé it to burn off the alcohol which causes it to flare up spectacularly – the flame can be pretty high! If using, warm the brandy in a small pan, set it alight and pour over the pheasants. When it dies down, transfer the pheasants and any pan juices to the casserole.

Deglaze the frying pan with a little of the wine – pour into the hot pan and let it simmer while you scrape up any tasty bits stuck to the bottom. Trickle this wine over the pheasants, then pour in the rest of the wine and 250ml water. Add the prunes. Bring to a simmer, cover and cook in the oven for 1½ hours.

Remove the pheasants from the casserole and place them on a large board or carving tray. Carve the birds (or simply joint them into thigh, drumsticks and chunky breast portions) and divide between warm plates. Spoon over the bacon, prunes and cooking juices. Serve with mash.

SWAP To make a fantastic rabbit stew, just replace the pheasant with two jointed rabbits.

Lamb, potatoes, mushrooms

Cooking a shoulder of lamb over sliced potatoes allows the meat juices to run into the potatoes as they cook, resulting in a wonderful, savoury alchemy. The lamb ends up fork-tender and the potatoes take on a gorgeous richness. Mushrooms give the dish a third, earthy dimension. This is a real winter warmer.

Serves 6–8

1 shoulder of lamb, hogget or mutton, on the bone (about 2kg)

A little olive oil

1.25kg large white potatoes

1 large onion, finely sliced

2–3 large garlic cloves, sliced

2 long stems of rosemary, leaves only, chopped (optional)

300g open cap mushrooms, thickly sliced

Sea salt and freshly ground black pepper

Preheat the oven to 220°C/Gas 7. Put the lamb in a large roasting tin. Trickle with a little olive oil and season well with salt and pepper. Roast for 25–30 minutes until golden. Meanwhile, peel the potatoes and cut into slices no thicker than a £1 coin.

Remove the lamb from the roasting tin and set aside on a plate. Turn the oven down to 150°C/Gas 2. Splash about half a glass of hot water into the hot roasting tin and use a spatula to loosen any bits stuck to the bottom. Spread a layer of potato slices over the base of the roasting tin, on the meat juices. Don't bother to make it too neat. Scatter over a little of the onion, garlic and rosemary, if using, then add a layer of mushrooms. Season with salt and pepper. Repeat this process to use up all the ingredients – aim for two or three layers, finishing with potatoes on the top.

Place the lamb on top of the potatoes. Cover with foil, sealing the edges well. Return to the oven and cook undisturbed for 3 hours.

Transfer the lamb to a warm plate to rest. The veg underneath should be completely tender – cooked in the juices and fat from the roasting lamb and transformed to a rich, meaty-flavoured potato and mushroom gratin.

To top it off with a lovely crisp golden crust, preheat the grill to high. Put the tin of veg under the grill for 5–6 minutes until golden brown and crisp on top.

Serve the lamb thickly sliced with the potatoes and some simply steamed greens, such as leeks and kale. Or a sharply dressed leafy salad will go well with, or after, the meat and potatoes.

SWAPS Try a small rolled shoulder of pork, instead of the lamb, and thinly sliced fennel instead of the mushrooms. Rub a few crushed fennel seeds into the pork skin, before the initial hot roasting, if you like.

Lamb, lettuce, vinegar

Breast of lamb is a flavourful and very inexpensive cut of meat. It is fatty, but that's precisely why the sharpness of vinegar and the crisp freshness of lettuce work so well alongside. It can be bought on the bone, or boned and rolled; either will work here.

Serves 2–3

1 large breast of lamb (about 500g)

About 1 tablespoon rapeseed or olive oil

6 garlic cloves (unpeeled), lightly bashed

1 large or 2 small Little Gem or other crunchy hearted lettuces

2 tablespoons red wine vinegar or cider vinegar

Sea salt and freshly ground black pepper

Preheat the oven to 220°C/Gas 7. Place the breast of lamb in a roasting tin, rub it with a little oil, then season all over with salt and pepper. Roast for 20 minutes, then lower the oven setting to 120°C/Gas ½ and add the garlic cloves. Cook for 2–3 hours until very tender. Set aside to rest in a warm place for 20 minutes.

Divide the lettuce leaves between serving plates, sharing out the inner heart leaves equally. Gently pull the lamb breast into pieces, including the crispy skin and fattier bits, and place on the lettuce leaves. Leave the bones (if there are any) and garlic cloves in the tin. Spoon out most of the lamb fat from the roasting tin.

Add the vinegar to the tin, place over a low heat and gently work the roasting juices together with the vinegar, squishing the garlic as you go. Let the mixture bubble and reduce a little, then taste it. Reduce it further if you like, then season with salt and pepper. Spoon this warm dressing over the lamb and leaves and serve, with warm bread.

PLUS ONE To make this a more substantial meal, add some just-cooked, waxy little new potatoes, cut into halves or quarters. Arrange these on the plate with the lettuce before adding the lamb and dressing.

Lamb, kale, quince

A winning combination of meat, fruit and greens. The spice marinade for the lamb is optional, but it does give the whole dish a lovely exotic undertone. Quinces are not easy to find in the shops, though they are easy to grow. Apples or pears make an easy straight swap.

Serves 2

500g lamb leg steak, sliced 1.5-2cm thick, trimmed

1 large quince (about 400g), well washed

2 tablespoons runny honey

Juice of 1 lemon

A sprig of rosemary (optional)

300g curly kale or cavolo nero, tough stems removed, leaves roughly shredded

Sea salt and freshly ground black pepper

For the marinade (optional)

1 teaspoon coriander seeds

1 teaspoon cumin seeds

Finely grated zest of 1 orange

A good pinch of dried chilli flakes

3 tablespoons extra virgin olive oil

For the marinade, if using, toast the coriander and cumin seeds in a small dry frying pan over a medium heat for a few minutes until fragrant. Tip into a mortar and allow to cool, then grind with the pestle to a rough powder. Mix with the orange zest, chilli flakes and olive oil in a large bowl. Add the lamb and rub well with the spice mix. Cover and leave to marinate in the fridge for 2-4 hours, turning once or twice.

Quarter and core the quince, then halve each quarter. Put into a small pan with the honey, lemon juice, rosemary, if using, and enough water to just cover. Bring to a simmer, partially cover and poach gently until tender – anywhere from 10-45 minutes, so keep checking. Remove the quince with a slotted spoon, let cool, then add to the marinade with the lamb, if using, turning to coat.

Bring a pan of salted water to the boil, add the kale and simmer for 4-5 minutes, until tender. Drain well and keep hot in the pan.

Heat a cast-iron griddle pan or heavy frying pan over a high heat. Season the lamb with salt and pepper and fry for 2-3 minutes on each side until well coloured (it will still be pink inside). Transfer to a warm plate to rest for 5 minutes while you griddle or fry the quince segments on both sides until starting to caramelise.

Thinly slice the lamb and arrange on warm plates with the quince. Add 2-3 tablespoons of the quince poaching liquid to the frying pan and let it bubble over a medium heat, stirring to deglaze. Pour these pan juices over the kale and toss well. Add to the plates, sprinkle with salt and pepper and serve immediately.

SWAPS If you can't get quince, use slices of slightly under-ripe pear or a crisp, tart dessert apple instead. There is no need to precook – just add the fruit to the marinade. Deglaze the frying pan with a splash of wine or water.

Lamb, tomatoes, feta

There's a lovely summery feel to this dish; indeed you could very well barbecue the chops rather than grill them indoors.

Serves 4

8 lamb chops

500g ripe tomatoes

150g feta cheese, crumbled

½ teaspoon finely chopped rosemary or thyme (optional)

Extra virgin olive oil to trickle

Sea salt and freshly ground black pepper

Preheat the grill to medium-high. Season the lamb chops well with salt and pepper all over. Place them on a baking tray or on the grill pan and grill for 4–5 minutes on each side or until done to your liking. Cook for the extra couple of minutes if you like your chops more crispy on the outside and less pink in the middle. Leave the chops to rest in a warm place for 5 minutes.

Meanwhile, quarter and deseed the tomatoes, then chop them roughly. Combine with the crumbled feta and rosemary or thyme, if using. Season with salt and pepper and dress with a trickle of extra virgin olive oil.

Serve the lamb chops with the tomato and feta, accompanied perhaps by new potatoes, or just good bread.

SWAPS You can make this with pork chops, instead of lamb, in which case a crumbly, mild blue cheese, like Dorset Blue Vinney or Harbourne Blue goat's cheese, works well instead of the feta.

Lamb, spinach, chickpeas

A fantastic leftovers dish, this is simple and very tasty. A hint of garlic and a spoonful of spice bring the compatible trio of ingredients alive. I suggest making up a North African inspired merguez spice mix, but you can use the teaspoonful of smoked paprika on its own to very good effect.

Serves 2

225g large leaf or baby spinach

3 tablespoons extra virgin olive oil

150–200g leftover cooked lamb, cut into broad strips

1 garlic clove, finely chopped

½ x 400g tin chickpeas, drained and rinsed

A squeeze of lemon juice

Sea salt and freshly ground black pepper

For the merguez spice mix

1 teaspoon cumin seeds

1 teaspoon fennel seeds

1 teaspoon coriander seeds

1 teaspoon caraway seeds (optional)

10–12 black peppercorns

1 teaspoon sweet smoked paprika

A pinch of cayenne pepper

For the merguez spice mix, combine the cumin, fennel, coriander, caraway seeds, if using, and the black peppercorns in a frying pan. Toast lightly over a medium heat for a minute or so, until fragrant. Tip into a mortar. Once cool, crush with the pestle to a powder, then combine with the paprika and cayenne. Set aside.

If you're using baby leaf spinach, you won't need to precook it, but for large leaf spinach, bring a pan of water to the boil. Remove any tough stems from the leaf spinach, then drop into the boiling water and cook for just a couple of minutes, until wilted. Drain in a colander. When cool enough to handle, squeeze all the water from the spinach with your hands, then chop it coarsely.

Heat 1 tablespoon extra virgin olive oil in a large frying pan over a medium heat. Add the lamb strips and fry for 2–3 minutes, stirring often, until nicely browned. Stir in precooked spinach now. Or, if using raw baby spinach, add it a handful at a time, keeping the heat fairly high and stirring often. As each handful of spinach wilts, add the next, until it is all wilted and combined with the lamb.

Add the other 2 tablespoons extra virgin olive oil, the garlic, chickpeas, 1 tablespoon of the merguez spice mix and some salt and pepper. Lower the heat a little and cook for a couple of minutes, stirring often, to heat the chickpeas and cook the garlic. Add a squeeze of lemon juice, taste and add more salt, pepper and/or spice mix as needed. Allow to cool a little before serving, finished with a final sprinkle of the spice mix. Warm pitta or flatbreads make an ideal accompaniment.

PLUS ONE This dish is beautifully enhanced with a few spoonfuls of thick, plain yoghurt, scattered with a little salt and pepper and a pinch more merguez mix, which you can save for the purpose.

Beef, shallots, tomato

Shin of beef is an inexpensive cut because when raw it is tough, with lots of connective tissue. That makes it perfect for a big slow-cooked stew such as this. As it cooks with the roasted tomato purée and shallots, the meat gradually softens to a lovely tenderness and the collagen within it becomes pleasantly gelatinous. It's a stew with a wonderfully rich flavour and lots of body.

Serves 4

About 3 tablespoons olive, rapeseed or sunflower oil

1kg shin of beef, cut into 4–5cm cubes

14–16 shallots, peeled and halved

1 garlic bulb, cloves separated and peeled but left whole

½ glass of red wine (optional)

250ml beef stock

250ml roasted tomato purée (see page 89) or tomato passata

2–3 bay leaves

1 star anise (optional)

Sea salt and freshly ground black pepper

Preheat the oven to 140°C/Gas 1. Brown the beef in batches. To do this, heat 1 tablespoon oil in a large non-stick frying pan over a fairly high heat. Season the beef with salt and pepper, then add a third of it to the pan. Fry for about 5 minutes, shaking the pan once or twice to turn the meat, until it has a good, golden brown colour on most of its surfaces. Transfer to a large flameproof casserole with a lid. Repeat with the remaining beef, adding a little more oil with each batch.

Reduce the heat under the frying pan. Add another 1 tablespoon oil, then the shallots and garlic cloves. Fry for about 5 minutes, stirring often, until they are golden. Tip them into the casserole with the meat.

You now need to deglaze the frying pan, using the red wine or a splosh of water. Pour the liquid into the frying pan over the heat and let it bubble for a few minutes, stirring to loosen all the bits of caramelised meat and seasoning stuck to the pan. Add this liquid to the casserole with the beef and shallots, then pour in the stock. Add the tomato purée, bay leaves, and the star anise, if using.

Bring it up to a simmer on the hob, over a medium heat, then put the lid on the casserole and transfer to the oven. Cook for 3–3½ hours, until the beef is beautifully tender.

Taste the stew and add more salt and pepper as needed, then serve in deep dishes. Creamy mashed potato (page 260) is very good with this, or polenta (page 314) or rice, and perhaps some steamed greens or cabbage.

Salt beef, cabbage, mash

Preparing your own salt beef requires several days' soaking and a few hours' cooking, but it's incredibly easy, involves little hands-on work and transforms a cheap, unglamorous cut of meat into something totally delicious. And you'll have enough beef left over for sandwiches, or the hash cakes over the page.

Serves 4 (with beef left over)

1.5–2kg piece of beef brisket, on or off the bone

2 bay leaves

A large sprig of thyme

A few parsley stalks

1 carrot, chopped

1 onion, chopped

1 celery stalk, chopped

1 leek, chopped

½ garlic bulb (sliced across)

Sea salt and freshly ground black pepper

For the brine

3 litres water

300g demerara or light brown sugar

900g coarse sea salt

½ teaspoon black peppercorns

½ teaspoon juniper berries

3 cloves

2 bay leaves

A sprig of thyme

For the mash

500g large potatoes, such as Maris Piper or King Edward

100ml whole milk

35g unsalted butter

For the cabbage

1 Savoy cabbage

A knob of butter

For the brine, put all the ingredients into a large saucepan and stir over a low heat until the sugar and salt have dissolved. Bring to the boil and boil for 1–2 minutes, then take off the heat. Leave to cool, then refrigerate. Put the beef in a non-metallic container, such as a large plastic tub or clay crock, and pour on the cold brine to cover. To keep the meat submerged it may be necessary to put a plate and a heavy weight on top. Leave in a cool place or the fridge for 4–5 days. Lift out the meat, rinse and pat dry. Wrapped in muslin, it will now keep for a few days in the fridge.

To cook the beef, put it in a large saucepan with all the aromatics and cover with cold water, by at least 2cm. Bring to a low simmer and cook for about 3 hours, or until the meat is very tender and can be torn into shreds with a fork. Remove it from the liquor and leave to rest in a warm place for 20 minutes.

Half an hour before the cooking time is up, peel the potatoes and cut into even-sized pieces, no smaller than a golf ball. Place in a saucepan, cover with water, add salt and bring to the boil. Simmer for 15–20 minutes or until tender. Drain, return to the pan and let the potatoes steam-dry for a few minutes. Heat the milk and butter together. Begin mashing the potatoes in their pan, then gradually add the hot milk and butter. Continue to mash until smooth and light. (Alternatively, put the potatoes through a ricer into the pan of milk and butter.) Season with salt and set aside to keep warm.

Remove the coarse stalks from the cabbage, then cut into thick ribbons. Either cook in a pan of boiling salted water or steam for 3–4 minutes until just tender, but retaining a bite. Toss with the butter and some salt and pepper.

Slice the warm salt beef thickly and serve on warm plates with the mash and buttered cabbage. Finish with a spoonful of hot horseradish sauce or English mustard if you like.

Salt beef, mash, duck egg

This is really a hash recipe – ideal for using up leftover mashed potato and salt beef, but also other cooked meats, even pressed ox tongue or tinned corned beef. And, of course, you can use hen's eggs, although duck eggs have a lovely richness that makes a glamorous treat out of a leftovers classic. If you've got suitable meat for this recipe, but no mash, it's well worth cooking the spuds from scratch.

Serves 3–4

About 300g leftover mashed potato OR floury potatoes, such as King Edward, Wilja or Maris Piper, plus butter and milk for mashing

2 tablespoons rapeseed, sunflower or olive oil, plus extra for frying

1 onion, finely sliced

1 garlic clove, finely chopped

About 300g cooked salt beef (see page 260), shredded or chopped

A good handful of flat-leaf parsley, leaves only, chopped (optional)

1 teaspoon English mustard

A small knob of butter

3–4 duck eggs (one per person)

Sea salt and freshly ground black pepper

If you're cooking spuds from scratch, peel them and cut into even-sized pieces. Put into a saucepan, cover with water, add salt and bring to the boil. Simmer for 15–20 minutes or until tender. Drain the potatoes, return to the pan and leave to steam-dry for a few minutes, then mash them, with a knob of butter and a dash of milk, if you like.

Place a frying pan over a medium heat and add the 2 tablespoons oil. Add the onion and fry for 10–12 minutes until soft and starting to colour. Add the garlic, shredded salt beef and parsley, if using, and fry for a further 2–3 minutes. Season well with salt and pepper. Fold this into the mashed potato, along with the mustard. Form the mixture into 3 or 4 large cakes, leave to cool on a large plate, then refrigerate for 1 hour.

Heat a thin film of oil in a non-stick frying pan over a medium heat. Add the hash cakes and fry gently for 5–6 minutes, turning occasionally, until nicely browned on each side.

Meanwhile, to fry the duck eggs, heat a touch more oil and a small knob of butter in another frying pan. Fry the eggs for 2–3 minutes to your liking, and serve with the fried hash cakes.

PLUS ONE Some might say it lowers the tone, but these cakes are pretty good served with baked beans!

SWAPS Pressed ox tongue and tinned corned beef are good straight swaps for the salt beef, as are hen's eggs for duck eggs.

Pork, celeriac, garlic

This pot-roast of unctuous, melting pork and layers of yielding celeriac has an incredible depth of flavour. To maximise your chance of getting some good crackling, leave the pork uncovered in the fridge overnight before roasting, to help dry out the skin.

Serves 6

1.5–2kg piece of boned and rolled spare rib of pork, skin removed and reserved for crackling

A little olive, rapeseed or sunflower oil

2 medium celeriac

A small bunch of thyme, leaves only (optional)

2 garlic bulbs, cloves separated and peeled

300ml water or vegetable, chicken or pork stock

2 bay leaves (optional)

Sea salt and freshly ground black pepper

Preheat the oven to 220°C/Gas 7. Season the pork all over with salt and pepper and rub with a little oil. Place in a large oven dish – a big cast-iron casserole with a lid is ideal, but a large roasting dish will work too. Score the skin, sprinkle with salt and lay it over the meat. Roast, uncovered, for 25–30 minutes until the joint is well coloured and golden and the skin is puffed and crackled.

Meanwhile, peel the celeriac and cut them into quarters. Cut each quarter into slices, the thickness of a £1 coin.

Take the casserole dish out of the oven and lower the oven setting to 140°C/Gas 1. Set the crackling aside. If the skin has failed to crackle completely, don't worry, you can crisp it up later. Put the pork joint on a plate.

Layer the celeriac in the casserole, sprinkling over some thyme leaves, if using, and seasoning with salt and pepper as you go. Place the pork on top. Scatter over the garlic cloves, pour over the stock or water and tuck in the bay leaves, if using. Place the lid on or cover very tightly with foil. Cook in the oven for a further 3 hours or until the pork is meltingly tender.

Allow the pork to rest in a warm place for 15–20 minutes. In the meantime, if you need to crisp up the crackling, place it under a hot grill for a few minutes; otherwise just warm it in the oven. Slice the pork and serve with spoonfuls of the melting celeriac, some sweet, soft garlic and the rich pan juices.

Pork, potatoes, apples

Pork and potatoes with apple sauce is, of course, an all-time classic Sunday roast. Here the same ingredients are combined in a much quicker way for an easy weeknight supper – or an effortless weekend feast.

Serves 2

About 500g fairly floury potatoes, such as King Edward or Maris Piper

3 tablespoons sunflower, rapeseed or olive oil, plus extra for frying

2 dessert apples

2 pork chops

8–10 sage leaves

Sea salt and freshly ground black pepper

Preheat the oven to 200°C/Gas 6. Peel the potatoes and cut into 2–3cm chunks. Put into a saucepan, cover with water, add salt and bring to the boil. Simmer for 5 minutes, then drain well and return to the pan. Add some salt and pepper. Put the lid on the pan and give it a good shake to roughen up the potatoes a little.

Put the oil into a large roasting tin and place in the oven for about 5 minutes until hot. Add the potatoes, toss in the oil and roast for 30 minutes.

Meanwhile, quarter and core the apples, then cut each quarter into 2 or 3 wedges. Take the potatoes out of the oven, add the apples and stir well. Roast for another 10–15 minutes until the potatoes are really crisp and the apples are soft.

While the potatoes and apples are roasting, heat a little more oil in a large frying pan over a medium heat. Season the chops with salt and pepper and add to the pan. Fry for 6–8 minutes on each side, or until nicely coloured and cooked through, adding the sage leaves for the last few minutes.

Nestle the cooked chops into the cooked potatoes and apples and leave in a warm place to rest for 5–10 minutes. Serve with a green vegetable such as kale or cabbage, or a leafy salad on the side.

SWAPS This works very well with lamb chops instead of pork, and plums in place of the apples. Cut the plums in half around the middle and remove the stones. Leave out the sage, but put a pinch of ground cinnamon on each plum half as you add them to the roasting spuds.

Ham, potatoes, parsley

Glazed baked ham and mashed potatoes with a good parsley sauce has always been a favourite trio of mine. This recipe uses those same ingredients in a rather different way, to make a lovely, hearty salad. If you don't want to cook your own ham hock, buy a ready-cooked one from your butcher, or use any good ham – even the leftovers from a baked ham. Just make sure it's in nice, thick chunks.

Serves 4–6

1 large bunch of flat-leaf parsley (about 50g)

1 ham hock (1.2–1.5kg)

1 onion, halved

1 carrot, roughly chopped

1 celery stalk, roughly chopped

500g new or waxy salad potatoes

Sea salt and freshly ground black pepper

For the dressing

2 teaspoons cider vinegar

4 tablespoons extra virgin olive oil

1 heaped teaspoon English mustard

½ teaspoon sugar

Pick the leaves from the parsley stalks and set aside, reserving the stalks.

Place the ham hock in a large saucepan with the onion, carrot, celery and parsley stalks. Pour on enough water to cover and bring to a simmer. Cover and cook at a very gentle simmer for 3 hours or until the meat is tender and comes away easily from the bone. Skim off any scum that rises to the surface and top the pan up with boiling water if you need to. Remove the ham from the pan and allow to cool. Scoop out and discard the onion, carrot, celery and parsley stalks. Bring the ham stock back to a simmer.

Scrub or scrape the potatoes and cut them into equal-sized pieces (about the size of a golf ball). Add them to the simmering ham stock and cook for 10 minutes or so, until they are tender but not breaking up. (If you're not cooking a ham hock yourself, just boil the potatoes in salted water.) Carefully scoop out the potatoes with a slotted spoon and set aside to cool. Strain the ham stock and save for another recipe (it makes a delicious soup with some finely chopped veg and beans or lentils).

Remove the skin from the ham hock. Pull the meat from the bone and trim away any sinew. Cut the meat into bite-sized pieces.

Put all the ingredients for the dressing in a jam jar with some salt and pepper, screw the lid on and shake to emulsify. Put the whole parsley leaves in a bowl with the chunks of ham and potato. Trickle over the dressing and toss lightly. Arrange on a platter or on individual plates and sprinkle with a little salt and pepper.

PLUS ONE A handful of Puy lentils, cooked as for the recipe on page 27, make a lovely addition to this substantial salad. Just throw in around 40–50g cooked lentils with the other ingredients.

Ham, squash, marmalade

You may think this sounds a little odd, but the delicate bitterness of marmalade is delicious with salty ham, and also cuts the creamy squash flesh. When choosing squash, go for a good eating variety, such as Sweet Mama or Crown Prince, or an acorn or red kuri, rather than the monstrous pumpkins used for Halloween celebrations. You can make this dish with cooked or leftover ham, but you want thick wedges or chunky pieces rather than thin slices.

Serves 6–8

3 gammon hocks

1 carrot, quartered

1 celery stalk, quartered

1 onion, quartered

1–2 squash (1.5–2kg in total)

2–3 tablespoons rapeseed or olive oil

Some leafy sprigs of thyme (optional)

6 bay leaves (optional)

6 tablespoons marmalade

Sea salt and freshly ground black pepper

Put the gammon hocks in a large pan with the carrot, celery and onion. Pour on enough cold water to cover and bring to the boil, then skim off any scum. Lower the heat to a gentle simmer. Cover and cook gently for about 3 hours, until tender.

An hour or so before the ham will be cooked, preheat the oven to 190°C/Gas 5. Cut the squash into wedges, scoop out the seeds and put into a roasting tray large enough to take the ham chunks as well (later on). Season the squash all over with salt and pepper, trickle with the oil and toss well. Roast for 25–30 minutes.

Once cooked, remove the ham hocks from the pan, reserving the liquor. When cool enough to handle, remove the skin and excess fat from the hocks. Take the meat off the bone in large chunks.

Add the ham chunks to the roasting tray with the thyme and bay, if using. Mix the marmalade with 3–4 tablespoons of the warm ham liquor (or water, if you haven't cooked the ham yourself); you want a thick coating consistency. Spoon this marmalade mixture over the ham and squash. Return the tray to the oven and bake for a further 20–25 minutes until glazed and bubbling.

Serve with something green, such as buttered Savoy cabbage or a salad of winter leaves.

Bacon, beans, tomato

This is essentially a homemade version of baked beans, though the beans are simmered, not baked. There are similarities – the rich tomato sauce, the touch of sweetness, the slight edge from the mustard and vinegar – but these beans are a world away from anything that comes out of a tin. They are good on toast, but also lovely with a hunk of bread or mashed potatoes and a robust green salad.

Serves 6–8

250g dried beans, such as haricot, cannellini or borlotti, soaked overnight in cold water (or 3 x 400g tins, drained and rinsed)

1 tablespoon rapeseed, sunflower or olive oil

250g smoked pancetta or streaky bacon, cut into cubes or lardons

1–2 bay leaves (optional)

4–6 garlic cloves (unpeeled), lightly bashed

400ml tomato passata or roasted tomato purée (see page 89)

200ml apple juice

1 tablespoon English mustard

2 tablespoons cider vinegar

Sea salt and freshly ground black pepper

If cooking the beans yourself, drain the soaked beans, rinse them and put into a large saucepan. Cover generously with cold water, bring to the boil and boil for 10 minutes, skimming off any scum that rises to the surface. Then reduce the heat to low, cover and simmer gently for about 50 minutes or until the beans are tender but not completely soft. Drain.

Heat the oil in a large, heavy-based casserole over a medium heat. Add the pancetta or bacon lardons and cook for about 10 minutes, stirring often, until they start to colour. Add the beans (home-cooked or tinned) and toss them in the bacon fat, then add the bay leaves, if using, garlic cloves, tomato passata or purée, apple juice, mustard and cider vinegar. Bring to a simmer, then cover the pan and cook gently for 30–45 minutes or until the beans are crushably soft and tender.

Taste and add pepper, and salt as needed (you may not need any salt as the bacon contributes a fair amount). The beans are now ready to serve, but will taste even better if cooled, chilled and reheated a day or two later.

Serve on toast, or with hunks of good bread, or as a side dish to sausages or grilled chops.

Bacon, radicchio, shallots

This wonderful combination of sweet, salty and bitter flavours makes a rich and delicious lunch for a cold day. You will find the radicchio darkens considerably when cooked, but don't worry, it tastes fantastic.

Serves 4

500g shallots or baby onions

200g thick-cut streaky bacon

3 tablespoons olive oil

A couple of sprigs of thyme (optional)

1 radicchio

Sea salt and freshly ground black pepper

Preheat the oven to 190°C/Gas 5. Peel and halve the shallots or onions, or quarter them if large. Cut each bacon rasher into 4 or 5 pieces. Put the shallots in a large roasting tray with 2 tablespoons olive oil, the thyme if using, and some salt and pepper. Toss well and roast for 10 minutes.

Meanwhile, cut the radicchio into 6 or 8 wedges, keeping the stalk end intact. In a large bowl, toss the radicchio wedges with the remaining 1 tablespoon olive oil and some salt and pepper. Add the bacon and radicchio to the shallots. Roast for a further 25–30 minutes, until the radicchio is soft and wilted and the bacon and shallots are nicely caramelised, giving it a stir about halfway through.

Serve hot, with plenty of bread for mopping up the juices.

PLUS ONE If you want to be a little bit greedy (and I often do), pour a good trickle of double cream over the finished dish and flash it under a hot grill for a few minutes until bubbling.

SWAPS If radicchio is hard to come by, a couple of heads of chicory will do equally well. Cut them in half, rather than into wedges.

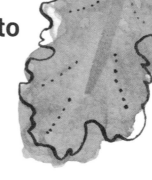

Bacon, lettuce, tomato

This is definitely not your average BLT. Lettuce and tomatoes both take on a whole new character when cooked, particularly when they are tossed in the salty fat left from frying a bit of bacon. This is an excellent super-quick brunch or supper.

Serves 2

2 tablespoons sunflower, rapeseed or olive oil

4 rashers of bacon

2 large or 3 small Little Gems, or other small, compact lettuce

200g small-medium tomatoes

Sea salt and freshly ground black pepper

Heat 1 tablespoon oil in a large, non-stick frying pan over a medium heat. Add the bacon and fry until cooked to your liking on both sides. Remove from the pan and keep warm.

Meanwhile, cut the lettuces lengthways into quarters and halve the tomatoes. Combine them in a large bowl with the remaining 1 tablespoon oil and some salt and pepper. Toss gently together to distribute the oil and seasoning.

Tip the lettuce and tomatoes into the hot bacon pan. Cook for about 4 minutes until the lettuce is wilted and browned and the tomatoes are soft and coloured, turning everything once or twice and returning the bacon to the pan for the last 30 seconds or so, to reheat.

Serve straight away, with some bread on the side to wipe up all the delicious juices.

SWAPS If you don't mind abandoning the BLT conceit, you can make a lovely version of this dish using spinach, kale, Brussels tops or pretty much any wilted greens, in place of the lettuce.

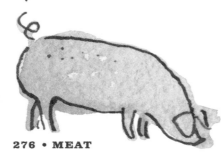

Sausages, parsnips, onions

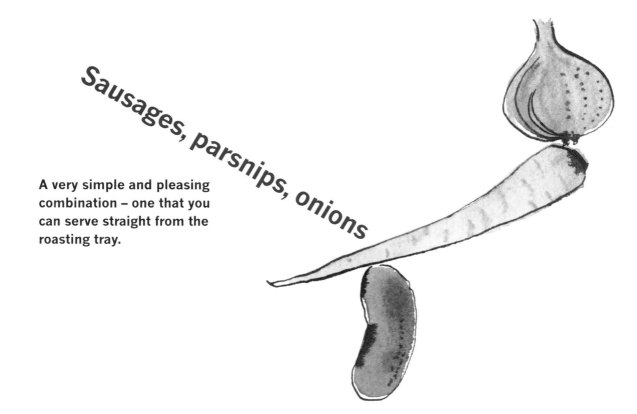

A very simple and pleasing combination – one that you can serve straight from the roasting tray.

Serves 4

4–6 parsnips

3 medium onions (red, white or a mixture)

1 tablespoon olive or rapeseed oil

1 tablespoon garam masala

8–12 pork sausages

50g unsalted butter

12 sage leaves (optional)

1 teaspoon thyme leaves (optional)

Sea salt and freshly ground black pepper

Preheat the oven to 200°C/Gas 6. Peel the parsnips and quarter them from root to tip. If they have very coarse, woody cores, cut them out. Peel the onions, but leave the root end intact. Cut each onion from root to tip into quarters or eighths, depending on size.

Place the parsnips and onions in a roasting tin, trickle over the oil, sprinkle with the garam masala and season well with salt and pepper. Cover the tin tightly with foil and cook in the oven for 30 minutes or until the onions are tender.

Lightly brown the sausages in a frying pan over a fairly high heat for 3–4 minutes.

Take the roasting tin from the oven and remove the foil. Add the sausages to the tin, dot the butter around and scatter over the sage leaves and thyme, if using. Return to the oven and roast, uncovered, for about 20 minutes until the sausages are cooked and everything is golden and starting to caramelise.

Allow to rest in a warm place for 5–10 minutes before serving, with a green salad.

SWAPS This works pretty well with potatoes instead of the parsnips – particularly a waxy, salady variety, like Charlotte or Pink Fir Apple, that can be roasted whole in their skins.

Liver, onion, mash

Assuming you like liver, as I certainly do, it's hard to beat the traditional partnership with fried onions. However, you do need time to cook the onions. A long, slow sweat will render them into a sweet, silky golden tangle that beautifully mellows the rich, strong tang of the liver. A pillow of creamy mash ties it all together nicely. Fresh sage is optional, but it does go brilliantly with liver.

Serves 2

4 tablespoons sunflower, rapeseed or olive oil

2 large onions, finely sliced

250g slice of very fresh pig's, calf's or lamb's liver, about 1cm thick

50g plain flour

About 6 sage leaves, chopped (optional)

25g unsalted butter

Sea salt and freshly ground black pepper

For the mash

500g large fairly floury potatoes, such as Maris Piper or King Edward

100ml whole milk

35g unsalted butter

Heat 3 tablespoons oil in a large pan over a medium heat. Add the onions and, as soon as they start to sizzle, give them a good stir and prod to break up the rings, then turn the heat down low. Cook, stirring often, at a very gentle sizzle, for at least half an hour – up to an hour if you have the patience – until really soft, sweet and golden. Season with salt and pepper and keep warm.

For the mash, peel the potatoes and cut into equal-sized pieces, no smaller than a golf ball. Place in a large pan, cover with water, add salt and bring to the boil. Simmer for 15–20 minutes or until tender. Drain the potatoes and leave to steam-dry in the colander for a few minutes. Meanwhile, gently heat the milk and butter together, with a few twists of pepper, in the empty pan. When the milk and butter are almost bubbling, tip the spuds back into the pan and start mashing. (Or, put the potatoes through a ricer into the hot milk and butter and stir to combine.) Either way, don't overwork the mash. Check the seasoning and keep warm.

If you can, remove the fine membrane that covers the liver and cut out any white tubes. Cut the slice of liver in half. Put the flour into a bowl, add most of the chopped sage, if using, and season with salt and pepper. Coat each piece of liver in the seasoned flour, shaking off the excess.

Heat a frying pan until very hot. Add the remaining 1 tablespoon oil to the pan, then the liver. Cook for 45 seconds–1 minute on each side, no more. A few seconds before you take them out, add the butter and remaining sage, if using, and toss with the liver.

Transfer the liver to warm plates and spoon over the buttery juices. Serve with the mash and golden onions.

Liver, onion, spice

This pairing of liver with onions is completely different to the one on the previous page, but equally delicious. I use some merguez spice mix – a favourite of mine – to give the dish a very intense, spicy flavour. Alternatively, you can just combine 1 teaspoon each of ready-ground caraway, coriander and cumin with a pinch each of smoked paprika and cayenne pepper.

Serves 2

300g very fresh pig's or lamb's liver, thinly sliced

1 medium red onion, thinly sliced from root to tip

1 garlic clove, finely sliced

½ tablespoon rapeseed or olive oil

About 4 tablespoons plain wholemilk yoghurt

A small knob of butter

Sea salt and freshly ground black pepper

For the merguez spice mix

1 teaspoon cumin seeds

1 teaspoon fennel seeds

1 teaspoon coriander seeds

1 teaspoon caraway seeds (optional)

10–12 black peppercorns

1 teaspoon sweet smoked paprika

A pinch of cayenne pepper

For the merguez spice mix, combine the cumin, fennel, coriander, caraway seeds, if using, and the black peppercorns in a frying pan. Toast lightly over a medium heat for just a minute or so until fragrant, then tip into a mortar. Once cool, crush with the pestle to a powder and combine with the paprika and cayenne.

Put 1 tablespoon of the merguez spice mix into a large bowl. Add the sliced liver, onion, garlic and oil. Toss together with your hands, then cover and leave in a cool place for 20–30 minutes.

Meanwhile, add ½ teaspoon of the merguez spice mix to the yoghurt, along with a pinch each of salt and pepper, and set aside.

When you're ready to serve, place a large frying pan over a high heat. When it's really hot, add the liver mixture, making sure it's well spread out. Let the liver sear for about a minute, then give it a good stir or toss, making sure all the slices are flipped. Cook for a minute or so more, then add the knob of butter and cook, tossing or stirring, for barely another minute.

Season the liver and onions with salt and pepper to taste and serve straight away, with rice or warm flatbreads or pitta and a good dollop of spiced yoghurt.

PLUS ONE For added deliciousness, cram some young spinach leaves into the wrap with the liver. You can use raw spinach, or wilt it gently in a smidge of butter first.

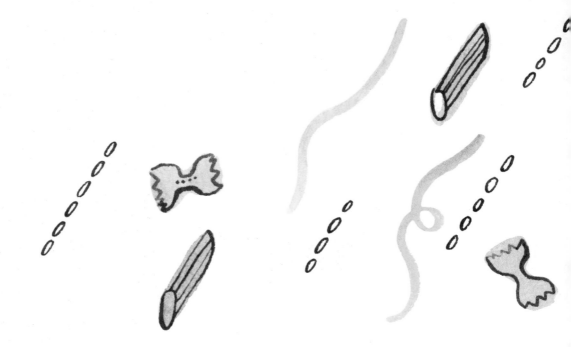

Pasta, Rice and Company

Here comes comfort food, pure and simple. And

I mean really simple. These are recipes for the end of a long, hard day. Easy to prepare and easy to eat, they are guaranteed to soothe both body and soul.

Pasta, noodles, rice, pearl barley and couscous: these inexpensive staples hark back to a rustic tradition of food for workers. The custom of seasoning a big plateful of these dependable tummy-fillers with a soupçon of something more flavoursome (and more pricey) has spawned some peasant food classics, such as Scotch broth, Italian spaghetti carbonara and Japanese ramen noodles. You don't get to be a nationally loved dish without delivering a winning combination of taste, energy and value.

In particular, pasta has become a default option when something fast and filling is needed. As long as it's not a default we resort to every night, and as long as we take our starchy ballast down a slightly different path each time, I don't think there's anything wrong with that at all. There's something honest and reassuring about straightforwardly energy-boosting, mood-enhancing dishes like these.

Nowadays, you can stay true to the thrifty spirit of this kind of cuisine by keeping it simple, but perhaps shifting the balance of the ingredients a little. If you haven't actually been tilling the fields all day, then your portion of pasta needn't be too mountainous, while you can perhaps be a little freer with the other elements: the luscious olive oil, the feisty cheese, the well-spiced sausage.

When it comes to choosing one or two complementary ingredients to top your pile of carbs, you'll be instinctively drawn to foods that carry a bit of oomph. I usually add some kind of fresh, lustrous vegetable, often a green one – asparagus, courgettes, cabbage, kale, broccoli, seaweed, sorrel, nettles even. Then I might embellish this pair with something pretty intensely flavoured – maybe a herb, spice, strong cheese or some kind of smoked or salted meat or fish. Improvisation is the order of the day, and as long as there's a shade more method than madness, the results invariably rock.

So, embrace the recipes that follow, and the spirit they embody, and you will never again look at your packet of penne or your panful of basmati as a same-old, same-old culinary cop-out. Rather, they will become the blank canvases for enjoyably stress-free creative outings. You'll be knocking out masterpieces without breaking a sweat.

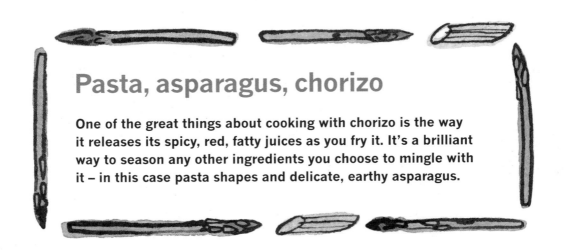

Pasta, asparagus, chorizo

One of the great things about cooking with chorizo is the way it releases its spicy, red, fatty juices as you fry it. It's a brilliant way to season any other ingredients you choose to mingle with it – in this case pasta shapes and delicate, earthy asparagus.

Serves 4

About 500g asparagus

150g cooking chorizo

300g pasta shapes, such as penne, fusilli or strozzapreti

1 tablespoon rapeseed, sunflower or olive oil

A good squeeze of lemon juice

Sea salt and freshly ground black pepper

A handful of flat-leaf parsley, leaves only, chopped, to finish (optional)

Snap the woody ends off the asparagus and cut the spears into roughly 3cm pieces. Remove the skin from the chorizo and cut the sausage into thick matchsticks.

Bring a large pan of water to the boil, salt it well and add the pasta. Cook according to the time suggested on the packet until al dente, adding the asparagus to the pan for the last 3–5 minutes. (Freshly cut asparagus will only take 3 minutes.)

Meanwhile, heat the oil in a frying pan over a medium heat. Add the chorizo and fry gently for 5–10 minutes until it is beginning to turn crisp and the spicy juices are running nicely.

Drain the pasta and asparagus well and immediately toss with the hot chorizo and the spicy oil in the pan. Taste and adjust the seasoning, adding more salt and pepper if needed and a good squeeze of lemon juice. Serve straight away, scattered with chopped parsley if you like.

SWAPS Any highly seasoned sausage will work well in place of chorizo, either cut into chunks or squeezed out of the skin and crumbled. Pancetta and bacon work too. When asparagus is not in season, try using green beans instead, or broad beans or peas. Shredded greens can also provide the green element.

Spaghetti, garlic, olive oil

It's a truism (but a very apt one) that the simpler the recipe the more crucial the quality of the ingredients. This minimalist classic proves the point. If ever you are to splash out on some top-quality, bronze-die pasta, this is the time to do it. It's also worth using a really good extra virgin olive oil and very fresh garlic. Tick these boxes, and you'll have a sublime, wonderfully quick supper.

Per person

100g spaghetti, linguine or tagliatelle

1 garlic clove

2 tablespoons extra virgin olive oil

Sea salt and freshly ground black pepper

Grated Parmesan or hard, matured goat's cheese to serve (optional)

Bring a large pan of water to the boil, salt it generously and add the pasta. Cook according to the time suggested on the packet until al dente.

Meanwhile, check your garlic clove: if it has even a touch of green shoot in the centre, nick this out as it will be bitter, then cut the garlic into thin slivers.

Heat the extra virgin olive oil very gently in a small pan over a low heat. When it is hot, add the garlic and cook for just 30 seconds or so. Don't let it colour more than the merest fraction. Remove from the heat.

Drain the pasta and toss with the garlicky oil. Season with salt and pepper and transfer to warm bowls. I like this just as it is, without any cheese. But I wouldn't begrudge you a few gratings of Parmesan or other hard cheese, if you feel the urge.

PLUS ONE Although this incredibly simple dish is authentic, it is often found on Italian menus with the addition of peperoncino (chilli). Add either finely chopped fresh red chilli or a pinch of dried chilli flakes to the olive oil with the garlic.

Pasta, tomatoes, blue cheese

Hot pasta, raw tomatoes, creamy blue cheese – this trio makes a delicious pasta dish. It really works best if you choose a fairly creamy blue cheese with a reasonably gentle flavour, such as Cornish Blue, Shropshire Blue or Dorset Blue Vinney, rather than something as strong as Stilton.

Serves 4

400g cherry tomatoes, quartered

4 tablespoons extra virgin rapeseed or olive oil, plus extra to serve

1 garlic clove, slivered

A good pinch of dried chilli flakes

300g pasta shapes (any will do)

200g blue cheese, crumbled

Sea salt and freshly ground black pepper

In a bowl, combine the tomatoes, oil, garlic and chilli flakes with a good pinch of salt and a few twists of pepper. Leave to macerate for 30 minutes, stirring once or twice.

Bring a large pan of water to the boil, salt it well and add the pasta shapes. Cook according to the time suggested on the packet until al dente.

Drain the pasta well. Add the tomatoes along with their juices and toss well. Lightly stir through the crumbled blue cheese. Serve at once, topped with a final splosh of oil and another twist or two of black pepper.

SWAP If blue cheese really isn't your thing, this works well with a tangy goat's cheese, such as a classic chèvre log.

Pasta, courgettes, mozzarella

Vegetable pasta bakes can be rather dreary, but not this one. These three simple ingredients combine to make a delicious and deeply comforting dish.

Serves 4

A knob of butter

500g courgettes, trimmed

3 tablespoons olive oil

2 garlic cloves, finely chopped

250g pasta shapes, such as penne or rigatoni

2 balls of buffalo mozzarella (250g in total)

2 tablespoons double cream

Freshly grated Parmesan, hard goat's cheese or other well-flavoured hard cheese

Sea salt and freshly ground black pepper

Preheat the oven to 190°C/Gas 5 and lightly butter an oven dish, about 1.5 litre capacity. Cut the courgettes into 3mm thick slices.

Heat the olive oil in a large frying pan over a medium heat and add the courgettes. Once they are sizzling nicely, but before they start to brown, turn the heat down and season with a little salt; this helps draw out their moisture. Cook the courgettes gently, stirring often and breaking them down a little with your spatula or wooden spoon as they become tender. Continue to cook until they have softened almost to the point of mushiness – up to half an hour. Add the garlic when you think they are almost done. You should end up with a fragrant, garlicky, rough courgette purée.

Meanwhile, bring a large pan of water to the boil, salt it well and add the pasta. Cook for a minute or two less than the minimum time suggested on the packet, so it is marginally underdone.

Drain the pasta well. Add the mushy, garlicky courgettes and stir to combine. Tear up the mozzarella with your hands and add it to the pasta, along with the cream. Season with salt and pepper and stir the whole lot together one more time.

Transfer the mixture to the prepared oven dish and give it a good grating of Parmesan or other hard cheese. Bake in the oven for 20 minutes or until piping hot and golden brown on top. Serve straight away.

PLUS ONE OR TWO Various optional extras work very well here, such as little matchsticks of chorizo or lardons of bacon, fried until crisp and stirred in with the courgettes. If you would prefer to keep the dish meat-free, try some roughly chopped oven-dried tomatoes (see page 114) and/or chopped stoned black olives.

Pappardelle, squash, sage

Long ribbons of pappardelle work beautifully in this lovely, warming autumnal dish, but smaller pasta shapes like fusilli, orecchiette or penne are good too.

Serves 4

About 750g squash, such as Crown Prince, butternut or kabocha

4–6 fat garlic cloves (unpeeled), lightly bashed

4 tablespoons rapeseed or olive oil

250g pappardelle, tagliatelle or pasta shapes of your choice

50g unsalted butter

About 15–20 sage leaves, cut into thin ribbons

Sea salt and freshly ground black pepper

Finely grated Parmesan or hard goat's cheese, to serve

Preheat the oven to 190°C/Gas 5. Peel and deseed the squash and cut into 2–3cm cubes. Put it into a roasting tin and add the garlic and some salt and pepper. Trickle over the oil and toss together. Roast for about 45 minutes, stirring once or twice during cooking, until the squash is completely soft and starting to caramelise at the edges.

When the squash is halfway through cooking, bring a large pan of water to the boil and salt it well. Add the pasta and cook for the time suggested on the packet until al dente.

While the pasta is cooking, heat the butter very gently in a small pan until foaming. Add the sage and cook gently over a low heat, without letting the butter brown, for about 3 minutes, then take off the heat.

When the pasta is cooked, drain it well and return to the pan. Tip the hot, roasted squash, along with any pan juices and the garlic cloves if they're not too burnt, into the pasta. Add the sage butter and toss the lot together, adding more salt and pepper if needed.

Divide between warm plates and add a grinding of pepper and a scattering of grated cheese. Serve at once, with extra Parmesan or other hard cheese on the table for people to help themselves.

PLUS ONE Toasted pine nuts or roughly chopped walnuts will add texture and flavour. Toss them into the pan of roasting squash for the last 10 minutes.

Pasta, sausage, cabbage

This is a wonderfully quick and satisfying pasta supper –
something you can put together in under half an hour and
a good way to entice the veg-shy into eating their greens.

Serves 4

1 tablespoon rapeseed,
sunflower or olive oil

4 large butcher's sausages
(or 8 smaller bangers)

300g pasta shapes, such as
fusilli or penne

½ green cabbage, such as
Savoy, tough ribs removed,
shredded

Sea salt and freshly ground
black pepper

Heat the oil in a large frying pan over a medium heat. Add the
sausages and fry them fairly gently, turning often, for at least
10 minutes, until golden brown all over and pretty much cooked
through. Take out the sausages and cut them into bite-sized
chunks, then return to the hot pan and fry for another 5 minutes
or so to crisp and rough up the cut surfaces.

Meanwhile, bring a large pan of water to the boil, salt it well and
add the pasta. Cook according to the time suggested on the packet
until al dente, adding the cabbage about 3 minutes before the end
of the cooking time.

Once cooked, drain the pasta and cabbage well and add to the
chunks of hot sausage and any juices in the frying pan. Toss well,
add some salt and pepper if needed, and serve straight away.

SWAPS You can use any greens in this recipe, including spring
greens, kale, cavolo nero and Brussels tops. Spinach is very good
too, but wilt it with the sausage chunks, rather than add it to the
pasta water.

Noodles, chicken, greens

This is the sort of dish I make whenever I have some good homemade stock to hand. The 'chicken' element is really the stock itself but if you have any scraps of meat left on your roast chicken carcass, they make a welcome addition.

Serves 3–4

1 small head of spring greens (about 200g), or use cabbage or kale

2 nests of fine egg noodles, broken

1 garlic clove, finely sliced

A dash of soy sauce (optional)

A squeeze of lime juice (optional)

For the chicken stock

1 roast chicken carcass

1–2 onions, roughly chopped

1–2 large carrots, roughly chopped

3–4 celery stalks, roughly chopped

½ large leek, roughly chopped

A few black peppercorns

2 bay leaves

1 sprig of thyme (optional)

A few parsley stalks (optional)

For the stock, use your fingers and a small, sharp knife to strip the chicken carcass of any remaining good meat. Set this aside. Tear the carcass into fairly small pieces and cram them, along with any skin, bones, fat, jelly or bits from the roasting tin, and all the stock vegetables, peppercorns and herbs, into a saucepan that will take them snugly. Pour in enough cold water to just cover everything – with a bit of luck you'll need no more than 1.5 litres.

Bring to a bare simmer and cook, uncovered, for at least 3 hours, or up to 5 hours, topping up the water once or twice, if necessary. Strain the stock through a fine sieve into a bowl and leave it to cool. The stock can be chilled or frozen, or you can cook your noodle dish straight way.

You'll need about 750ml stock: bring it to a simmer. Meanwhile, remove the tough stems from the greens and roughly shred the leaves. Add the shredded leaves to the stock and bring back to a simmer, then add the noodles and garlic. Cook for 3–4 minutes, stirring a few times, or until the noodles are just tender. If you have any reserved chicken, add this a couple of minutes before the end of the cooking time.

Taste and season well with salt and pepper, then pour into warm bowls. Finish, if you like, with a dash of soy sauce and a squeeze of lime juice.

SWAPS Try cooking a handful of rice in the broth, instead of the noodles. Or pearled barley or spelt. These will all take longer, of course – 20–25 minutes simmering in the stock, so add the greens about 5 minutes before they will be cooked.

ANOTHER TAKE If you don't have any chicken meat but you would like to add a little protein to the dish, cook a simple egg 'pancake' – just pour a couple of beaten eggs into a hot pan and cook for a few minutes until set, then roll it up and cut into slices. Add these egg ribbons to the stock just before the end of the noodle cooking time.

Rice, saffron, tomatoes

A golden, saffron-infused risotto and intense, oven-roasted tomatoes look stunning together on the plate. The flavours complement each other extremely well too, with the delicate, floral bitterness of saffron beautifully offsetting the sweetness of the tomatoes.

Serves 4

A little rapeseed or olive oil

25g unsalted butter, plus extra to finish

1 large onion, finely chopped

About 800ml chicken or vegetable stock

A large pinch of saffron strands

250g risotto rice

150ml dry white wine

A bay leaf and/or a sprig of thyme (optional)

Sea salt and freshly ground black pepper

For the roasted tomatoes

500g small or medium tomatoes

2 garlic cloves, finely chopped

3 tablespoons olive oil

1 teaspoon sugar

Preheat the oven to 190°C/Gas 5. For the roasted tomatoes, lightly oil a medium roasting dish. Halve the tomatoes or cut into quarters, depending on size, and place them in the dish. They should fit reasonably snugly in one layer. Scatter over the garlic and lots of salt and pepper, then trickle over the olive oil and sprinkle on the sugar. Roast for about 30 minutes until golden, juicy and bubbling. Keep warm.

Meanwhile, make the risotto. Heat a dash of oil with the butter in a large saucepan over a medium heat. Add the onion and sauté gently for 10 minutes or until soft but not coloured. Meanwhile, put the stock and saffron in another saucepan and bring to a simmer, then keep warm over a very low heat.

Add the rice to the soft onions and cook, stirring, for a minute or two. Pour in the wine and cook until it is all absorbed, then add the bay leaf and/or thyme, if using. Now add the saffron-infused stock, about a quarter at a time, keeping the rice at a low simmer and stirring often. Let each batch of stock be absorbed by the rice before you add the next. Continue until the rice is tender and the risotto is creamy and slightly soupy. This should take 20–25 minutes; you may not need quite all of the stock. Take off the heat. Dot a little butter over the surface of the risotto, cover and leave to rest for a couple of minutes.

Remove the bay leaf and/or thyme, if used. Fork through the melted butter and season the risotto to taste with salt and pepper. Spoon into warm bowls and top with the juicy roasted tomatoes. Give an extra grinding of black pepper, then serve.

Rice, seaweed, avocado

This is a kind of laid-back vegetarian sushi. It can be a lovely light lunch or supper dish and it also makes a good starter for sharing. I like to use a 'sea salad', which is a mix of dried seaweeds, but you can use any ready-to-eat dried seaweed.

Serves 4–6

200g sushi rice

30ml rice vinegar

10g sugar

½ teaspoon salt

1–2 ripe avocados, depending on size

2 tablespoons ready-to-eat flaked dried seaweed

To serve

Wasabi

Soy sauce

Put the rice in a sieve and wash it several times under cold water. Transfer to a large, heavy-based saucepan and pour on 250ml water. Bring to the boil, turn the heat down low and put the lid on. Simmer for 18 minutes, keeping the pan covered. Remove from the heat and leave to stand, lid on, for a further 15 minutes.

Meanwhile, mix the rice vinegar, sugar and salt together in a small saucepan. Heat gently until the sugar dissolves, stirring frequently. Remove from the heat and set aside to cool.

Take the lid off the rice pan and use a wooden spatula or spoon to 'cut and fold' the rice gently. The idea is to release steam and separate the grains. Be as gentle as possible so as not to damage the cooked rice grains. After a minute or two of this, turn the warm rice out into a large shallow bowl or platter and gradually work in the vinegar mixture, using the spatula or spoon as before, and being as gentle as possible. A proper sushi chef would now fan the rice to cool it further. I don't see this as being essential, but I do sometimes put the rice outside in the breeze. Allow the rice to cool to room temperature, or just a shade warmer.

Halve, stone and peel your avocado(s). Cut each avocado half into 5 or 6 slices and arrange them over the rice. Put the seaweed in a dry pan and toast over a medium heat for 1 minute. Scatter the seaweed over the rice and avocado.

Stir a smidge of wasabi into a little dish of soy sauce – better still, make a little saucer of the mix for each guest – to serve alongside the sushi as a sauce/dressing.

PLUS ONE Try sprinkling some toasted sesame seeds over the avocado slices, as well as the seaweed.

Rice, lentils, sorrel

This is a wonderfully simple, honest sort of dish – by which I mean you can really taste each ingredient. It's perfect for a chilly spring day when sorrel will be unfurling its bright green leaves. Adding this lemony herb to an earthy lentil risotto has an amazing lightening effect. If you don't have sorrel in your garden (and it's very easy to grow), you may find some growing wild, or in a supermarket or greengrocer if you are very lucky.

Serves 4

1 tablespoon olive oil

50g butter

1 onion, finely chopped

100g Puy lentils

About 1 litre chicken or vegetable stock

250g risotto rice

150ml dry white wine

A good bunch of sorrel leaves (about 75g), stalks removed, shredded

Sea salt and freshly ground black pepper

Heat the olive oil and half the butter in a large saucepan over a medium-low heat. Add the onion and sweat gently for 7–8 minutes until softened.

Meanwhile, put the lentils into a bowl, cover with boiling water and leave for 5 minutes, then drain. Bring the stock to a simmer in a small pan and keep it hot over a very low heat.

Add the rice and drained lentils to the soft onion in the pan. Cook for a couple of minutes, stirring often. Add the wine and simmer until it is all absorbed. Now add the stock, about a quarter at a time, keeping the risotto at a low simmer and stirring it often. Let each batch of stock be fully absorbed by the rice before you add the next. Continue until the rice is tender. This should take 20–25 minutes; you may not need quite all of the stock.

Stir in the sorrel and cook for just a minute or two, so it wilts into the risotto. Take off the heat. Season the risotto well with salt and pepper and dot the remaining butter over the top. Cover and leave for a couple of minutes, then stir the melted butter through the risotto. Taste to check the seasoning, then serve.

PLUS ONE If you are making this in the spring and you happen to come by some wild garlic leaves, shred them finely and add with the sorrel. A sprinkling of snipped chives or garlic chives will have a milder but similarly delicious effect.

SWAPS Instead of, or as well as, sorrel, you can use nettle tops (the top 4 or 6 leaves of young, early spring nettles). Wash well, blanch in boiling water for a minute, then drain and squeeze out most of the water. Roughly chop and add to the risotto 5 minutes before the end (or 2 minutes before the sorrel).

Sprouted lentils, cashews, coriander

I love the flavour and texture of sprouted lentils – not to mention the fact that they're bursting with vitamins, minerals and other good things. Sprouting your own is incredibly easy. It takes a few days to get them going, but your hands-on work time can be counted in minutes. Apart from in a simple stir-fry like this, sprouting lentils are great scattered over buttered new potatoes, sautéed with a little chorizo and garlic, or added raw to a grated cheese sandwich with a dollop of mayo.

Serves 2

100g green or Puy lentils

50g cashew nuts

1 tablespoon sunflower oil

1 garlic clove, very thinly sliced

Juice of 1 lime

1 tablespoon soy sauce

A couple of large handfuls of coriander (leaves only), to finish

To get your lentils sprouting, place them in a large glass jar and cover with cold water. Cut a square of muslin or cheesecloth and use an elastic band to fasten it over the jar. Don't use a lid because you want the lentils to be able to breathe.

After about 24 hours, drain off the water. After that, you simply need to rinse and drain the lentils twice a day, morning and night, for a further 4–5 days, keeping them in their jar under the muslin cover. On the second or third day, you will see tender, pale shoots. In another couple of days these will have grown into little wiggly tails of 2cm or so, and you'll have what looks like a jar of little lentilly tadpoles. Give them a final rinse, drain well and they are ready to eat, raw or cooked. Store them in a clean container in the fridge and use within 5 days.

To make the stir-fry, set a frying pan over a high heat. Add the cashews and toss them quickly in the dry pan for 2–3 minutes to toast evenly. Add the oil and garlic and cook for a matter of seconds. Then, before the garlic gets a chance to burn, add the sprouted lentils. Toss them around in the pan for 1–2 minutes before adding the lime juice and soy sauce.

Immediately transfer to warm plates, scatter over lots of coriander and serve, with rice if you like.

Spelt, partridge, dried pears

Partridge is a delicious little bird – ideal for those who don't like their game too gamey. It's particularly good enhanced with a hint of fruity sweetness. I like it when pears and partridges come together in the festive season, and luscious dried pears work brilliantly here too.

Serves 2

2 oven-ready partridges

About 25g butter, softened

A few sprigs of thyme

Sea salt and freshly ground black pepper

For the spelt or barley mix

1 tablespoon rapeseed, sunflower or olive oil

1 onion, finely chopped

1 garlic clove, finely chopped

150g pearled spelt or pearl barley, rinsed

About 600ml chicken, game or vegetable stock (or use plain water)

50g dried pears, roughly chopped

Grated zest of 1 lemon, plus the juice of ½ lemon

Sea salt and freshly ground black pepper

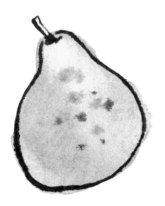

Preheat the oven to 200°C/Gas 6. For the spelt or barley mix, heat the oil in a large saucepan over a medium-low heat. Add the onion and garlic and fry gently for about 10 minutes until soft. Add the spelt or barley and stir well. Pour in 450ml stock or water, bring to the boil, then lower the heat. Simmer, uncovered, until the grain is tender and most of the liquid is absorbed – about 20 minutes for spelt, a bit more for barley. If it looks in danger of boiling dry, top up with a little boiling water. Take off the heat and stir in the dried pears, lemon zest and juice, and plenty of salt and pepper. Spread the mixture over the base of a smallish oven dish.

Smear the partridges with the butter and season well with salt and pepper. Push the thyme sprigs inside the birds as best you can – it's fine if some of it sticks out! Put the partridges into the oven dish, nestling them gently in the hot grain mix. Trickle 125ml hot stock or water over the spelt or barley. Roast in the oven for 30–35 minutes or until the partridges are cooked. To check, insert a skewer into the thickest part – the juices should run clear. Leave to rest in a warm place for 10–15 minutes.

Tip up the partridges so any juices inside them run into the spelt or barley. Place a bird on each warm serving plate with spoonfuls of the fruity grains. Serve with shredded greens or broccoli.

SWAPS Pretty much any dried fruit will work in place of pears. Try roughly chopped prunes or dried apricots, or raisins or sultanas.

ANOTHER TAKE Use a whole chicken instead of the partridges to serve 4, and double up the spelt or barley mix. Smear butter over the chicken, season and place in the oven dish. Roast the bird alone at 220°C/Gas 7 for 20 minutes. Now spoon the hot grain mix around it, trickle over the stock or water and roast for a further 40 minutes at 180°C/Gas 4. Turn off the oven and leave the tray inside with the door ajar for 20 minutes. Now check that the chicken is cooked with a skewer – the juices should run clear.

Couscous, lamb, courgettes

A very quick and simple way to use up leftover lamb, this is
a lovely supper, or a delicious thing to find in your lunchbox.
You can use standard 'white' couscous or big, nutty grains
of 'giant' wholewheat couscous.

Serves 2

125g couscous

About 250g small courgettes

2 tablespoons olive oil

1 garlic clove, finely slivered

A good spritz of lemon juice

2 tablespoons shredded mint

About 150g cold, leftover
lamb, shredded

Sea salt and freshly ground
black pepper

Prepare the couscous according to the packet instructions.

Meanwhile, cut the courgettes into roughly 3mm slices, on an
angle. Heat the olive oil in a large pan over a medium heat and
add the courgettes. Cook, tossing frequently, for 10–15 minutes
until tender and lightly coloured, adding the garlic for the last
few minutes of cooking.

Take the courgettes off the heat, season with salt, pepper and lots
of lemon juice, and stir through half of the shredded mint.

Toss the lemony, minty courgettes into the couscous, along with
the lamb. Check the seasoning and serve, warm or at room
temperature, sprinkled with the remaining mint.

PLUS ONE/SWAP Some toasted nuts – pine nuts, slivered almonds
or cashews – make this dish extra delicious. Use the nuts as well
as the lamb, or, if you want to turn this into a vegetarian dish, use
plentifully instead of the meat.

Polenta, blue cheese, greens

Hearty, comforting and filling, this simple threesome is just the ticket on a chilly day. If blue cheese doesn't appeal to you, use a soft goat's cheese instead.

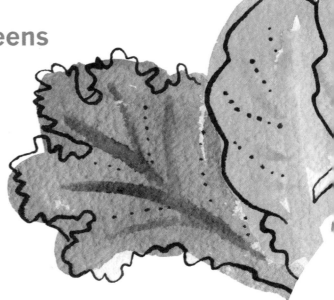

Serves 4

400g spring greens, kale
or cavolo nero

A large knob of butter

200g fairly soft blue cheese,
or goat's cheese, crumbled
into small chunks

Sea salt and freshly ground
black pepper

For the polenta

400ml milk

1 bay leaf

½ onion

A sprig of thyme (optional)

150g quick-cook polenta

20g butter

Put the milk for the polenta in a saucepan along with 400ml water. Add the bay leaf, onion, and thyme if using. Bring to just below the boil, then take off the heat and set aside to infuse for 20 minutes.

Strip the spring greens or kale leaves away from their tough stalks. Roll the leaves up and slice across them to produce thick ribbons. Steam them for about 3 minutes until tender, or add to a pan of boiling salted water and simmer for just 2 minutes until tender, then drain well. Squeeze or press the greens in the colander to remove as much water as you can. Toss with the knob of butter and some salt and pepper and keep warm.

For the polenta, strain the infused milk and water into a clean pan. Bring to a simmer, then add the polenta in a thin stream, stirring as you do so. Stir until the mixture is smooth and let it return to a simmer. Cook for just 1 minute, then remove from the heat. Stir in the butter and season generously with at least ¼ teaspoon salt.

Scoop the soft polenta into warm bowls. (If you have to leave it standing for any time in the pan, and it seems to be thickening too much, you can loosen it with a splash or two of hot water.) Top with the crumbled cheese and put a heap of buttered greens alongside. Grind over some pepper and serve.

Polenta, beans, kale

This is my take on farinata – a traditional Tuscan peasant dish of kale and beans thickened with polenta. It's somewhere between a vegetable stew and a soup, the grain thickening the liquor without detracting from the flavours of the veg and beans. As with all very simple dishes, the quality of the ingredients is paramount. Use a good stock – homemade if possible – and finish with some really top-notch olive oil.

Serves 4

2 tablespoons olive oil

1 onion, chopped

2 garlic cloves, chopped

About 200g kale, cavolo nero or spring greens

850ml vegetable or chicken stock

400g tin white beans, such as cannellini, drained (or 200g home-cooked beans)

100g quick-cook fine polenta

Sea salt and freshly ground black pepper

Extra virgin olive oil to serve

Heat the olive oil in a large saucepan over a medium-low heat. Add the onion and sweat for 10 minutes, until really soft and golden. Add the garlic and cook gently for another 5 minutes.

Meanwhile, strip the kale, cavolo or spring green leaves away from their tough stalks. Roll the leaves up and slice across them to produce thick ribbons.

Add the stock and beans to the soft onion and garlic and bring to a simmer. Add the shredded leaves, return to a simmer and cook for 3–5 minutes, or until they are just tender. Now pour in the polenta, stirring it in well so it doesn't form lumps. Return to a simmer and cook for 3–4 minutes until thickened. When you taste the dish, it should be velvety and smooth, not at all gritty. Season with salt and pepper to taste.

Ladle into warm bowls, trickle generously with good extra virgin olive oil, grind over some pepper and serve straight away.

As the dish cools, the polenta will begin to set and once cold, it will be less soupy and more solid. To serve leftovers, you can loosen it back down with some more stock and/or water and reheat it, stirring often, until piping hot again.

SWAPS Spinach or even nettle tops (see page 174 for preparation) can be used instead of kale. And chickpeas can happily stand in for the beans.

Polenta, mushrooms, cheese

The nutty 'goat Cheddar' made by Quickes is my first choice cheese for this, but any firm, well-flavoured cheese would work, including Parmesan or regular Cheddar. You can ring the changes with the mushrooms too: large, flat, dark-gilled varieties are ideal, but you could include some fresh wild mushrooms, or a small handful of dried porcini or ceps, rehydrated in boiling water.

Serves 4

For the polenta
400ml milk
A few black peppercorns
½ onion and/or 2 bashed garlic cloves
1 bay leaf (optional)
A sprig of thyme (optional)
150g quick-cook polenta
20g butter
2 tablespoons olive oil

For the mushrooms
2 tablespoons olive oil
A large knob of butter
About 500g mushrooms, trimmed and sliced
1 teaspoon thyme leaves (optional)
1 large garlic clove, chopped
A squeeze of lemon juice
Sea salt and freshly ground black pepper

To serve
Goat's Cheddar or other firm cheese

Put the milk for the polenta and 400ml water into a saucepan. Add the peppercorns, onion and/or garlic, and bay leaf and thyme if using. Bring almost to the boil, then take off the heat. Set aside to infuse for 20 minutes.

Strain the infused liquid into a clean pan. Bring to a simmer, then add the polenta in a thin stream, stirring as you do so. Stir until smooth and let it return to a simmer. Cook for 4–5 minutes, then take off the heat. Stir in the butter and season well, adding at least ¼ teaspoon salt. Mix well, then tip the polenta on to a cold plate or marble slab. Smooth into an even disc, about 2cm thick, and leave to cool completely. When cold, cut into wedges or thick fingers.

Heat 2 tablespoons olive oil in a large, non-stick frying pan over a medium-high heat and fry the chunks of polenta for 2–3 minutes each side, until they form a light, golden brown crust. Keep hot while you cook the mushrooms, using the same pan.

It's best to cook the mushrooms in two batches (to ensure they fry rather than stew). Heat 1 tablespoon olive oil and half the butter in a large frying pan over a medium-high heat. When foaming, add half the mushrooms and thyme, if using, and a pinch of salt. Fry briskly, stirring often, until the liquid released has evaporated and the mushrooms are starting to colour. Add half the garlic and cook for another minute or two. Season with more salt and pepper and a tiny squeeze of lemon juice and then transfer to a warmed dish. Keep warm while you cook the rest of the mushrooms in the remaining oil and butter.

Put the polenta wedges on warm plates and add the mushrooms. Finish with fine shavings of goat's Cheddar or other cheese and a sprinkling of salt and pepper.

Oatmeal, nettles, bacon rind

Savoury porridge may not sound exactly glam, but it's certainly warming and delicious. Chunky pinhead oatmeal cooks to a lovely texture not unlike risotto rice and carries the punchy flavours of nettles and bacon well. I like the way bacon rind makes this a really parsimonious dish, but you can use whole rashers or snippets of crisply fried bacon.

Serves 2

Rind from 6–7 rashers of bacon, or 4 rashers of streaky bacon

75g pinhead oatmeal

50g young nettle tops (the top 4–6 leaves only)

450ml chicken, vegetable or ham stock

35g butter

3 shallots or 1 medium onion, finely chopped

1 garlic clove, finely chopped

Sea salt and freshly ground black pepper

Preheat the grill. Lay the bacon rind or rashers on a small baking tray and cook under the grill for 4–5 minutes until crisp, turning as necessary to ensure even colour and crackling. Keep warm.

Put the pinhead oatmeal in a sieve and give it a good shake to get rid of the smaller grains. Give the oatmeal in the sieve a quick rinse under the cold tap and set aside.

Wearing rubber gloves, wash the nettle tops thoroughly in a sink full of cold water, removing any unwanted plant matter or insect life. Pick the leaves from their stalks and place in a large bowl.

Bring the stock to the boil in a pan, then pour it over the nettle leaves to cover them. Leave to stand for 1 minute, then drain the nettles in a sieve over the pan to save the nettle stock. When cool enough, squeeze out any stock from the nettles into the pan.

Heat half the butter in a small saucepan over a gentle heat. When it is foaming, add the shallots or onion and garlic and cook for 2–3 minutes. Add the oatmeal and cook for a minute, then pour in the stock and bring to a simmer. Cook gently, stirring occasionally, for 15–20 minutes, or until the oatmeal is tender and the stock absorbed. If it is too dry, add a splash more stock. You want a loose consistency like that of traditional porridge. Finely chop half the nettles and add to the porridge. Season well with salt and pepper.

Melt the remaining butter in another small pan and add the rest of the blanched nettle tops. Cook them gently for a minute or two and season well with salt and pepper.

To serve, spoon the porridge into warm bowls, top with the buttered nettles and finish with the crispy bacon rind or rashers.

SWAP Nettles are an early spring wild green. If you want to make this dish at another time of the year, try spinach instead.

Fabulous Fruity Puds

It's in the arena of simple fruit puds that I think the purest and most successful manifestations of my 'three good things' idea can be found. I could keep on dreaming up easy, gorgeous fruity threesomes forever. In fact, I found it very hard to stop putting this chapter together.

My recipes fall into two loose categories. There are those that have two, or even three different fruits, with something to balance out the acidity of the fruit. So a tangy blackberry and apple granita is calmed with a cap of cool cream (page 354), while rhubarb and oranges are tempered with the nutty sugariness of candied chestnuts (page 330), and in one case it's a third fruit – creamy, sweet banana – that answers the gentle acidity of apples and pears (page 328).

Then there are those recipes that are based around just one fruit, that follow a reliably delicious formula: sweet-tart fruit, a starchy, crisp or crunchy carb element and a luscious, creamy dollop of something on top (or underneath, or in the middle). Trifle, in its simplest form, is a good example, comprising fruit, cake, custard/cream. Raspberries, panna cotta, shortbread (page 347); strawberries, amaretti, ricotta (page 336, swap); pears, custard, ginger cake (page 357) – these are tremendous treaty trinities in which each element points up the loveliness of its partners. It's a formula that works brilliantly at teatime too – scones, cream, strawberries; and even at breakfast – muesli, blueberries, yoghurt.

I hope you will particularly turn to these recipes during the prime season for British fruit: summer and early autumn. From the strawberries, gooseberries and outdoor rhubarb of June, through the raspberries, blueberries, cherries, currants, juicy plums and gages of high summer, and the first pears and apples in September, there is always a fruity harvest for the taking.

So often this homegrown bounty is overlooked in the posh pud stakes, passed over for imported kiwis and passion fruit, or superseded by lemon tarts and mango mousses. We can run a bit low on inspiration when it comes to cooking our native fruit, stuck down a cul-de-sac of crumbles and pavlovas. Both of these are fine puds, but there's so much more to explore and relish.

It pays to stock up on some of these perfect partners, so you always have them handy: a little honey and various shades of sugar; pud-worthy biscuits such as shortbread and gingernuts; a tub of vanilla ice cream, or a carton of wholemilk yoghurt, or just plain cream. Then, when the ripe fruit starts dropping into your lap, you're just minutes away from a luscious fruity plateful!

Apple, orange, lemon

This is a delicious way to make a compote of Bramleys or any other collapsing cooking apple – scented with citrus zest and juice. You can serve it hot or cold, for breakfast or pudding, with yoghurt, cereal, custard or cream, or use it in another recipe – with my independent crumble (page 360), for example.

Makes about 800g (up to 8 servings)

1 orange, halved

1 lemon, halved

1kg Bramleys or other cooking apples

50g caster sugar, plus extra to taste

Finely grate the zest from one orange half and one lemon half into a saucepan. Squeeze all the juice from both fruits into the pan too. Peel, core and thinly slice the apples, dropping the slices directly into the pan and tossing them in the juice to stop them browning. Add the sugar.

Bring to a simmer, stirring regularly to help dissolve the sugar. Then cook gently, stirring occasionally but vigorously, for about 20–30 minutes, until the apples have collapsed into a tender, but still slightly chunky purée. Alternatively, cook for a little longer, until the compote is smooth, translucent and golden, breaking up the last of the apple pieces with the back of a wooden spoon. Do be careful, though, that it doesn't catch on the bottom of the pan.

Taste and add more sugar if you fancy a sweeter compote. Serve either hot or cold.

SWAP I have tried this using a few clementines instead of the orange and lemon. It's a bit tricky to grate the zest, because the skin is softer and more delicate, but the flavour is excellent.

Apples,
bananas,
pears

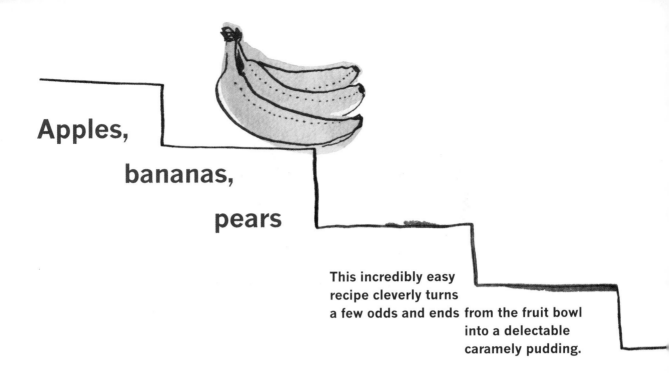

This incredibly easy recipe cleverly turns a few odds and ends from the fruit bowl into a delectable caramely pudding.

Serves 4

2 large or 3 medium bananas

2 medium-large crisp dessert apples

2 pears

A knob of butter

1 tablespoon sunflower oil

2 tablespoons soft brown sugar

Preheat the oven to 190°C/Gas 5. Peel the bananas, halve them lengthways and cut each half in two. Put into an oven dish. Peel the apples and pears, halve or quarter them and remove the cores, then add to the dish. Add the butter, then the oil (which will stop the butter burning) and place in the oven for 10 minutes.

Take the dish from the oven and give the whole thing a gentle stir to distribute the butter over all the fruit. Return to the oven for 10 minutes, then take it out again.

Sprinkle over the sugar, stir gently and return to the oven for a further 10 minutes or until everything is soft and the buttery, sugary juices are starting to caramelise. Serve at once, with plain yoghurt, cream or ice cream, and shortbread if you like.

PLUS ONE A few toasted nuts – roughly bashed walnuts, pecans or slivered almonds, toasted in a hot oven for 5–10 minutes until lightly browned – make an extra delicious finishing touch.

SWAPS The above version of this dish is very much an autumn/winter affair. For a high-summer alternative, replace the apples and pears with sliced peaches and halved strawberries, adding the strawberries with the sugar for the final 10 minutes, as they require less cooking.

Orange, rhubarb, chestnut

An indulgent treat, marrons glacés (candied chestnuts) are drenched in a sugar syrup that endows them with an almost fudgy character. They turn a very simple fruit compote into a luxurious pudding.

Serves 4

500g rhubarb

3 oranges

About 50g caster sugar

8–12 large marrons glacés

Trim the rhubarb, cut into 2–3cm chunks and place in a pan large enough to take it pretty much in a single layer. Finely grate the zest from one of the oranges over the rhubarb.

Slice all the peel and pith away from all 3 oranges. To do this, cut a slice off the base of each and stand the orange on a board. Then use a sharp knife to cut down through the peel and pith, slicing it away completely, in sections. Now, working over a bowl to catch the juice, slice the segments of orange out from between the membranes, dropping them directly into the bowl. Discard any pips as you go.

Squeeze out the remaining juice from the orange membranes into the pan of rhubarb and add the juice from the bowl of segments too. Add the sugar, stir together and leave for 15 minutes so the sugar starts to dissolve and draw some juice from the rhubarb.

Place the pan over a medium-low heat and bring to a very gentle simmer. Cook until the rhubarb is tender, stirring carefully once or twice. This can take as little as 8–10 minutes, but it might be a bit longer. Ideally you want the rhubarb to hold its shape, but don't worry if it starts to break down a bit.

Leave the rhubarb to cool completely, then combine with the orange segments. Taste and add a little more sugar if needed, then refrigerate.

To serve, spoon the rhubarb and orange compote into a large glass serving bowl or individual bowls and crumble over the marrons glacés.

PLUS ONE A spoonful of thick, plain yoghurt or crème fraîche goes well here.

MINUS ONE Leave out the marrons glacés and have the rhubarb and orange as a healthy breakfast, with granola, muesli and/or plain wholemilk yoghurt.

Apricots, tea, mascarpone

Another lovely recipe from Nikki Duffy. The fragrance and delicate, tannic bitterness of Earl Grey tea makes it a good foil to the rich sweetness of dried apricots. A dollop of creamy, sweetened mascarpone turns the aromatic fruit compote into a satisfying pudding.

Serves 6

250g organic dried apricots, halved

500ml hot, strong Earl Grey tea

200g mascarpone

20g icing sugar, or to taste

A splash of cream (optional)

Put the dried apricots into a bowl and pour the hot tea over them. Leave to soak for at least 6 hours; overnight is ideal.

Drain off the liquid that remains into a small saucepan and boil until it has reduced by about half, then pour this light syrup back over the apricots. Leave to cool, then cover and refrigerate. Leave in the fridge for several hours at least, or up to 2 days. The apricots will become even more plump and juicy as they soak.

Beat the mascarpone with the icing sugar until smooth. If the mixture becomes unmanageably stiff, thin it down with a splash of cream or a trickle of the tea liquor.

Serve the apricots, chilled, in glass dishes, with the syrup trickled over and a dollop of sweet mascarpone on top.

PLUS ONE/SWAP You can use other dried fruit as well as, or instead of, the apricots – try prunes, sultanas or figs.

Blueberries, yoghurt, lemon curd

I hope you can find the time to make a batch of your own lemon curd for this exquisite little threesome (the curd recipe comes from the brilliant Pam Corbin and makes five small jars). If not, a good bought lemon curd will do. When it comes to serving this trio, I'm not giving you exact quantities – the beauty of it is that precision is unnecessary. Just put the three ingredients on the table and let everyone tuck in.

For the lemon curd

Finely grated zest of 3 lemons

200ml strained lemon juice (5–6 large lemons)

125g unsalted butter, softened

450g granulated sugar

200ml strained, beaten egg (4–5 large eggs)

To serve

Blueberries

Thick, plain wholemilk yoghurt

To make the lemon curd, first prepare your jars by washing thoroughly in hot soapy water, rinsing well then putting them upside down in a very low oven to dry out and warm up.

Put the lemon zest and juice, butter and sugar into a heatproof bowl over a pan of simmering water. Stir until the butter has melted and the mixture is smooth. Take off the heat for a minute (if it is too hot when you add the eggs, they will scramble). Pour in the strained beaten eggs, whisking all the time. Return the pan to a gentle heat and stir the mixture until thick and creamy; this will take 9–10 minutes (the temperature should register 82–84°C on a sugar thermometer). If the curd gets too hot and starts to scramble, take off the heat and whisk vigorously until smooth.

As soon as it has thickened, pour the lemon curd into the warm jars and seal. Leave to cool completely, then label. Store in the fridge for up to 4 weeks. Once opened, use within a week.

To serve, just put a bowl of blueberries, a dish or carton of yoghurt and a jar of lemon curd on the table and invite your guests to serve themselves to roughly equal volumes of each.

SWAPS Try raspberries or blackberries, or a combination of the two, instead of blueberries.

Strawberries, cream, shortbread

Freshly baked shortbread has an unbeatable flavour and just the right melting, crumbly texture you want for this gorgeous summery assembly. Of course, you don't have to make your own, but it is very easy.

Serves 4

400g strawberries

1 tablespoon caster sugar

300ml double cream

1 vanilla pod

2 tablespoons icing sugar

For the shortbread

100g unsalted butter, well softened

50g caster sugar, plus extra for dusting

50g rice flour

100g plain flour

A pinch of salt

First make the shortbread. Preheat the oven to 160°C/Gas 3. Line a baking sheet with baking parchment or a silicone liner. Beat the soft butter and sugar together in a bowl until thoroughly blended. Sift the rice flour, flour and salt over the mixture and incorporate with a wooden spoon, bringing it together into a crumbly dough.

Gather the dough into a ball with your hands and place on the lined baking sheet. Pat it out gently into a disc, about 1cm thick. Bake for 30 minutes, until a very pale golden brown. Leave the shortbread to cool completely.

Meanwhile, hull the strawberries, cut them into smallish pieces and place in a bowl. Sprinkle with the caster sugar and leave to macerate for at least an hour.

Just before you're ready to serve, pour the cream into a bowl. Split open the vanilla pod and scrape out the seeds with the tip of a small knife on to the cream. Sift over the icing sugar. Beat with a balloon whisk or handheld electric whisk until the cream thickens and holds very soft peaks (don't overdo it or it will become too firm).

Break up the shortbread into smallish pieces and put a couple of spoonfuls into the base of large serving glasses or sundae glasses. Top with a layer of whipped cream, then the strawberries. Finish with another dollop of cream and a little more shortbread. Serve straight away.

SWAPS For an Italianesque change of scene, roughly crush about 100g amaretti biscuits and use instead of the shortbread. Replace the cream with 400g ricotta, beating it with 3 tablespoons icing sugar and the vanilla seeds until soft.

Rhubarb, ginger, cream

**This is a wonderfully indulgent pudding –
a classic fool, really, spiked with ginger.
You can make it with early forced rhubarb
or the later outdoor-grown crop.**

Serves 6

500g rhubarb

150g caster sugar

4 balls of preserved stem
ginger, plus 2 tablespoons of
the ginger syrup from the jar

250ml double cream

250g plain wholemilk
yoghurt

1 vanilla pod (optional)

Trim the rhubarb, cut into 2–3cm chunks and place in a pan large
enough to take it pretty much in a single layer. Add 100g of the
sugar and 50ml water. Cover and cook gently over a low heat for
8–10 minutes until soft – if the rhubarb pieces aren't in a single
layer, they'll take a bit longer and you'll have to stir them a little,
but go carefully: you want them to retain some of their shape.

Drain the rhubarb in a sieve over a bowl to catch the juices. Set
the rhubarb pieces aside to cool, then chill in the fridge.

Combine the strained juices with the ginger syrup in a small pan.
Bring to the boil and let bubble until reduced by half. Allow this
syrup to cool completely, then chill.

Combine the cream, yoghurt and remaining 50g sugar in a bowl.
Chop the stem ginger very finely and add to the bowl. Split open
the vanilla pod, if using, and scrape the seeds on to the cream
mixture. Whisk the mixture until you have fairly soft peaks.

Very carefully fold the cooled rhubarb pieces into the whipped
cream mixture, trying not to break them up too much. Divide the
fool between glass dishes and trickle over a little of the rhubarb
and ginger syrup. Serve straight away.

PLUS ONE To turbo-charge the gingery element of this pud, add
a good old gingernut – standing it upright in the fool just before
serving (as shown). Alternatively, scatter some independent
crumble (see page 360) over the top of the fool – and you have
yourself a fine fumble!

Gooseberries, custard, honey

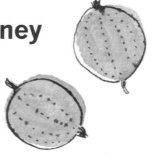

This is another great combination of the tart, the creamy and the sweet. The saffron in the custard is optional, but it makes the dish especially fragrant and delicious. You can serve the poached gooseberries warm, at room temperature or chilled.

Serves 4

400g gooseberries, topped and tailed

6 tablespoons runny honey

For the custard

200ml whole milk

300ml double cream

1–2 pinches of saffron strands (optional)

4 large egg yolks

100g caster sugar

1 heaped teaspoon cornflour

Start with the custard. Put the milk, cream and saffron, if using, into a saucepan. Slowly heat the mixture to just below boiling, then leave to cool a little and infuse.

Whisk the egg yolks, sugar and cornflour together in a bowl, then pour on the hot creamy milk, whisking as you do so to keep the mixture smooth. Return to a clean pan. Cook gently, stirring all the time, until the custard thickens. Don't let it boil or it will split. Pass the custard through a sieve into a bowl and cover the surface closely with cling film or greaseproof paper to stop a skin forming as the custard cools. Once cold, chill in the fridge.

Put the gooseberries into a heatproof bowl with half the honey and cover the bowl with cling film. Set over a pan of simmering water to cook the fruit very gently for 45 minutes until it is soft but still retaining its shape. Remove the bowl from the pan. Strain off the juice into a small pan, bring to the boil and let bubble to reduce to about 2 tablespoons. Pour the reduced juice over the gooseberries and leave to cool.

To serve, pour the custard into bowls, spoon the gooseberries on top and finish with a trickle of the remaining honey.

PLUS ONE Toasted flaked almonds are a nicely textured addition.

ANOTHER TAKE Gooseberries are particularly good cooked this way as they retain their shape, yet they are sweet, intense and tender. However, if you prefer, you can simply poach the berries in a small pan with the honey and 1 tablespoon water for about 5 minutes, giving them an occasional stir. You'll have a wetter, mushier compote, but still a very tasty one.

Cherries, chocolate, cream

This is a great pud to make during the all-too-short cherry season. If, like me, you view a couple of bars of good-quality dark chocolate as storecupboard staples, you can knock up this chocolate mousse, almost certainly to loud applause, at the drop of a hat. Combine it with a little cloud of whipped cream and briefly cooked fresh cherries, and you have a very sophisticated and indulgent pudding.

Serves 4

500g ripe cherries, halved and stoned

25g caster sugar

For the chocolate mousse

150g dark chocolate, broken into small chunks

30g unsalted butter, cut into small cubes

3 large eggs, separated

20g caster sugar

To finish

200ml double cream

Put the cherries into a pan with the sugar. Cook over a very gentle heat, stirring occasionally, for a few minutes until the cherries are starting to soften and release some of their deep red juices. Set aside to cool.

To make the mousse, put the chocolate and butter into a heatproof bowl and place over a pan of barely simmering water. Leave to melt, stirring once or twice. Set aside to cool a little, then stir in the egg yolks.

In a large, clean bowl, whisk the egg whites with the sugar for a few minutes, until they form a soft meringue. Fold this into the chocolate mixture. Spoon into glasses and chill for an hour or so.

Lightly whip the cream until it just holds soft peaks. Put a dollop of cream on each mousse, add the cherries and serve.

SWAPS Instead of poached cherries, use fresh strawberries – hulled, thickly sliced and briefly tossed in a little caster sugar. Or raspberries, again with a sprinkling of caster sugar, and very lightly crushed until the juices run.

Strawberries, meringue, cream

These three ingredients combine to form some of our loveliest summer puds, including pavlova and gloriously smashed-up and marbled Eton mess. A roulade is another pretty way of marrying them to wonderful effect. Note the shorter, hotter cooking time compared to normal meringues – this achieves a softer meringue sheet that rolls without shattering.

Serves 8–10

250g strawberries, plus extra to serve

2 tablespoons caster sugar

400ml double cream

100g plain wholemilk yoghurt

½ vanilla pod

For the meringue

5 medium egg whites

275g caster sugar

To finish

Icing sugar for dusting (optional)

Preheat the oven to 200°C/Gas 6. Line a 33 x 23cm Swiss roll tin, or a baking tray with similar dimensions, with lightly greased baking parchment.

Hull the strawberries and halve, quarter or cut into thick slices, depending on size. Sprinkle with the sugar and leave to macerate.

To make the meringue, whisk the egg whites in a clean bowl until they hold stiff peaks. Gradually add the sugar, 1 tablespoon at a time, whisking well between each addition. Continue until all the sugar has been added and the meringue is very stiff and glossy.

Spread the meringue evenly into the lined tin. Bake for about 8 minutes until golden, then lower the setting to 160°C/Gas 3 and bake for a further 15 minutes until the meringue is crisp and firm to the touch. It will rise a lot, but don't worry. Carefully turn it out upside down on to a sheet of baking parchment or a clean tea towel. Peel away the lining paper and leave to cool for 10 minutes while you prepare the filling.

Put the cream and yoghurt into a bowl. Split open the vanilla pod and scrape out the seeds with the tip of a small knife into the bowl. Whip until the mixture just holds its shape. Spread evenly over the meringue, to about 1cm from the edges. Layer the sugared berries on top. Roll up the meringue firmly from a long edge, using the paper or tea towel to help you. Don't worry if the surface of the meringue cracks and tears – it will, but it's all part of the fun. Wrap the roulade in baking parchment and chill thoroughly.

Cut the roulade into thick slices to serve and scatter over a few halved or quartered strawberries.

PLUS ONE I sometimes scatter a few fresh raspberries, whole or lightly crushed, over each slice of roulade as I serve it.

Raspberries, panna cotta, shortbread

A perfect panna cotta should be softly set and wobbly. In order to achieve this the gelatine quantity needs to be a good bit lower than it would be to set, say, a jelly. I haven't been specific about the number of gelatine leaves here because different brands vary. But if you use the number of leaves stated on your pack to set 400ml of liquid (as opposed to the 700ml or so in this recipe), then you'll be spot on. And your wibbly wobbly, creamy panna cotta will be perfectly offset by tangy raspberries and shortbread.

Serves 4–6

For the panna cotta

500ml double cream

150ml whole milk

100g good-quality white chocolate, broken into pieces

30g caster sugar

Gelatine leaves, enough to set 400ml liquid (see above)

To serve

400g raspberries

150–200g shortbread (see page 336)

A little caster sugar (optional)

For the panna cotta, heat the cream and milk in a pan over a medium heat until the mixture is hot, but not quite boiling. Reduce the heat to low and stir in the chocolate and sugar until melted and the mixture is well combined.

Meanwhile, calculate how many gelatine leaves you need to set 400ml liquid. Put them in a shallow bowl of cold water to soak for a few minutes.

Remove the pan from the heat. Squeeze the gelatine leaves to remove excess water, then add them to the panna cotta mixture and stir until melted. Cover the surface closely with cling film or greaseproof paper to prevent a skin forming and set aside to cool.

Give the cooled panna cotta mixture a good stir, then pour into ramekins or moulds. Chill in the fridge for 6–8 hours, or until set.

To serve, dip each mould very briefly in warm water to loosen the panna cotta, then carefully turn out on to a plate. Serve with the raspberries and shortbread. You can either scatter whole fresh raspberries around the panna cotta, or crush the berries lightly with a little caster sugar and dab blobs around the plate.

SWAPS All kinds of tart fruits work here: the blackcurrants from page 352; the gooseberries on page 340; the rhubarb compote from page 330. Or replace the raspberries with strawberries that have been sliced and macerated in orange juice and a little sugar.

Peaches, praline, cream

If you have perfectly ripe, fragrant peaches, you can use them raw here, but peaches that are a little firm and under-ripe will benefit from a brief, sugar- and butter-enhanced roasting. The praline adds a delectable crunch and sweetness to the peaches and cream pairing, but also – with its nuts and burnt sugar – a balancing hint of bitterness. Making praline isn't difficult, but you can buy ready-made, if you wish, or even use peanut brittle.

Serves 4

4 large peaches
A small knob of butter
A little soft brown sugar
250ml double cream

For the praline
100g caster sugar
50g skinned hazelnuts or blanched almonds

To make the praline, cover a baking sheet with a non-stick liner or baking parchment. Put the sugar into a heavy-based saucepan (with a light interior so you will be able to see the colour of the caramel). Place over a medium heat and move the sugar around a little with a spatula from time to time, until melted. Continue to cook until the melted sugar has turned to a golden caramel, watching it closely all the while. As soon as it has reached a deep golden brown, remove from the heat and sit the pan in a bowl of cold water to stop the cooking, otherwise the caramel can start to burn very quickly. Stir in the nuts, then pour the mixture on to the prepared baking tray.

Leave the praline to cool completely and harden, then bash into small pieces with a rolling pin or heavy pestle.

Preheat the oven to 190°C/Gas 5. Halve the peaches and remove the stones. Place them, cut side up, in an oven dish and put a knob of butter and a pinch of sugar on each. Bake for about 30 minutes until soft and starting to colour at the edges. Leave to cool slightly.

Whip the cream in a bowl until it holds soft peaks. Place the peach halves on individual plates and add a dollop of cream and a generous scattering of praline shards to serve. (Any leftover praline can be stored in an airtight container.)

PLUS ONE Take this to another level with a trickle of raspberry sauce. Crush 150g raspberries, whisk in 40g icing sugar, then sieve to remove the pips. Trickle some over the dish, and serve more on the side.

SWAPS Use large plums instead of peaches, allowing two or three per person.

Rhubarb, strawberries, shortcrust

Based on an idea from my friend and former River Cottage head gardener Mark Diacono, this is a very simple tart to make. You don't have to worry about lining a tin or blind-baking the pastry, and I like the fact that there's no pastry wastage.

Serves 4

For the sweet shortcrust

200g plain flour

1 heaped tablespoon icing sugar

Pinch of salt

120g cold unsalted butter, cut into cubes

1 egg yolk

About 50ml cold milk or water

For the filling

200g rhubarb, trimmed

200g strawberries, hulled and halved or quartered (depending on size)

75g caster sugar

Finely grated zest of 1 lemon

3 tablespoons ground almonds

To finish

1 egg white, lightly beaten, to glaze

A little caster sugar

To make the sweet shortcrust pastry, put the flour, icing sugar and salt into a food processor and blitz briefly to combine. Add the butter and blitz until the mixture resembles breadcrumbs. (Or you can make the pastry by hand, rubbing the butter into the flour and icing sugar with your fingertips.) Add the egg yolk and enough milk or water to bind, pulsing or mixing just enough to bring the dough together in large clumps. Tip out on to a lightly floured surface and knead lightly into a ball. Wrap in cling film and chill for 30 minutes.

For the filling, cut the rhubarb into 2–3cm lengths and combine with the strawberries, sugar and lemon zest in a bowl. Set aside for 30 minutes to macerate.

Preheat the oven to 200°C/Gas 6. Line a large baking tray with baking parchment or a non-stick liner.

On a floured surface, roll out the pastry to a rough circle, 2–3mm thick and about 35cm in diameter. Lift it on to the baking sheet. Sprinkle the ground almonds evenly over the pastry, without going right to the edges. Spoon the macerated fruit and any juices over the pastry, leaving a good 3–4cm border around the edge. Fold this border inwards over the fruit, to make a rough square.

Brush the folded pastry edges with egg white and sprinkle with caster sugar. Bake for 30 minutes or until the pastry is a deep golden colour. Serve warm, with cream or ice cream.

PLUS ONE/SWAP If you fancy a change from strawberries, use blueberries instead – or a mixture of the two.

Blackcurrants, goat's cheese, digestives

Halfway between a pudding and a cheese course, this lovely
combination functions as a very cool take on either. I've given
a simple and delicious recipe for homemade digestive biscuits,
but of course you could use a good ready-made variety.

Serves 4

400g ripe blackcurrants

50–100g caster sugar

300g light, fresh, unrinded
goat's cheese (unsalted
if you can get it)

Finely grated zest of
½ lemon

For the digestives

125g porridge oats

125g wholemeal flour

125g cold unsalted butter,
diced

75g soft light brown sugar

A generous pinch of salt

1 teaspoon baking powder

50–75ml milk

Start with the digestives, if you are making your own. Put the oats
into a food processor and blitz briefly to break them down a bit.
Add the flour, butter, sugar, salt and baking powder and blitz
again until the mixture forms crumbs. With the motor running,
trickle in just enough milk to bring the dough together. Tip it out
on to a lightly floured surface and shape into a thick disc.

Wrap the dough in cling film and chill for 30 minutes (this makes
a very firm dough, so if you chill it for longer you will need to take
it out of the fridge for a little while before rolling out).

Preheat the oven to 180°C/Gas 4 and grease two baking sheets
or line with baking parchment. Roll out the dough to a thickness
of 3–4mm – as it's slightly crumbly, you may find it easiest to do
this between two sheets of cling film or baking parchment. Cut
out the dough using whatever shape cutter you like or, as I do for
this dish, just tear it into in large rough pieces that you can break
up before serving. Bake for 10–15 minutes until brown around the
edges and golden in the middle. Transfer to a wire rack to cool.

Place the blackcurrants in a pan with 50g caster sugar. Cook for
1–2 minutes over a low heat until you have a very lightly cooked
compote that is still on the sharp side. Add more sugar only if you
really think it necessary.

Break the biscuits into pieces and place on serving plates (you'll
have some left over for the biscuit tin, to serve with cheese). Top
with the goat's cheese and a sprinkling of lemon zest, spoon over
some blackcurrant compote and serve straight away.

SWAPS Use fresh cream cheese or ricotta instead of goat's cheese,
and feel free to replace the blackcurrants with gooseberries.

Blackberries, apple, cream

The divine pairing of blackberries and apples is usually served hot, but you can also turn these fruits into a gorgeous granita – the simplest of all frozen puds. I like to enrich it with a slosh of cream, which takes on a wonderful, slightly chewy texture as it freezes on the ice crystals.

Serves 6

2 large Bramley or other cooking apples (450–500g in total)
700g blackberries
50–75g icing sugar, sieved
Double cream, to serve

Peel, quarter and core the apples, then cut into thin slices. Put into a saucepan with 4 tablespoons water and bring to a simmer. Cook for about 5 minutes, stirring often, until the apple starts to break down. Add a splash more water if necessary, but keep it to a minimum. Add the blackberries and continue to cook, stirring often, for about 20 minutes, until the fruit breaks down and you have a soft, juicy, coarse purée.

Give the fruit a quick blitz in the saucepan with a handheld stick blender (or in a freestanding blender). Tip the purée into a sieve over a bowl and rub through using the back of a wooden spoon, to remove the seeds. Leave the purée to cool completely, then whisk in enough icing sugar to make it taste just a little too sweet – it will taste less so once frozen.

Transfer the purée to a shallow, freezerproof container (an empty ice cream carton will do) and freeze for several hours at least, until solid. Take it out of the freezer about 30 minutes before serving to soften slightly.

To serve, use a fork to scratch the frozen purée into crystals; the finished granita should have a texture rather like a coarse sorbet. Pile the granita into serving glasses, top with a generous, snowy cap of cream and serve straight away.

MINUS ONE You can make a pure blackberry granita, if you prefer, with no apple at all. You'll need about 1kg blackberries.

SWAPS You can replace the blackberries with an equal quantity of late summer/early autumn raspberries. Or use blackcurrants (fresh or frozen); these have a more intense flavour, so you won't need as many – use about 350g blackcurrants and 1kg Bramleys.

Pears, custard, ginger cake

The sweetness of ripe pears is always good when spiked with ginger and this recipe delivers a spicy triple-whammy: the ginger is used to flavour the pears as well as a rich custard, while a chunk of ginger cake turns the whole thing into a gingery, trifle-ish delight.

Serves 6

250g ginger cake

4 ripe pears

2 balls of preserved stem ginger in syrup, plus 2 tablespoons of the syrup from the jar

For the custard

200ml whole milk

300ml double cream

50g caster sugar

2–3 tablespoons syrup from the ginger jar

1 heaped teaspoon cornflour

4 large egg yolks

Start with the custard. Pour the milk and cream into a saucepan, bring to a simmer, then remove from the heat. Put the sugar, ginger syrup, cornflour and egg yolks into a bowl and whisk until well combined. Pour on the hot creamy milk, whisking as you do so to keep the mixture smooth. Return to a clean saucepan. Cook gently, stirring all the time, until the custard thickens. Don't let it boil or it will split. Pass the custard through a sieve into a bowl and cover the surface closely with cling film or greaseproof paper to stop a skin forming. Leave to cool completely.

Cut the ginger cake into 6 equal slices. Place each one in a glass serving dish and press it so it curves and more or less lines the base, without squishing it too much. (Alternatively, just break the cake into chunks and distribute between the bowls.) Pour the ginger custard over the cake, distributing it evenly, and chill in the fridge to allow the custard to set.

Peel, quarter and core the pears. Cut each quarter into roughly 1cm cubes. Finely chop the stem ginger and add to the pears with 2 tablespoons of ginger syrup. Stir together.

When you're ready to serve, spoon the gingery pears and their syrup on to the custard and bring to the table.

SWAPS For a slightly less gingery pud, replace the cake with some of my independent crumble (page 360). Sprinkle on top of the custard and pears, rather than in the bottom of the bowls.

Plums, yoghurt, honey

The rich, tangy taste of this reduced plum purée is, I find, completely addictive. Resist the urge to sweeten it too much – you may find you don't need to at all. Served like this with yoghurt and honey, it makes a gorgeous breakfast but it's also very good as a simple pudding.

Serves 4–5

About 500g plain wholemilk yoghurt

Honey, to taste

For the plum purée

1kg plums

A little honey or sugar (optional)

To make the purée, halve the plums and remove the stones. Put them in a large saucepan with a little water – just enough to give a film over the base of the pan. Begin heating very gently, then, as the juices start to flow, increase the heat a little to bring to a simmer. Cook for about 10 minutes, stirring often, until the plums are completely collapsed.

Tip the plums into a sieve and rub them through with the back of a ladle or a wooden spoon into a clean pan. Put the plum purée back on the heat and bring to a simmer. Cook, stirring often so that it doesn't catch, until reduced to a thick saucy purée – 10–20 minutes, depending on the juiciness of the plums.

Leave the plum purée to cool completely (it will thicken a little more as it cools). Now taste and sweeten with a little honey or sugar if you like, keeping it quite tart and tangy though. Cover and chill the purée until needed.

To serve, divide the yoghurt between small serving dishes. Add the plum purée beside the yoghurt, then top with a generous swirl of honey.

PLUS ONE Scatter over some crushed ginger biscuits or my independent crumble (page 360) and this combination becomes a rather fancy and delicious pudding. Or, to boost the breakfast version, sprinkle over a handful of muesli or granola.

Plums, crumble, ice cream

Plum crumble is a favourite of mine. To make the crumble more versatile, I cook it separately, so I can layer it on thickly, scatter it lightly, or even eat it on its own. I make a big batch to use on all kinds of fruity/creamy puddings and store it in an airtight container – it keeps for a couple of weeks but rarely lasts that long in our house.

Serves 4

For the 'independent crumble'
225g plain flour
A pinch of fine sea salt
200g cold, unsalted butter, cut into cubes
150g granulated or demerara sugar
100g medium oatmeal, ground almonds or porridge oats

For the fruit
30g butter, softened
8 large plums
2 tablespoons soft brown sugar or honey
4–8 star anise (optional)

To serve
4 generous scoops of vanilla ice cream

For the crumble, which you can make ahead, preheat the oven to 180°C/Gas 4. Put all the ingredients into a large bowl and rub together with your fingertips until you have a crumbly dough. Squeeze the mixture in your hands to form clumps, then crumble these on to a large baking tray and spread out evenly. Bake for about 25 minutes, giving the whole thing a good stir halfway through, until golden brown and crisp. Leave to cool completely then transfer to an airtight container. (You'll have more than you need for this recipe, so keep the rest for other puds.)

Heat the oven to 190°C/Gas 5 and use some of the butter to grease a roasting dish. Halve the plums and remove the stones. Put them, cut side up, in the dish, dot with the remaining butter and sprinkle with the sugar or honey. Scatter the star anise, if using, on top. Bake for 20–30 minutes, until the plums are bubbling and juicy. Leave to cool for a few minutes, or completely: the plums can be served warm or cold, or even chilled. (As an alternative to roasting, you can simply stew the plums with a little water and the sugar for about 10 minutes until juicy and tender.)

Transfer the plums to a large serving platter or individual bowls and add a generous sprinkling of crumble. Top with scoops of ice cream and spoon over any juices from the dish.

'FUMBLE' SWAPS Some tart fruit, roughly mixed with cream, whipped or otherwise, and/or a little yoghurt, then topped with 'independent crumble' is a classic combination in our house, with almost infinite variations. I call it a 'fumble', because it's really a cross between a fool and a crumble. Its main incarnations are with fresh strawberries and raspberries or cooked gooseberries (see page 340) in the summer, with a compote of Bramley apples or plums in the autumn, and with rhubarb in winter and spring.

Rhubarb, Champagne, cream

This elegant pud takes jelly and cream to a whole new level. Made with rhubarb and Champagne, it's full of bubbles and fizzes on the tongue. Topped with a swirl of vanilla-infused cream, it is decadent and exciting – perfect for a party.

Serves 6–8

500g trimmed rhubarb

175g caster sugar

1 vanilla pod (optional)

500ml Champagne or sparkling white wine, well chilled

Enough sheets of leaf gelatine to set 850ml liquid (as advised on the packet)

150ml double cream

Cut the rhubarb into 2cm chunks and put into a pan with the sugar and 500ml water. Split the vanilla pod, if using, scrape out the seeds and set these aside. Add the pod to the pan with the rhubarb. Bring to the boil, then lower the heat and simmer for 10 minutes. Leave to cool for half an hour or so.

Line a sieve with muslin and set this over a bowl. (Or use a jelly bag.) Pour the rhubarb and its juice into the sieve (or jelly bag) and leave it to drip. Don't force the juice through or you will make it cloudy. You want to end up with 350ml of pale, pink, clear juice. (Any excess can be added to the rhubarb pulp, chilled and stirred into yoghurt and/or muesli for breakfast.) If you don't have quite enough juice, you'll have to add a touch more Champagne later to make up the difference. Shame. Pour your 350ml rhubarb juice into a small pan.

Soak the gelatine in a shallow bowl of cold water to soften for 5 minutes. Bring the rhubarb juice almost to a simmer and take off the heat. Squeeze the soaked gelatine leaves to remove excess water, then add to the rhubarb juice and stir until fully melted. Pour into a large jug and leave to cool to room temperature.

Open your chilled Champagne and very, very slowly pour 500ml into the syrup – I tilt the jug and trickle the Champagne down the side. This painstaking step will maximise the number of bubbles held within your jelly. Stir the mixture as carefully as you can to make sure the rhubarb liquid and wine are completely combined. You will find a frothy head forms on top of the liquid – just skim it off with a spoon. Carefully pour the fizzy jelly into wine glasses, skim again if necessary and place in the fridge to set. This should take 2–3 hours.

When you are ready to serve, add the reserved vanilla seeds, if using, to the cream, and whip until it holds soft peaks. Put a little spoonful of this on top of the jellies and serve.

Sweet Treats

I've never been one for an over-worked plate, and though sweet treats and fancy puds are sometimes decorated most artfully, they so often under-deliver on their visual promise. I've learned to see it coming, and now when I look through the window of posh pâtisseries, I'm wary of confections that have clearly been created with enormous technical skill, and look amazing, but somehow fail to make me salivate. Of course an 'assiette' of desserts in a top-notch restaurant can be absolutely delicious – but when ice cream, hot fudge and a scattering of almonds tastes so good, I wonder why they bothered? The mouthwatering recipes that follow are my antidote to all that artifice.

Puddings, for me, are all about straight-down-the-line indulgence. The kind delivered by a slice of steaming treacle sponge and fridge-cold cream, or a slab of good old-fashioned millionaire's shortbread (chocolate, caramel, biscuit – in other words, a homemade Twix). One of my favourite recipes in the whole book is the affogato (page 378). A spoonful of ice cream, a splash of strong coffee, a shot of brandy. It's so easy, it's pushing my luck to call it a recipe. (Even the brandy is optional – a classic affogato is just coffee and ice cream.) But it's definitely one of the most enjoyable ways I know to finish a meal.

As you'd expect, you'll find plenty of sugar here, and plenty of honey. But look closely and you will see they are used with some restraint. Often the sugar is a mere seasoning, brightening the flavour of its partners. A sprinkling is all that's required to bring out the richness of eggy bread and fruit (page 386), and you don't need much to lighten the creamy softness of a rice pudding (page 382).

Sure, there are some puds – that awesome fudge sundae (page 375) springs to mind, as do good old meringues filled with cream (page 369) – where the sugar is central and gratuitous, almost a homage to the sugar rush. But a good sweet treat in my book is never just about the sugar. It must have depth – sometimes even a hint of danger or darkness. A really fine caramel, like the one used for the praline on page 370, has a hint of bitterness from the almost-burnt sugar – and I like to add a pinch of salt too. Other sharp, sour or bitter 'edgy' ingredients feature prominently in this chapter: brandy, dark chocolate, coffee, dried fruits, citrus zest. Add to that sweet/not-sweet tension something soft, milky, pillowy (cream or eggs, say), or something snappy (nuts or biscuit), or a yielding background texture (pastry or cake) and you're there. Unfettered indulgence is duly delivered.

Meringue, coffee, blackcurrants

Super-sweet meringue tempered by bitter, aromatic coffee and spiced up with tart, fragrant blackcurrants: this is such a winning combination. A dollop of smooth cream wraps it all up nicely.

Serves 4

For the coffee meringue
2 egg whites
100g caster sugar
1 tablespoon very strong espresso coffee (or use 1 tablespoon instant coffee dissolved in 1 tablespoon boiling water)

For the blackcurrant sauce
500g blackcurrants
About 75g icing sugar, to taste

To serve
125ml double cream

Preheat the oven to 120°C/Gas ½. Line a large baking sheet with baking parchment.

Put the egg whites in a clean bowl and whisk with an electric whisk until they hold soft peaks. Start adding the sugar, a couple of spoonfuls at a time, whisking well after each addition. The mixture will become thick and shiny. Keep whisking until the meringue holds firm peaks and is so thick that you can turn the bowl upside down without anything sliding out. Carefully fold in the coffee, leaving it very slightly streaky if you like.

Spoon the meringue on to the lined baking sheet in 8 equal blobs, spacing them apart and shaping as well as you can into neat, even swirls. Place in the oven for 1½–1¾ hours, until the meringues are light and crisp on the outside and can be lifted off the paper easily (they should still be a touch gooey in the middle). Remove to a wire rack and leave to cool completely.

Meanwhile, for the sauce, put the blackcurrants into a pan with 50ml water and cook until soft – 10 minutes or so. Rub through a sieve into a bowl, using a wooden spoon. If the purée seems very thick, add a little more water. Sweeten to taste with icing sugar, then chill until needed.

When you're ready to serve, whip the cream until it holds soft peaks. Sandwich the meringues together in pairs with spoonfuls of cream and place on serving plates. Spoon over some of the blackcurrant sauce and serve the rest in a jug on the side.

SWAPS Any good meringues, homemade or bought, served with whipped cream and some tart fruit, will be scrumptious. In place of the blackcurrant sauce, try lightly crushed raspberries and strawberries, or gooseberries, or rhubarb cooked with a little sugar into a compote, or even my apple compote (see page 327).

Apples, praline, ice cream

Although it's very elegant and completely delicious, this is actually a corner-shop standby pudding – the ingredients are all widely available. You can even buy the praline instead of making it – or use peanut brittle or sesame snaps.

Serves 4

For the salted walnut praline
100g granulated sugar
50g walnut halves, roughly broken up
½ teaspoon flaky sea salt

For the apples
3 medium, crisp dessert apples, such as Cox
30g butter

To serve
4 good scoops of vanilla ice cream

To make the praline, lightly oil a baking sheet (or line with baking parchment or a non-stick liner). Put the sugar into a heavy-based saucepan (ideally with a light interior, so you will be able to see the colour of the caramel). Place over a medium heat and heat, moving the sugar around a little with a spatula from time to time, until melted. Continue to cook until the melted sugar has turned to a golden caramel, watching it closely all the while. As soon as it has reached a deep golden brown, remove from the heat and sit the pan inside a bowl of cold water to stop the cooking, otherwise the caramel can start to burn very quickly. Stir in the walnuts with a fork and immediately pour on to the prepared baking sheet. Sprinkle the salt over the top and leave to set.

When set, break the praline into small pieces by bashing it with a rolling pin. Store in an airtight container until needed.

Shortly before you are ready to serve, quarter the apples and remove their cores. Peel if you like. Cut each quarter into 2 or 3 wedges. Heat the butter in a frying pan over a medium heat. Add the apples and fry gently for 10 minutes or so, turning now and again, until golden and tender but still retaining their shape.

To serve, divide the warm apples between individual plates, then top with a ball of ice cream and a liberal scattering of walnut praline. You may have a little left over, in which case store it in an airtight container until next time.

Ricotta, honeycomb, hazelnuts

You probably won't get honeycomb at your local supermarket, but good delis often stock it, and a small local honey-producer will be able to sell to you direct; it's also available on the internet. It's worth getting hold of some because it is such a treat: honey in its purest form, straight from the hive, untreated and pretty much as the bees intended it. The idea is to eat the whole thing, comb and all. The comb has a chewy, waxy texture and is perfectly edible, but you can discreetly discard it once you've sucked all the honey from it, if you prefer.

Serves 4

100g hazelnuts (skin-on)
250g ricotta
About 200g honeycomb

Preheat the oven to 180°C/Gas 4. Spread the hazelnuts out on a baking sheet and toast them in the oven for about 5 minutes, until they are lightly coloured and their skins are starting to split. Tip them on to a clean tea towel, fold the towel over them and give them a vigorous rub. This will remove most of the skins – don't worry if a few bits remain. Alternatively, you can remove the skins by tipping the hazelnuts into a sieve and rubbing the tea towel over them, so the bits of skin fall through the sieve.

Divide the ricotta between shallow serving bowls. Break or cut your honeycomb into 4 roughly equal pieces and place on the ricotta, trickling over any honey that has escaped from the comb too. Scatter over the hazelnuts. Admire the irresistible tripartite simplicity of what you have just compiled, and serve with a smile.

SWAPS You can certainly use a thick, rich natural yoghurt instead of the ricotta, or plain fromage frais. And, of course, you can use a good runny honey without the comb.

Ice cream, fudge, nuts

A slab of decent fudge – used two ways, hot and cold – can turn plain ice cream into a sumptuous sundae treat. This is monumentally indulgent, but what the heck? We all need a little sweetness sometimes.

Serves 4

350g vanilla ice cream

250g vanilla fudge, roughly chopped or crumbled

25ml whole milk

50g walnuts, flaked almonds, chopped hazelnuts or other nuts, lightly toasted

Leave the ice cream out of the freezer for 15–20 minutes, until it is just soft enough to mash.

Transfer the ice cream to a shallow freezerproof container (an empty ice cream carton will do), crumble over 100g of the fudge and mash it in to the ice cream. Put the lid on the container and return to the freezer while you make the sauce.

Put the remaining crumbled fudge into a small saucepan and add the milk. Heat gently, stirring constantly and crushing the fudge pieces with a spoon, until the fudge has melted completely into the milk, making a smooth, pourable sauce. Leave to cool a little, so the sauce is warm rather than boiling hot.

Put two scoops of the fudge-studded ice cream into each serving glass or sundae dish. Top with some warm fudge sauce and finish off with a generous scattering of nuts.

SWAPS You can totally choccify this recipe, using chocolate ice cream and/or chocolate fudge, and adding plenty of grated chocolate to top it off, along with the nuts.

PLUS ONE To zing this up a bit and cut the sweetness a little, add a spoonful of dried sour cherries or dried cranberries along with the nuts.

Egg yolks, sugar, cider brandy

This is my version of zabaglione: the heady but light-as-air Italian dessert. It does take a bit of whisking – an electric whisk is essential, unless you have the arms of Hercules – but it uses only three storecupboard ingredients to produce something very delicious and elegant. I'm assuming your storecupboard includes a bottle of brandy, as mine does – Somerset cider brandy lends a special flavour here. Rich and creamy (although actually dairy-free), this pud is lovely served alone, or with fairly plain little biscuits, such as a langues de chat or savoiardi, for dipping. It's also stunningly good heaped over raspberries.

Serves 6

8 large egg yolks
75g caster sugar
100ml cider brandy

Pour a 4–5cm depth of water into a large saucepan and set it to simmer on the hob.

Put the egg yolks and sugar in a large heatproof bowl and whisk together with an electric whisk for 2–3 minutes, until thick and creamy. Stand the bowl over the pan of gently simmering water and slowly whisk in the brandy. Continue whisking until the mixture is pale, thick and billowy, and roughly quadrupled in volume. If you lift the beaters, the 'trail' that falls on to the mixture should hold its shape for a few seconds, before slowly sinking back in. This will take at least 10, more likely 15 or 20 minutes, so you might want to make sure you have a glass of wine, or a cup of tea at the very least, by your elbow. Ensure that the water in the pan is only just simmering and that the bowl doesn't get too hot, or the eggs will start to cook and the mixture may split.

Serve straight away or at least within minutes, while still warm, in elegant glasses. After 20–30 minutes, it will start to separate.

PLUS ONE For an espresso version, pour a tablespoon or two of very strong coffee over the finished zabaglione. It messes it up a bit, but the taste is exquisite.

SWAPS If you don't want to use cider brandy, any good brandy or Calvados will do. Traditionally, zabaglione is made with the Italian fortified wine marsala, which is also lovely.

Ice cream, brandy, espresso

The classic Italian affogato – ice cream doused in a shot of espresso – is a very simple and very fine pudding. Some cooks also add a snifter of brandy or amaretto. This version, which I like to make using my favourite Somerset cider brandy, is my nod to that divine three-way combination.

Per person

1 large scoop of vanilla ice cream

1 tablespoon cider brandy or Calvados

1 shot of hot espresso (or 2 tablespoons extremely strong, hot filter coffee)

Put a scoop of ice cream into each small serving dish. Pour over the brandy, then the hot coffee and eat without further ado.

MINUS ONE If you're not a coffee lover, you can leave it out and just go for the booze.

SWAPS Instead of the cider brandy, try any of the following: whisky (a good single malt is not wasted on this), grappa, mirabelle or Poire William.

Chocolate, prunes, brandy

Little chocolate 'fondants' – oozy-middled chocolate puddings – are divine, if somewhat ubiquitous these days. I love the combination of chocolate, prunes and brandy so I doctored the original idea a little. Timing is important here – a minute too long in the oven, or even waiting around to be served, and these little puds lose their lovely gooey centres. But you can prepare them in advance, ready to bake when you want to serve them.

Makes 6

100g prunes, roughly chopped

40ml brandy

A little cocoa powder for dusting

150g dark chocolate, broken into small pieces

150g unsalted butter, diced, plus extra for greasing

3 large eggs

75g caster sugar

35g plain flour

Soak the prunes in the brandy in a small bowl for at least 2 hours (overnight is fine), to absorb most of the liquid.

Preheat the oven to 200°C/Gas 6 and put a baking tray inside to heat up. Butter 6 dariole moulds well and dust with cocoa.

Melt the chocolate and butter in a heatproof bowl over a pan of simmering water. Stir gently to blend and leave to cool a little.

Beat the eggs and sugar together with an electric whisk for at least 5 minutes until the mixture is thick and moussey and 'holds a trail' (when a little is dropped from the whisk it should sit on the surface of the mixture and only slowly sink back in).

Fold the melted chocolate and butter lightly into the egg mousse. Sift the flour over the mixture, then fold it in carefully. It needs to be thoroughly incorporated, but don't overwork the mix. Fold in the prunes and brandy – again, carefully.

Divide the mixture between the dariole moulds. You can prepare the puds ahead to this point, if you like, and refrigerate them for up to 2 hours.

Bake the puds on the hot tray in the oven for 10–12 minutes. Go for the shorter time if your oven is very efficient or if your puds will be sitting around for a few minutes before serving. Go for the longer time if your oven is on the cool side or if they have been in the fridge. Turn out immediately into shallow bowls and serve at once, with chilled cream.

SWAPS Soak raisins in whisky, dried cherries in Calvados, or even dried cranberries in vodka to replace the prunes in brandy.

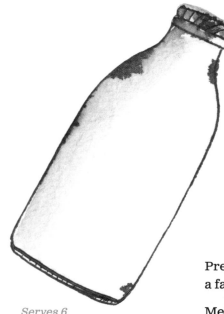

Rice, milk, sugar

Rice pudding is one of my all-time favourites and a brilliant example of the three-key-ingredients principle. The vanilla isn't essential, nor is the cream – you can make the pud with just a litre of milk if you prefer.

Serves 6

A large knob of butter (30g)

100g pudding rice

800ml whole milk

200ml double or single cream (or an extra 200ml milk)

½–1 vanilla pod (optional)

50g caster sugar

Preheat the oven to 140°C/Gas 1. Use half the butter to grease a fairly deep oven dish, about 2 litres capacity.

Melt the remaining butter in a saucepan over a low heat and add the rice. Heat very gently for a minute or two, stirring, until the rice is lightly coated with butter. It shouldn't fry or even sizzle.

Add the milk and cream, if using, to the pan, and stir well. Split the vanilla pod, if using, and scrape out the seeds, adding these and the pod to the milk. Add the sugar and stir, keeping the heat very low, until the sugar is dissolved and the milk warm. Transfer the mixture to the buttered dish.

Cook in the oven for 2½ hours, stirring the pudding gently every 30 minutes – separating the grains and working the surface skin back into the pudding – but don't stir for the final half hour, to allow a golden skin to form. Turn the oven up to 170°C/Gas 3 for the last 10 minutes to brown the skin a little.

Allow the rice pudding to cool for a while before serving. It's good warm or at room temperature rather than piping hot. Try serving it with one of the added-extras suggested below.

PLUS ONE OR TWO A dollop of raspberry jam and/or a sprinkling of toasted flaked almonds is an easy way to jazz up this classic pud. Caramelised apples are lovely served with rice pudding: fry some fairly thin apple slices in butter until tender and lightly browned, then add a shake of sugar and cook for another couple of minutes until glazed. (If it's for grown-ups, I add a splash of apple brandy or Calvados to the apples and let it reduce for a minute or two.) Caramelised bananas are also scrumptious with rice pud: slice a couple of not-too-ripe bananas thickly on the diagonal and cook as for the apples, above. Rum is the optional booze.

Condensed milk, lemon, gingernuts

This is an incredibly easy and deliciously retro pud. The idea of 'setting' condensed milk with lemon juice goes back to recipes-on-the-back-of-the-tin in the 1970s, or earlier. It's a neat trick, and a yummy one. The lemon cuts the intense sweetness of the condensed milk perfectly and the crushed biscuits on top give a sort of upside-down-cheesecake effect.

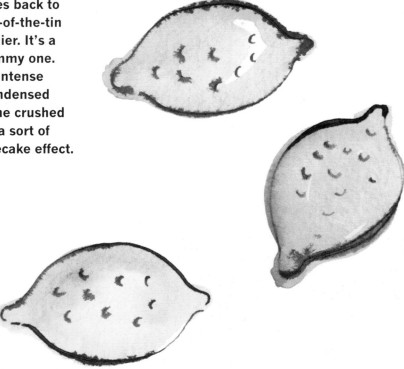

Serves 6

4 large lemons

400g tin sweetened condensed milk

150ml double cream

About a dozen gingernut biscuits

Finely grate the zest of two of the lemons. Squeeze the juice from all of them and strain it to remove any pips and fibres. Measure out 150ml strained juice.

Tip the condensed milk into a large bowl and stir in the cream. Add the lemon zest and juice and stir until the mixture is thick and smooth.

Divide evenly between 6 small cups or glasses and chill for several hours, until set.

Crush the biscuits to fine crumbs and scatter thickly over the lemony puds to serve.

Egg, bread, apple

Eggy bread, or French toast, is a favourite breakfast in my house: quick, filling and the perfect partner to some kind of fruit. I love its slightly dense, eggy sweetness with the sharpness of a citrussy apple purée. And, as you will see from the suggestions below, it can easily be elevated to posh pud status.

Serves 2

For the eggy bread

2 large eggs

2 tablespoons milk

1 tablespoon caster sugar

2 slices of white bread (dry or fresh), about 1cm thick

A large knob of butter

1 tablespoon sunflower oil

To serve

About 200g apple compote (such as the one on page 327)

For the eggy bread, beat the eggs and milk together with about ½ tablespoon sugar, then pour into a shallow dish (one that is wide enough to take both slices of bread is ideal).

Add the slices of bread to the dish and leave them to soak for at least 10 minutes (ideally half an hour if the bread is dry), turning them a few times so they thoroughly absorb the egg. You really want it to penetrate right to the centre of the bread – so there's almost no eggy liquid left in the dish.

Heat a non-stick frying pan over a medium-low heat and add the butter and oil. When foaming, transfer the soaked bread slices to the pan. Pour any remaining egg in the dish over the bread. Cook for about 2–3 minutes, until the base of the eggy bread is golden brown, then flip over and cook for 2 minutes more.

Transfer the eggy bread to plates for serving. Sprinkle a touch more sugar over each piece, then add a generous dollop of apple compote before you take the plates to the table.

PLUS ONE Yoghurt balances the dish nicely with its creamy-but-light sauciness. Ice cream, on the other hand, especially a good vanilla, will elevate humble eggy bread to an elegant pud.

SWAPS If I haven't got an apple compote to hand, I peel, quarter, core and slice a couple of tart, crisp eating apples and fry them in a little butter, finishing with a sprinkling of soft brown sugar. Other fruits work well too, especially roasted plums (see page 360) or roasted peaches (see page 348), or a compote of rhubarb. In the summer try using fresh strawberries and/or raspberries. In this case, lightly crush the fruit and mix with a little sugar before serving on the eggy bread.

Drop scones, maple syrup, ice cream

Wicked... there's no other word for it. Without the ice cream, these peanut butter drop scones – topped lavishly with maple syrup – are an unashamedly indulgent weekend brunch. Add a scoop of the cold stuff, and it's a lovely, easy pud.

Makes about 25

For the drop scones
200g plain flour
2 rounded teaspoons baking powder
35g caster sugar
150g crunchy, no-sugar-added peanut butter
300ml milk
2 large eggs, lightly beaten
A little sunflower oil

To serve
Maple syrup
Vanilla ice cream

Preheat your oven to a very low setting for keeping the cooked drop scones warm.

Sift the flour and baking powder into a large bowl and then stir in the sugar.

Put the peanut butter in a bowl with about 100ml of the milk and work the two together with a fork or small whisk to a loose paste. Gradually stir in the remaining milk and beaten eggs. Now slowly whisk this liquid into the flour to make a batter that is smooth apart from the chunks of peanut.

Heat a large, non-stick frying pan over a medium heat and add a little oil. You will need to cook the drop scones in batches. When the pan is hot, drop in dollops of the batter, each 1–1½ tablespoons – I use a small ladle as this makes it easy to control how much batter I drop each time. Cook for 1–1½ minutes each side, until the drop scones are golden brown, puffy and light. Transfer them to an oven dish and keep warm in the oven while you cook the rest.

When all the drop scones are cooked, serve them on warm plates. Put the maple syrup on the table for everyone to help themselves, along with a tub of vanilla ice cream, if you're going down the greedy pud route.

SWAPS Maple syrup is extraordinarily good here but golden syrup will stand in very well as an alternative trickly, sticky sweet stuff, and so will runny honey. Instead of the ice cream, you could have thick plain yoghurt – and just about keep the whole thing in the realms of a credible breakfast treat.

Puff pastry, cream, chocolate

This is ridiculously easy, yet comes out looking pretty elegant. The only vaguely tricky bit is splitting the pastry into two – and that requires just a modicum of care. The end result is a sort of cross between a mille feuille and giant chocolate éclair. And who could resist that?

Serves 8

1 ready-rolled puff pastry sheet (about 200g), or roughly the same weight of ready-made block puff pastry

300ml double cream

4 tablespoons icing sugar

100g dark chocolate

Preheat the oven to 200°C/Gas 6 and lightly butter a baking sheet, or line with baking parchment.

Your ready-rolled pastry sheet should measure about 22 x 30cm. If you are using a block of pastry, roll it out on a lightly floured surface to roughly these dimensions and 4–5mm thick. Trim the edges to neaten. Lift the pastry on the prepared baking sheet and bake for 15–20 minutes until puffed up and golden brown. Carefully transfer to a wire rack to cool (this won't take long).

Using a long, sharp, serrated knife, carefully split the pastry in two horizontally. You should find a natural 'in' where the layers of pastry are thinner and weaker. Carefully insert the knife and work it gently all the way around the pastry rectangle until you have completely freed the upper layer from the lower.

In a bowl, whisk the cream together with the icing sugar until it holds soft peaks. Spread the cream over the base piece of puff pastry. Using a fine grater, grate about half the chocolate over the cream. Carefully put the second piece of pastry on top.

Melt the remaining chocolate: break it into a small bowl or tea cup and stand this inside a larger bowl of just-boiled water. When the chocolate is melted and smooth, trickle it lavishly over the top of the pastry. I like to do this going back and forth diagonally across the pastry, but you can make any pattern you like.

As soon as the chocolate is set, the pud is ready to serve. Use a sharp, serrated knife to cut it into portions at the table.

PLUS ONE A little fruit, such as poached cherries (see page 342), whole or lightly crushed fresh raspberries or sliced strawberries, provides a nice contrast. You can either scatter the fruit over the cream before you put the pastry lid on, or just serve it on the side.

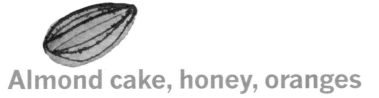

Almond cake, honey, oranges

Almonds, honey, oranges... there is a touch of the Med about this fragrant trio. And if you use a gluten-free baking powder for the cake, you'll have a gluten-free pud – and a very good one at that. Should you find yourself with some cake left over and no more honeyed oranges, don't worry – it's lovely on its own.

Serves 8–10

For the almond cake

225g unsalted butter, softened, plus extra for greasing

225g caster sugar

Finely grated zest of 1 lemon (optional)

225g ground almonds

3 large eggs

125g polenta or fine cornmeal

1 teaspoon baking powder

A large pinch of salt

100g honey

For the honeyed oranges

5 large oranges

3 tablespoons honey

Preheat the oven to 170°C/Gas 3. Butter a 20cm round springform tin and line it with baking parchment.

Beat the butter, sugar and lemon zest, if using, together using a mixer, or with a handheld electric whisk, for several minutes until pale, fluffy and light. Stir in the ground almonds until well combined. Beat in the eggs, one at a time, incorporating each fully before you add the next. Thoroughly combine the polenta, baking powder and salt, then fold into the cake mixture.

Spoon into the prepared tin and bake for 45–50 minutes or until a skewer inserted in the centre of the cake comes out clean. Warm the honey in a small pan until it is very loose and liquid. Make holes all over the top of the hot cake with a skewer, then trickle the warm honey over the surface. Leave to cool completely in the tin.

For the honeyed oranges, finely grate the zest from one of the oranges into a small pan. Slice the peel and pith away from all 5 oranges. To do this, cut a slice off the base of each and stand the orange on a board. Then use a sharp knife to cut down through the peel and pith, slicing it away completely, in sections. Now, working over a bowl to catch the juice, slice the orange segments out from between the membranes, dropping them into the bowl. Squeeze the juice from the orange membranes on to the zest and strain the juice from the bowl of segments into the pan too. Add the honey, stir over a low heat to combine, then boil for 1 minute. Leave to cool, then pour over the orange segments and stir gently.

Serve the cake in slices with spoonfuls of the honeyed oranges and their fragrant syrup.

PLUS ONE Crème fraîche or thick yoghurt is good on the side.

Filo, walnuts, honey

This honey-soaked pastry, jam-packed with walnuts, is my super simple version of baklava, a sweetmeat you will find in differing guises in Greece, Turkey and many parts of the Middle East and Central Asia.

Makes about 24 pieces

250g walnuts

50g caster sugar

Finely grated zest of 1 lemon (optional)

Finely grated zest of 1 orange (optional)

175g unsalted butter, melted

250g ready-made filo pastry

For the honey syrup

150g honey

150g caster sugar

Juice of 1 lemon

Juice of 1 orange

Preheat the oven to 160°C/Gas 3. Put the walnuts, sugar and citrus zests, if using, in a food processor and pulse a few times until well combined and the nuts are fairly finely chopped.

Brush a little of the butter over the base of a baking tin, about 30 x 20cm. Layer half the filo sheets in the tin, brushing each layer with butter, folding them over and tucking them so that each layer fits neatly. Now spread the chopped walnut mixture in a thick, even layer over it.

Layer the remaining filo over the walnuts, buttering it well as you go. Cut the last couple of sheets of filo so they fit the top of the tin exactly, giving you a neat, smooth top. Brush the top layer with butter (you may not use quite all of it). Use a sharp knife to mark the top couple of layers of pastry into neat diamonds, triangles or squares. Bake for 50 minutes–1 hour, until the filo is crispy and golden on top.

While the baklava is baking, for the honey syrup, put the honey and sugar in a pan. Squeeze the orange and lemon juice into a measuring jug and make up to 300ml with water. Strain through a sieve into the pan and bring slowly to the boil, stirring to dissolve the sugar. Boil for 10 minutes to reduce and thicken.

When you take the baklava from the oven, slowly pour the hot syrup all over the surface. Leave in the baking tin for at least 8 hours to soak and settle.

To serve, use a serrated knife to cut right through the baklava, following the marked lines, and carefully remove the pieces from the tin. Baklava is very good with a cup of coffee. It's also delicious as a pud, with vanilla ice cream.

Chocolate, ginger, digestives

This is a very simple 'tiffin', or chocolate 'refrigerator cake'. It's one of the easiest chocolate treats you can make and endlessly adaptable. A generous chunk is lovely in a lunchbox or picnic hamper, while smaller squares make good petits fours.

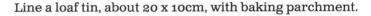

Makes 12 pieces

200g dark chocolate, broken into pieces

100g unsalted butter, cubed

1 tablespoon golden syrup or honey

75g crystallised ginger

150g digestive biscuits

Line a loaf tin, about 20 x 10cm, with baking parchment.

Put the chocolate, butter and syrup or honey into a heatproof bowl. Stand this over a pan of just-simmering water and leave, stirring occasionally, until melted and smooth. Keep the heat low and don't let the water in the pan touch the bowl.

Meanwhile, roughly chop the ginger and crush the biscuits to very coarse crumbs – you want some nice chunky bits still in the mix. Combine the ginger and biscuits in a large bowl.

Pour the melted chocolate into the ginger and biscuits and mix thoroughly. Tip this chocolatey mix into the prepared loaf tin and smooth it out. Leave to cool, then transfer to the fridge for several hours to allow it to set completely.

Lift the 'tiffin' out of the loaf tin in its parchment, then carefully peel the paper away. Use a sharp, heavy knife to cut the cake into 12 pieces, or smaller bites if you prefer. Put them into an airtight container and store in the fridge until needed.

PLUS ONE/SWAPS The sky's the limit on this one. If you don't like ginger, try chopped candied peel or chopped marshmallows in the mix. If you *do* like ginger, you could use gingernuts in place of the digestives. In fact, any decent biscuit, including a nice oaty one or even shortbread, can form the sweet, biscuity element. This kind of refrigerator cake is excellent with dried fruit added too – anything from raisins to dried cranberries or chopped dried apricots. And of course nuts can be a delicious extra element... hazelnuts are my favourite.

Fudge, honey, seeds

Fudge is never going to be a health food, but packing it full of wonderful seeds does at least mean that every gorgeous mouthful is delivering a few good things. Choose a honey with a reasonably strong, aromatic flavour so it can shine through. A blossom honey or chestnut honey is good.

Makes about 20 squares

A drop of sunflower oil

250g caster sugar

50g honey

100g unsalted butter, cut into chunks

100ml double cream

75g mixed sunflower, sesame, hemp and pumpkin seeds (or a seedy mixture of your choice)

Lightly oil a small square or rectangular dish – I use one that is 14 x 17cm; use a piece of kitchen paper to apply the oil sparingly.

Put the sugar, honey, butter and cream into a deep saucepan. Heat gently, stirring often, until the sugar is dissolved and everything is melted and smooth. Stop stirring, put a sugar thermometer into the pan and increase the heat. Let the fudge boil steadily until it registers 116°C on the thermometer. Remove from the heat and leave to stand for 10 minutes.

Add the seeds to the molten fudge, reserving a small handful for finishing. You now need to beat the fudge vigorously, ideally with a handheld electric whisk, until it thickens and becomes less glossy and more grainy. It should be thick enough that, if you scrape a spoon through it, you can see the bottom of the pan for several seconds and the fudge only sinks back slowly. If you're using an electric whisk, this will probably take 3–5 minutes. If you're using a wooden spoon, you'll need to beat it for longer – more like 10 minutes. If it isn't beaten enough, the fudge will not set firm with the right, smooth-but-grainy texture (though it will still taste pretty good).

Pour the thickened fudge into the prepared dish and smooth the surface. Scatter the remaining seeds over the top and leave overnight to set. Cut into small squares to serve.

PLUS ONE/SWAPS You can use chopped or flaked almonds and/or raisins instead of, or as well as the seeds. Chopped dried cherries are very good too.

Chocolate, fruit, nuts/seeds

I can't claim to be the first to have mingled chocolate with dried fruit and something nutty, but I do think these simple treats are particularly good. Broken into rough chunks and shards, they make lovely petits fours and great little gifts.

Chocolate, peanuts, raisins

200g best-quality milk chocolate

50g salted peanuts, very roughly chopped

50g raisins

Line a baking tray with baking parchment or silicone paper. Break the chocolate into pieces and put into a heatproof bowl. Place inside a larger bowl containing some just-boiled water (or over a pan of simmering water if you prefer). Leave, stirring from time to time, until the chocolate is melted and smooth. Remove from the heat and leave to cool slightly.

Stir about one-third of the peanuts and raisins into the chocolate. Carefully pour the melted chocolate on to the lined tray, then use a palette knife to spread it fairly thinly – aim to get it to roughly the area of a piece of A4 paper. Scatter the remaining peanuts and raisins all over the top of the chocolate (quickly, before it sets). Leave to set in the fridge, then carefully remove from the paper and break into shards with your hands or a knife.

White chocolate, poppy seeds, cranberries

200g white chocolate

4 teaspoons poppy seeds

75g dried cranberries

Line a baking tray with baking parchment or silicone paper. Melt the chocolate (as above) and leave to cool slightly. Proceed as above, stirring about one-third of the poppy seeds and dried cranberries into the chocolate first, then spreading the chocolate thinly on to the lined tray, and scattering over the remaining seeds and cranberries. Leave to set in the fridge, then carefully remove from the paper and break into shards.

Dark chocolate, apricot, coconut

200g dark chocolate

50g fresh or toasted, dried coconut flesh, finely sliced

50g dried apricots, roughly chopped

Line a baking tray with baking parchment or silicone paper. Melt the chocolate (as above) and leave to cool slightly. Proceed as above, stirring about one-third of the coconut and dried apricots into the chocolate first, then spreading the chocolate thinly on to the lined tray, and scattering over the remaining coconut and apricots. Leave to set in the fridge, then carefully remove from the paper and break into shards.

Storecupboard standbys

The better stocked your kitchen, the easier and more pleasurable your cooking will be. These are the foods I like to keep on hand most of the time.

STORECUPBOARD

Oils The essentials for me are a flavourless sunflower oil and a light olive oil for frying; an extra virgin rapeseed oil for frying and dressings; and a good, peppery extra virgin olive oil for finishing dishes.

Salt, pepper and spices Fine-grained sea salt is indispensable and I'd never be without a flaky, crystalline sea salt either (Cornish or Maldon). A mill filled with black peppercorns for grinding is a must. I keep other spices but cumin, coriander, fennel and caraway seeds, cayenne pepper and smoked paprika are those I use most frequently. Dried chilli flakes and a good blended curry powder or paste are other key flavourings.

Vinegars I use organic cider vinegar pretty much every day. I also like the rich apple balsamic made by Aspall's, and a decent red wine vinegar is extremely useful.

Mustard Good old English mustard is all I really need, but I also keep a pot of Dijon and/or wholegrain mustard.

Capers, olives and anchovies These salty flavouring ingredients are always to hand.

Tinned tomatoes I favour whole rather than chopped tinned tomatoes. Bottled passata (sieved tomatoes) is equally useful.

Coconut milk I turn to this lovely, creamy stuff increasingly often for curries and soups.

Pasta I stock long pasta, such as spaghetti or linguine, and a few pasta shapes, such as penne and fusilli. And I am particularly fond of the small, rice-shaped risoni or orzo.

Rice I prefer basmati or long-grain brown rice for simple side dishes, and arborio or carnaroli for risottos.

Pearled spelt or pearl barley I use these grains in everything from soups and stews to salads.

Dried lentils You'll find simply cooked Puy lentils in many recipes in this book; I couldn't be without them. Dried split red lentils are also a favourite standby.

Tinned pulses Chickpeas, cannellini beans, borlotti beans, kidney beans, lentils... you can base a meal around any of them.

Stock cubes Homemade stock is the ideal but I regularly use organic stock cubes too. My default choice is Kallo's organic, yeast-free veg stock cubes.

Nuts and seeds I often use walnuts, pecans, cashews, pine nuts and almonds, as well as pumpkin, sunflower and sesame seeds.

Dried fruit Raisins, sultanas, prunes and unsulphured dried apricots are the ones I use most frequently.

Flour Plain white and strong bread flours are everyday essentials. I like light brown flour for cakes.

Sugar and honey I keep a fine golden caster sugar and a soft brown sugar to hand. Lovely, fragrant, runny honey is an essential too – I get mine from local beekeepers.

Dark chocolate I like mine with roughly 70% cocoa solids – Green & Black's and Montezuma's organic chocolate are my two favourites.

Biscuits Good-quality all-butter shortbread, digestives and gingernuts stand me in good stead for quick puddings and treats.

Brandy The Somerset cider brandy produced by Julian Temperley is my favourite.

LARDER, FRIDGE AND FREEZER

Bread I'm a sourdough addict and we bake our own regularly. Nevertheless, I still always have some good bought bread stashed in the freezer – ready-sliced so I can take out just what I need.

Stock vegetables No cook should ever be without a bag of onions, but I like to have carrots and celery too: these form a holy trinity for stocks, soups and stews.

Herbs and garlic I try to never be without bay leaves, fresh thyme and garlic. Flat-leaf parsley is also a fairly constant presence in my garden, and kitchen.

Fresh red chillies A medium-sized, medium-hot variety such as a red jalapeño or fresno is great for general use.

Unwaxed lemons and oranges As a seasoning, I regard lemon juice as essential as salt and pepper. And, as I very often use the zest, I always buy unwaxed fruit. I also use a fair amount of fresh orange juice and zest in cooking.

Butter I buy mostly unsalted butter – it has a higher burning point than salted butter so it's good for gentle frying, and it gives the best flavour to cakes and puds.

Eggs Free-range, of course.

Double cream or crème fraîche Greedy, but gloriously useful.

Plain wholemilk yoghurt Less greedy and just as useful.

Mayonnaise I make my own, but also keep a jar of good ready-made, free-range egg mayo, such as the one made by Riverford.

Cheese There are hundreds of great British cheeses and I enjoy cooking with many of them. However, if I had to pare it right down, I would always want a fairly mild, firm goat's cheese for crumbling, a mature (but not too strong) Cheddar and a hard Parmesan-type cheese for grating – either a chunk of proper Parmigiano Reggiano or, my favourite alternative, a hard, matured goat's cheese called Capriano. A good creamy blue, such as Dorset Blue Vinney or Cornish Blue, is pretty useful too.

Salted/cured pork By which I mean any of the following: streaky bacon, pancetta, ham (cooked or air-dried) and spicy chorizo. They are some of the most useful 'good things' and 'plus ones'.

Frozen puff pastry I always go for an all-butter type; there are now organic ones too.

Frozen peas or petits pois If you can't get very fresh peas in the pod, then frozen can be a better choice – and of course they can be used all year round.

Frozen breadcrumbs I often process semi-stale bread and discarded crusts into crumbs and freeze them in smallish portions.

Index

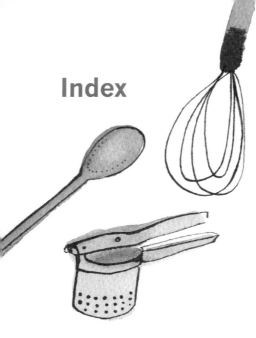

F

farinata 317
fennel
   fennel, apple, goat's cheese 22
   fennel, orange, watercress 18
   fennel, tangerine, pumpkin
      seeds 37
   potato, fennel, onion 131
feta cheese
   beetroot, feta, walnuts 62
   lamb, tomatoes, feta 255
filo pastry
   filo, walnuts, honey 395
fish 186–231
   brandade, tomatoes, toast 114
   bream, olives, couscous 220
   fish, bread, capers 215
   fish, coconut, coriander 219
   fish, lime, mint 74
   fish, onion, olives 222
   mackerel, oatmeal, rhubarb 210
   mackerel, celery, orange 208
   mackerel, juniper, bay 76
   mackerel, new potatoes,
      shallots 212
   sardines, garlic, leaves 206
   smoked fish, spinach, béchamel
      227
   smoked fish, sweetcorn, batter
      224
   smoked mackerel, beetroot,
      horseradish 228
   sole, lemon, potato 216
   trout, watercress, spelt 204
   see also shellfish
flatbreads
   broad beans, meatballs,
      flatbread 110
flour 402
fool
   'fumble' 360
   rhubarb, ginger, cream 339
French toast
   egg, bread, apple 386
fruit 322–63
   see also apples, strawberries
      etc

fudge
   fudge, honey, seeds 398
   ice cream, fudge, nuts 375
'fumble' 360

G

gammon
   ham, squash, marmalade 270
garam masala
   egg, purple sprouting, garam
      masala 64
   sausages, parsnips, onions 279
garlic 403
   beef, shallots, tomato 259
   clams, tomatoes, garlic 190
   garlic toast 114
   lamb, lettuce, vinegar 250
   parsnips, garlic, blue cheese
      94
   pork, celeriac, garlic 264
   sardines, garlic, leaves 206
   spaghetti, garlic, olive oil 291
gherkins
   steak, Cheddar, gherkins 106
ginger
   chocolate, ginger, digestives
      396
   condensed milk, lemon,
      gingernuts 384
   pears, custard, ginger cake 357
   rhubarb, ginger, cream 339
globe artichokes
   artichoke, egg, capers 69
   artichoke, yoghurt, lemon 70
gnocchi
   squash, gnocchi, cheese 172
goat's cheese
   beans, ham, tomatoes 44
   blackcurrants, goat's cheese,
      digestives 352
   fennel, apple, goat's cheese 22
   nettles, cheese, puff pastry 174
   peppers, sourdough, goat's
      cheese 118
   polenta, mushrooms, cheese
      318
   squash, gnocchi, cheese 172

gooseberries
   gooseberries, custard, honey
      340
granita
   blackberries, apple, cream 354
green beans
   squash, coconut, chilli 169
greens
   duck, blackberries, greens 242
   noodles, chicken, greens 300
   polenta, beans, kale 317
   polenta, blue cheese, greens 314
Gruyère cheese
   cabbage, onion, bread 165
guacamole 147
gurnard
   fish, onion, olives 222

H

haddock *see* smoked haddock
halloumi
   asparagus, new potatoes,
      halloumi 160
ham 403
   asparagus, egg, ham 60
   beans, ham, tomatoes 44
   ham, potatoes, parsley 269
   ham, squash, marmalade 270
   squash, ricotta, ham 46
haricot beans
   bacon, beans, tomato 272
hazelnuts
   peaches, praline, cream 348
   ricotta, honeycomb, hazelnuts
      372
herbs 403
   new potatoes, herbs, olive oil
      159
   see also basil, parsley *etc*
honey 403
   almond cake, honey, oranges
      392
   filo, walnuts, honey 395
   fudge, honey, seeds 398
   gooseberries, custard, honey
      340
   plums, yoghurt, honey 358

Acknowledgements

I've been very excited about this book from the off, and I would like to say a massive thank you to all those who have shared my enthusiasm, and whose hard work has helped bring the project to fruition.

Honing and testing this many new recipes is no easy task, and I've been very lucky to have two amazingly talented and dedicated collaborators. Gill Meller, head chef and dynamic driving force of the River Cottage kitchen, has brought his extraordinary creativity to many of the recipes, as well as preparing most of them for photography with his dependably superb skill and lightness of touch. And the brilliant and inexhaustible Nikki Duffy has offered up many delicious and original ideas, as well as tirelessly testing and tweaking my own nebulous notions until they actually work on the page and the plate.

Of course, these pages would be barren without the gorgeous photography of Simon Wheeler. His knack for capturing the rough-edged charm of easy-going food, so it is both irresistible and approachable, has been at the heart of all my books for over a decade now, and I still think he has no equal. Thank you, Simon.

Turning these recipes and photographs into a well-buffed book has taken a good deal of work. Thanks to everyone who has put so much time in, especially my editors at Bloomsbury, Richard Atkinson and Natalie Hunt, who took on the project with such relish and whose enthusiasm never waned as they guided it through to the last full-stop; and to Xa Shaw Stewart who so ably assisted them.

Four other tremendous talents have also helped to make this book what it is: Lawrence Morton, whose brilliantly sharp design work and good-humoured hosting of our layout meetings has brought it all together with such effortless élan; Mariko Jesse, whose lovely, lively, witty illustrations have once again given the book a wonderful extra dimension; Janet Illsley, my project editor, whose attention to detail and clarity of vision have kept us all on track from start to finish; and to Marina Asenjo, whose eagle eye has steered the book through the production process, kept it looking just as good as we all hoped it would. Thank you all.

For her tireless work in supporting me not just in this project, but in all the work I do, I thank the lovely Jess Upton, my brilliant PA. As ever, she has done a sterling job of organising not just my crazy schedule, but the crucial photo shoots for this book. She's a fantastic person to have on my side.

To my partners at Keo Films, Andrew Palmer, Zam Baring and Debbie Manners, thank you for all your support for the TV interpretation of *Hugh's Three Good Things*. And thanks to the brilliant production team who made it happen, especially Paula Trafford and Stephen Leigh.

And a big thank you to the whole team at River Cottage, particularly Simon Dodd, Tim Maddams, Lucy Brazier, Sally Gale, Steve Lamb, Craig Rudman, Graeme Roy and of course head honcho, Rob Love.

To my agent, Antony Topping, my heartfelt thanks, as always. Those with whom you deal on my behalf say you're the nicest agent they ever talk to – and yet somehow this doesn't worry me.

Finally to my wonderful family – Marie, Chloe, Oscar, Freddie and Louisa – whose love, support and patience (not to mention constructive criticism of the working contents of this book) have kept me sane and steady throughout. I couldn't do it, any of it, without you.

For Antony, Richard and Simon, who are definitely Three Good Things

HUGH FEARNLEY-WHITTINGSTALL is a writer, broadcaster and campaigner. His series for the BBC and Channel 4 have earned him a huge popular following, while his books have collected multiple awards including the Glenfiddich Trophy (twice), the André Simon Food Book of the Year (three times), the Michael Smith Award (twice) and, in the US, the James Beard Cookbook of the Year. Hugh lives in Devon with his family.

First published as *Three Good Things* in Great Britain 2012
This edition first published 2017

Text © 2012 by Hugh Fearnley-Whittingstall
Photography © 2012 by Simon Wheeler
Photographs on pages 65, 211 and 235 © 2012 by Marie Derôme
Illustrations © 2012 and 2017 by Mariko Jesse

Bloomsbury Publishing Plc
50 Bedford Square
London WC1B 3DP
Bloomsbury Publishing, London, Oxford, New York, New Delhi and Sydney

A CIP catalogue record for this book is available from the British Library

ISBN 978 1 4088 8849 0

Project Editor: Janet Illsley
Designer: Lawrence Morton
Cover design for this edition: Greg Heinimann
Photographer and stylist: Simon Wheeler (www.simonwheeler.eu)
Illustrator: Mariko Jesse (www.marikojesse.com)
Indexer: Hilary Bird

10 9 8 7 6 5 4 3 2 1

Printed and bound in Italy by Graphicom

www.bloomsbury.com
www.rivercottage.net